SOCIAL PHILOSOPHY

MW01174724

VOLUME 27

Edited by
Nancy E. Snow

Social Philosophy Today is published by the Philosophy Documentation Center.

For information regarding subscriptions or back issues, please contact:

Philosophy Documentation Center
P.O. Box 7147
Charlottesville, VA 22906-7147
804-444-2419 (U.S. & Canada); 434-220-3300
Fax: 434-220-3301
E-mail: order@pdcnet.org
Web: www.pdcnet.org

ISBN: 1-889680-85-0, ISBN 13: 978-1-889680-85-9
ISSN 1543-4044 (print)
ISSN 2153-9448 (online)

Recent issues of *Social Philosophy Today*:

Social Philosophy Today is indexed in *Academic Search Premier, American Humanities Index, Bibliographie de la Philosophie, Current Abstracts, Index Philosophicus, Index to Social Sciences & Humanities Proceedings, International Bibliography of Periodical Literature (IBZ), International Bibliography of the Social Sciences, Philosopher's Index, Reference and Research Book News, Sociological Abstracts*, and *Worldwide Political Science Abstracts*. Electronic access to the full text of Social Philosophy Today is provided through POIESIS: Philosophy Online Serials.

Designed and produced by the Philosophy Documentation Center,
Charlottesville, Virginia

Table of Contents

POVERTY, JUSTICE, AND MARKETS

Volume 27

Table of Contents

Introduction

NANCY E. SNOW

I was honored to be asked by Professor Margaret Crouch, the current President of the North American Society for Social Philosophy (NASSP), to guest edit volume 27 of *Social Philosophy Today* on "Poverty, Justice, and Markets." As is the tradition of the NASSP, each volume of *Social Philosophy Today* publishes a selection of papers from those presented at the annual conference held the preceding year. Volume 27 presents papers from the conference that was held in Toronto, Ontario, Canada, at Ryerson Polytechnic University in July, 2010. This year, we are pleased to present three additional sections—a keynote address from the 2009 NASSP conference given by David Schweickart at the 2009 conference held at St. Joseph's University in Philadelphia, Pennsylvania; the 2010 Presidential Address of outgoing NASSP President Alistair M. Macleod; and contributions to an "author meets critics" session at the 2010 conference on the co-authored book of James P. Sterba and Jan Narveson, *Are Liberty and Equality Compatible?*

Part I of this volume features David Schweickart's 2009 keynote address: "Reading *Legitimation Crisis* During the Meltdown," a trenchant analysis of the current economic malaise in the United States read in the light of Jürgen Habermas's *Legitimation Crisis* and other resources, and replete with bold suggestions for a way out of the crisis. Economic themes are continued in part II, which is devoted to Macleod's Presidential Address, entitled, "The Voluntary Transactions Principle and the Free Market Ideal." Drawing on a wide range of literature in both classical and contemporary philosophy and economics, Macleod argues that the implementation of free markets requires that voluntary transactions be regulated by principles of justice and fairness. His intriguing case for this position references the arguments of figures as diverse as Adam Smith, Milton Friedman, F. A. Hayek, G. A. Cohen, and the contemporary economist Joseph Stiglitz. The contributions of parts I and II offer penetrating and refreshing philosophical insights into the economic crisis that continues to afflict the U. S. economy.

Part III of this volume is comprised of a selection of peer reviewed conference papers. The policy of program committees for NASSP conferences is to accept worthy abstracts on all topics of philosophical interest, not just those on the conference theme. The essays of part III, entitled, "Explorations in Social Justice," reflect this topical diversity. Of these essays, Gunderson's and Johnston's take on the timely issue of justice in health care. Jenkins critiques George Sher's theory of desert. Long makes a case for "luck egalitarianism," the theory that seeks to neutralize inequalities arising from brute luck. Bramer applies Kant's ethical theory to the problem of domestic violence. Nenadic uses Heidegger's theory to expose the flawed ontological and epistemological assumptions that render ethically invisible the epidemic of sexual violence and sexual harassment suffered by women and girls. Finally, Silliman and Johnson explore, in trialogical form, tensions between an Enlightened, rationalist approach to pedagogy and the "critical" pedagogy advocated by Paolo Freire. Each side is taken by a character in the conversation, and a third seeks to resolve tensions between them.

Parts I, II, and III offer rich fare in terms of the range of theoretical and practical investigation they cover. Part IV adds to this cornucopia by introducing a novel format into NASSP conferences and publications: an "author meets critics" session. The authors are James P. Sterba and Jan Narveson, and their co-authored book is *Are Liberty and Equality Compatible?* Sterba takes the position that "equality is compatible with and required by liberty," and Narveson, that "The right to liberty is incompatible with the right to equality."[1] Published here is a brief co-authored précis of their book, followed by a response by Alistair M. Macleod. Each author then responds to critics.[2]

Part V concludes volume 27 with contributions from a traditional NASSP event: the annual book award session. The 2010 book award winner is Amartya Sen, the Thomas W. Lamont University Professor and Professor of Economics and Philosophy at Harvard University and winner of the 1998 Nobel Prize in Economic Sciences. Sen's magisterial work, *The Idea of Justice*, was the book award committee's choice. As is customary at NASSP conferences, book award committee members comment on the chosen work, and the author responds. Included here are commentaries by Deen Chatterjee, Helga Varden, and a response by Sen.

I am very proud to have edited this exciting volume. I am confident that readers will enjoy and profit from their engagement with the ideas presented herein. Many thanks to all who have helped: our contributing authors; NASSP and other reviewers; Alistair M. Macleod for managing the book award session contributions; and finally, Margaret Crouch, the NASSP President, and George Leaman of the Philosophy Documentation Center, for help and advice with the editing process.

Nancy E. Snow, Marquette University

Notes

1.   Narveson and Sterba, "Précis of *Are Liberty and Equality Compatible?*," this volume.

2.   Helga Varden, who also commented on Sterba and Narveson, chose to publish her commentary in an online journal. Consequently, it has not been included here.

Part I:
Keynote Address
2009 NASSP Conference

Reading *Legitimation Crisis* During the Meltdown

DAVID SCHWEICKART

In 2003 Robert Lucas, professor at the University of Chicago and winner of the 1995 Nobel Memorial Prize in Economics gave the presidential address at the annual meeting of the American Economics Association. After explaining that macroeconomics began as an intellectual response to the Great Depression, he declared that it was time for the field to move on: "the central problem of depression prevention," he declared, "has, for all practical purposes, been solved, and has, in fact, been solved for many decades."[1]

Paul Krugman, a more recent Nobel laureate, points out, in his 2009 best seller, *The Return of Depression Economics and the Crisis of 2008*, that Lucas was hardly alone in holding this view. Indeed, it has been the prevailing wisdom of the profession for nearly half a century. As you may surmise from the title of his book, Krugman dissents. "Looking back from only a few years," he writes, "with much of the world in the throes of a financial and economic crisis all too reminiscent of the 1930s, these optimistic pronouncements sound almost incredibly smug."[2]

"All too reminiscent of the 1930s." Let us recall for a moment that momentous decade, which began with a bang and then got really ugly. As John Kenneth Galbraith remarked, "The singular feature of the Great Crash of 1929 was that the worst continued to worsen."[3] The world was transformed.

For one thing, the Great Crash seemed to confirm Marx's theoretical conclusion that capitalism is inherently prone to economic crises, and that these would tend to worsen over time. This confirmation invigorated the international communist movement, which developed active parties in virtually every country in the world.

The economic crisis also invigorated the fascist movement, whose virulent anti-communism garnered the support of wealthy, threatened backers throughout Europe, and gave us, not only a vicious anti-semitism that resulted in the Holocaust, but World War II as well.

The Great Depression also set the stage for a new form of capitalism, eventually called "welfare-state capitalism, or "social democracy" or by Jürgen Habermas, in the work I happened to be teaching in the fall of 2008, "advanced" capitalism.

I. Legitimation Crisis

Before diving into *Legitimation Crisis*, some background. In 1923 in Frankfurt, Germany the Institute for Social Research was established, which brought together a remarkable collection of independent Marxist intellectuals, among them Max Horkheimer, Theodor Adorno, Herbert Marcuse, Erich Fromm, and, as a member of the Institute's outer circle, Walter Benjamin. Most relocated to the United States, following the accession of Adolf Hitler to power in 1933. (Benjamin was not so fortunate. He remained in Europe, then committed suicide in 1940 to avoid being taken prisoner by the Nazis.) Horkheimer and Adorno returned to Frankfurt after the war.

Several key questions dominated the thinking of these "first generation" critical theorists:

- Why had Communism, which held out such hope for liberation, degenerated into rigid, dogmatic, ruthless Stalinism?

- Why had the working class *not* emerged victorious from capitalism's most severe crisis—as Marx had predicted?

Then later, after the war,

- Is technology truly liberating, as Marx believed, or is it, having greatly enhanced the ruling elites' powers of mass indoctrination, ushering in a new, "happy" totalitarianism, creating a "one-dimensional man" so captivated by advertising, mass entertainment and the titillating sexualization of everyday life as to be incapable of revolt?

The first-generation critical theorists, apart from Marcuse in his later writings, tended to answer this latter question in the affirmative—a grim, disheartening conclusion. Jürgen Habermas, who had been a "Hitler Jugend" during the war, and who later became Adorno's assistant, was not so pessimistic.

Legitimation Crisis came out in 1973. (The English translation followed two years later.) Although Habermas self-identified as a Marxist at the time, he didn't think Marx had gotten everything right.[4] Marx is right, he thinks, that there is a direction to history, and that there are various stages of development. Marx is right that technological development and class struggle are key factors in explaining the development and transformation of social systems.

Marx is wrong, however, to think that moralities and worldviews are simply reflections of underlying, more basic, economic conditions. Worldviews and moralities, Habermas insists, have their own rationally-reconstructable, stage-like development trajectories, which set limits on the range of options available to particular societies when they come under stress. In his words, the change from one social system to another is "a function of forces of production and degree of systems autonomy, but [such change] is limited by the logic of the development of worldviews, *which is relatively independent of political and economic forces*" (8, my emphasis).[5]

Marx is wrong, also, to think that a severe economic crisis will more or less automatically generate a revolutionary class consciousness among the working class, inspiring them to bring down the old system and set up a new one. The transition from an "objective" crisis to a "subjective" one is more complicated than Marx supposed. For a socio-economic system to be radically transformed, a "systems crisis" must become an "identity crisis," that is to say, an economic crisis must ultimately change the self-identity of enough people in such a way as to allow/compel them to become agents of change. Whether or not this happens depends on an array of psychological and cultural factors quite distinct from the severity of the economic crisis.

Habermas is not only critical of Marx. He is also critical of certain tenets of first-generation critical theory. Advanced capitalism has not solved the problem of economic crisis, as the first-generation theorists (along with virtually all mainstream economists) seem to have concluded. More precisely, "I do not exclude the possibility that economic crisis can be permanently averted—but only in such a way that contradictory steering imperatives that assert themselves . . . would produce a series of *other* crises" (40).

Habermas is also less pessimistic than first-generation theorists as to the efficacy advertising, mass entertainment and mass communication in turning us all into mindless robots incapable of questioning the legitimacy of the given socio-economic order. This *might* happen—but it hasn't happened yet. For a very important reason. Certain crucial areas of life are highly resistant to administrative control. Habermas emphatically insists: "*There is no administrative production of meaning*" (70).

For Habermas, it is crucial to distinguish "systems" from "the lifeworld." There are two basic "systems" in a modern society, an economic system, where interactions are mediated by money, and a political system where interactions are mediated by hierarchical power. A very different set of interactions characterizes the "lifeworld." The lifeworld is the realm of personal interactions mediated by language. It is the locus of our normative structures and our sense of meaningfulness. It is the source of personal identity. Although the systems regularly attempt to "colonize" the lifeworld, the latter tends to resist these attempts.

In assessing the relevance of Marx's critique of capitalism, it is important, Habermas insists, to keep in mind the fact that "advanced capitalism" is significantly different from the "liberal capitalism" of Marx's day. One difference, noted by Habermas, is particularly important to our present concerns. The state now assumes responsibility for the economy. It is held responsible by an electorate that demands government intervention when the economy sours. We are certainly witnessing this demand today.

But will these interventions work? If not, how might things play out? These are the questions we are facing at the present moment. They are also the questions with which Habermas grappled thirty-eight years ago.

According to Habermas, we must distinguish various kinds of crises. He delineates four distinct "crises tendencies in advanced capitalism": economic crises, rationality crises, legitimation crises and motivation crises. The economic crises are the ones with which we are all familiar: serious inflation and/or deep recession. A "rationality crisis" occurs at the political-administrative level, when, given the conflicting demands of various constituencies, the government is unable to resolve the economic crisis it is expected to handle. A "legitimation crisis" occurs when the people lose faith in their government and begin to raise deep questions about the political or economic structures of their society. A "motivation crisis" occurs when motivational patterns important for the functioning of the system break down.

As a striking illustration of these various crisis tendencies, consider a world-historic example that occurred more than a quarter-century after *Legitimation Crisis* was published. Consider the collapse the Soviet Union.

First we had an economic crisis: seemingly permanent stagnation. Rather than overtaking the West, as its citizens had hoped, and as many in the West, among them influential economists, had feared, the gap between the Soviet Union and the West, which had narrowed significantly from the time of the Russian Revolution to the mid-1970s, suddenly began to widen, becoming ever larger—and, due to enhanced communication technologies, ever more apparent. (My 1973 edition of Paul Samuelson's *Economics*—by far the most widely used undergraduate economics textbook of the time—includes a graph, based on "plausible assumptions," showing the Soviet economy overtaking our own by 1990.[6]) The government responded by attempting various reforms. The basic economic structure—centralized planning instead of markets—had produced some triumphs, particularly in nuclear catch-up and the "space race," but it was realized that its earlier period of rapid economic growth had been due mainly to "extensive development" (building more factories, moving more labor from the countryside to cities), and that this source of growth had been exhausted. "Intensive development" (grounded in technological innovation) lagged far behind the capitalist West. So the state tried to change the incentive structures, first trying to get managers of state-run enterprises to run their enterprises according to profit and loss criteria, as opposed to simply fulfilling mandated quotas, then introducing more direct market mechanisms. The political structure was also opened up. We had both *perestroika* (restructuring) and *glasnost* (openness)—but nothing seemed to work.

The system became engulfed in a full-blown rationality crisis, which rather quickly devolved into a legitimation crisis. I got a first-hand taste of the latter when I visited Russia (my first and only visit) in 1987. I was startled by the virulence and extent of the criticisms now openly expressed in the newly freed press. (I remember in particular a column denouncing, of all things, Russian food: communism, it was claimed, had destroyed the fine traditions of Russian cuisine.) This legitimation crisis coincided with a motivation crisis. Factory production continued to deteriorate. The Russian joke at the time: "They pretend to pay us. We pretend to work." Soon enough, the Soviet system came crashing down.

II. The Current Economic Crisis

Let us leave Habermas for awhile. We'll come back to him. Let us now take a closer look at where we are today. We're in an economic crisis. Why?

Let us set aside the immorality and illegality that have garnered so much attention:

- Unscrupulous real estate brokers enticing people to sign contracts they didn't understand,

- Corrupt rating agencies giving triple-A ratings to high-risk securities,

- Lax regulators,

- Investment banks concocting securities they knew were rotten, then buying "credit default swaps" so as to bet against them.

Let's begin with the standard story: the subprime mortgage debacle caused a general liquidity crisis, which, in turn, provoked a recession. But what is a "liquidity crisis"? Let us back up for a moment. As everyone knows, the stock market collapse on that notorious "Black Tuesday," October 29, 1929 ushered in the Great Depression. But how could a collapse of the stock market—the devaluation of pieces of paper held mainly by the rich—lead to an economic collapse that lasted a decade? After all, this was not a natural disaster. We are not talking here of war or pestilence or drought, but of pieces of paper suddenly losing value. How could this "accounting fact" lead to massive misery?

The answer lies with banks—where the rubber meets the road, where finance meets the "real" economy. A stock market crash, in and of itself, need not cause much damage. Witness the Crash of 1987, which saw the stock market plunge 23 percent on October 19—nearly twice the 12 percent drop on Black Tuesday. The real economy barely blinked this time. The Federal Reserve rushed cash to the banks. Within a couple of months the stock market itself had recovered.

It is when banks get in trouble that the real economy is affected. Businesses need regular access to credit, since, typically, labor and raw materials must be purchased before the finished product is sold. Consumers, too, need access to credit, particularly for big-ticket items like homes and cars. If access to credit dries up, spending contracts, production contracts, workers are laid off, effective demand contracts further—the now-familiar downward recessionary spiral.

Back to the present: the standard story. A "housing bubble" led to a proliferation of subprime mortgage lending. (With house prices going up, where's the risk? Who cares if the borrower can't afford the mortgage? If the borrower defaults, the house can be resold—for even more.) These subprime mortgages, along with most other home mortgages, were sold to investment banks, which sliced and diced them, repackaged them as "mortgage backed securities," and sold them to eager investors everywhere. (A "mortgage-backed security" is essentially a contract to receive small pieces of the repayments of a great many loans.) These mortgage-backed securities were highly liquid, i.e., easy to sell on short notice if the buyer needed cash—at least they were before the crisis.

When housing prices stopped rising, and when "teaser" interest rates gave way to market rates, homeowners began to default in large numbers, especially those who had insufficient income in the first place, those to whom the "subprime" mortgages had been granted (NINJA loans, for example: no income, no job). Suddenly no one could tell what mortgage-backed securities were worth, since it was virtually impossible to ascertain, for a given security, how much income it could be expected to generate, given that many of its many-thousand pieces (how many?) were in or near default. So the markets for these securities, and indeed for most other "collateralized debt obligations," froze. There were no buyers at all for these particular pieces of paper.

Okay, but so what? Investors can't sell certain pieces of paper. So what? Now we get to the banks. Commercial banks, which make loans to individuals and businesses, held many of these "pieces of paper." When money is deposited in a bank, as you know, it is not simply stashed in a vault. A bit of it is (as is required by law), but most of it is either loaned out to customers *or* used to purchase securities. (After all, it makes no sense for a bank to keep idle cash on hand, when it could be "put to work" making more money.) If extra cash is needed to make new loans or to return to depositors who want to take their money out, the banks can simply sell their securities to raise the cash. Or at least they could *before* the crisis. Suddenly they couldn't. No one would buy these "toxic" securities (unless the taxpayers agree to assume the risk). Thus a "liquidity crisis." (I'm oversimplifying some, but this is the basic picture.)

But we know how to resolve a liquidity crisis, don't we? Isn't that what Robert Lucas was telling us? Here's Krugman again:

> Most economists, to the extent that they think about the subject at all, regard the Great Depression of the 1930s as a gratuitous, unnecessary tragedy. If only the Herbert Hoover hadn't tried to balance the budget in the face of an economic slump, if only

the Federal Reserve hadn't defended the gold standard . . . if only officials had rushed cash to threatened banks, . . . then the stock market crash would have led to only a garden variety recession, soon forgotten. And since economists and policymakers have learned their lesson . . . nothing like the Great Depression can ever happen again.[7]

But consider: We're not defending the gold standard anymore. We didn't try to balance the budget—at least not then. We did rush cash to threatened banks. So, from the point of view of current orthodoxy, we did everything right. Yet the unemployment rate remains painfully high and shows no sign of coming down. To be sure, the panic seems to have subsided, and the stock market has rebounded, but as Mortimer Zuckerman, Editor-in-Chief of *U.S. News and World Reports* wrote two years ago, in a prescient article entitled, "Nine Reasons the Economy is Not Getting Better, "The appropriate metaphor is not the green shoots of new growth. A better image is to look at the true total of jobless people as a prudent navigator looks at an iceberg. What we see on the surface is disconcerting enough. . . . The job losses are now equal to the net job gains over the previous nine years, making this the only recession since the Great Depression to wipe out all employment growth from the previous business cycle."

Beneath the surface, things look even worse—people not counted as unemployed who are, people working part time who want full-time work, people taking unpaid leaves, little prospect of job creation, etc. As a result, "we could face a very low upswing in terms of the creation of new jobs, and we may be facing a much higher rate of joblessnesss on an ungoing basis."[8]

Why haven't the standard remedies worked? It's time for a deeper, more Marxian-Keynesian analysis. From this perspective, the fundamental problem is not the housing bubble, or subprime lending, nor is it Wall Street greed nor excessive speculation nor even deficient regulation.

Let's begin with Marx's basic insight: The seemingly irrational "overproduction" crises of capitalism are rooted in the defining institution of capitalism: wage labor. The commodification of labor gives rise, over time, to a contradiction. Since labor is a cost of production, capitalists strive to keep its price (the wage rate) low. At the same time capitalists need to *sell* their products, so they need wages to be high. Hence an ever-present crisis tendency: if workers don't have the money to buy what is produced, production is cut back, workers are laid off, demand drops further . . . the downward spiral.

"But wait!" you might say, "Not so fast. Workers aren't the only ones that purchase goods. So do capitalists. If the gap between what is produced and what workers can buy is filled by the purchases of capitalists, recession can be avoided."

We are touching here on a key difference between Marx's analysis and Keynes's. Whereas Marx focuses on the constraints to workers' consumption, Keynes focuses on the behavior of the capitalists. Let's follow the Keynesian trail at this point.

What do capitalists buy? Consumer goods, to be sure, but not nearly enough to close the gap. It is a fundamental feature of a capitalist society that capitalists do *not* simply consume the surplus that workers have created. Feudal lords might have routinely consumed all the surplus their peasants produced, but what gives capitalism its fundamental dynamic is the fact that capitalists routinely *reinvest* a portion of their profits, so that they can reap even greater rewards in the future.

But what does "reinvestment" mean in real, material terms? Well, it means buying capital goods, not consumer goods—the extra machinery and raw materials to be utilized during the next production period to produce more than was produced in the preceding period. So long as the capitalists keep reinvesting, the economy can keep growing, can remain healthy, can avoid recession. But if the capitalists don't invest, then the economy slumps.

Moreover, as Keynes emphasized, the market's invisible hand will not automatically turn things around. To the contrary, market incentives often make matters worse: if the economy begins to slump, prices drop, companies go bankrupt, workers are laid off, demand drops further, etc. The downward spiral has no built-in counter-tendencies. An external event, or series of events, can sometimes turn things around, something that inspires investors to begin investing again, but there is no guarantee that such events will occur. Therefore, governments must intervene when a recession threatens. If government action isn't swift and substantial, a recession can turn into to a full-blown depression.

What can governments do? The received wisdom of the past three decades has focused on monetary policy: keep the money supply growing so that credit for business expansion is always available. When a recession threatens, cut interest rates, so as to make business and consumer borrowing (and hence business and consumer spending) more attractive, and provide structurally sound banks with liquidity (cash) in times of trouble so they can keep lending.

This is suitably Keynesian, but as Keynes himself pointed out, monetary policy alone may not be enough. Making money available to banks or to consumers doesn't guarantee it will be loaned out or spent. Monetary policy may amount to pushing on a string. Keynes—and his more radical followers—also argued for something more, namely fiscal policy: large-scale government employment and purchases, the costs of which should be allowed to exceed tax revenues when recessions threaten. Governments should provide the stimulus of public employment and purchases when private employment and purchases fall off. This, of course, was a significant part of the Obama stimulus package. It was also Paul Krugman's recommendation—although Krugman argued that the package should be much larger and more aggressive than it was.[9]

But notice, neither monetary nor fiscal policy addresses Marx's insight. What if wages are too low? Habermas has characterized "advanced capitalism" as involving a "quasi-political class compromise" that permits labor to organize and bargain collectively, so that workers can share in the productivity gains. For several decades following WWII, this development, combined with Keynesian monetary and fiscal policies, worked. It produced what is sometimes referred to as capitalism's "Golden Age." Here's Krugman's description:

> Postwar America was, above all, a middle-class society. The great boom in wages that began with World War II had lifted tens of millions of Americans—my parents among them—from urban slums and rural poverty to a life of home ownership and unprecedented comfort. The rich, on the other hand, had lost ground. They were few in number and, relative to the prosperous middle, not all that rich. The poor were more numerous than the rich, but they were still a relatively small minority. As a result, there was a striking sense of economic commonality: Most people in America lived recognizably similar and remarkably decent material lives.[10]

Soon enough, however: trouble in paradise. In the mid-1970s, real wages stopped rising—and have been flat ever since; that is to say, right about the time *Legitimation Crisis* was published, the social democratic compromise came to an end (at least in the U.S.). Median household income has grown only modestly since 1973, up only 16 percent in thirty-five years—and this increase is due primarily to the large influx of women into the workforce, greatly increasing the number of two-income households. As Krugman notes, "For men ages 35–44—men who would a generation ago, often have been supporting stay-at-home wives—we find that inflation-adjusted wages were 12% *higher* in 1973 than they are now." Yet worker productivity has increased steadily. "The value of the output an average worker produces in an hour, even after you adjust for inflation, has risen almost 50% since 1973." GDP has more than tripled.[11] Here's a picture of what has happened, taken from a lecture by then U. Mass./Amherst (now New School) economist Richard Wolff:[12]

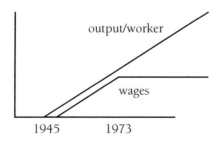

Where has all the money gone—the difference between those productivity gains and workers' wages? Who has been buying the products? Why hasn't the economy been in recession for the last quarter-century or so—as the Marxian analysis would suggest should have been the case?

Some of the money has been invested in the real economy—hence productivity has continued to grow. Much of the "surplus," however, went into paper assets (stocks and bonds) and real estate, inflating asset values. As a measure of these paper "investments," consider the following sequence: in 1956 the Dow Jones Industrial Average reached 500; sixteen years later, 1972, it reached 1000; fifteen years later, 1987, it hit 2000, then exploded to 8000 ten years later (1997), then to 14,000 ten years after that (2007). That is to say, the Dow only doubled during the "Golden Age" (during which period wages doubled as well); it then increased fourteen-fold between during the flat-wage period.

The real estate boom was later in coming. Housing prices increased only 1 percent per year between 1975 and 1997,[13] but then the rate of increase jumped six-fold, to 6 percent/year between 1997 and 2006.[14]

This explosion of asset values produced what economists call the "wealth effect." When people feel richer, they spend more. And major asset holders have become very much richer in recent times. Between 1995 and 2004 the number of millionaires (in 2004 dollars) more than doubled, as did the number of households worth more than $5million, more than $10 million, more than $25 million. Krugman notes that if we define a "billionaire" as someone whose wealth is greater than the output of 20,000 average workers ($1billion in mid-1990s), there were 16 in 1957, 13 in 1968. There are 160 now.[15]

In recent years, the wealthy have increased their own consumption dramatically, purchasing private jets, ever larger yachts, ever more spectacular villas, etc., creating what *Wall Street Journal* reporter Robert Frank has labeled "Richistan," a separate country within our country. (Three unnamed members of this country provided Frank with their annual expense statements. To cite but one: yachts—$20 million; air charters/private jets—$3 million; house staff—$2.2 million; personal beauty/salon/spa—$200,000, including $80,000 for massages.[16])

But still, even with their yachts and villas and private jets and massages, the upper one or two percent of the population can't consume nearly enough to keep the economy humming. Another large portion of total surplus—far more important than the portion consumed by the *über*-rich—has been loaned to working people. In effect, instead of raising wages, the capitalist class has lent out a large piece of their profits to the working class—to be repaid with interest, of course. The "debt explosion," which parallels the asset-value explosion, has been striking. Consider two statistics: (1) In 1975 outstanding household debt stood at 47 percent GDP. It currently stands at 100 percent. That is to say, the amount of debt people are in, adjusted for inflation, is twice what it was thirty years ago. (2) Personal outlays as share of disposable income was 88% in 1981—i.e., the average household saved 12% of its income). Today it is 100%—i.e, zero net savings.[17] (This doesn't mean that nobody saves. It means that massive amounts of the social surplus have been loaned out to finance consumer spending.) Over the last several decades there has been a massive increase in debt: home equity loans, credit card debt, students loans, automobile loans. Never before have so many borrowed so much.[18]

Consider this logical truth: What can't go on, won't. This applies full force to the situation in which we find ourselves today. Debt levels cannot keep increasing indefinitely when incomes are stationary, especially when compound interest begin taking its toll. Moreover, as we have begun to realize, when debt levels are high, monetary stimulus doesn't work. Tax cuts or rebates are used to pay down debts, not buy more stuff. Banks may be given cash, but they are reluctant to lend it out, since borrowers are already over-leveraged.

Might we be able to reform the system so as to return to a high wage, social democratic, post-WWII-type economy? This possibility would seem to be out of reach. We are now living in a global economy. High wages drive businesses abroad. Indeed, this need to stay globally competitive was a key factor in ending the social democratic "class compromise" in the first place.

What is to be done? It is sobering to realize that Keynesian stimulations of the standard sort, the kinds undertaken by the Roosevelt administration and now by the Obama administration, did not bring an end to the Great Depression. Although the recovery officially began in March of 1933 as the economy began to expand again, the unemployment rate, which had dropped from 25% in 1933 to 14% in 1937, shot up again to 19% the following year. (It had been 3.2% in 1929.) It wasn't Roosevelt's welfare and employment provisions that ended the Great Depression. As Krugman reminds us, "it took the giant public works project known as World War II—a project that finally silenced the penny pinchers—to bring the Depression to an end."[19]

But for us—there isn't going to be a World War III. Nuclear war is too destructive for even our most jingoistic to contemplate seriously, and our embarrassing, tragic debacles in Iraq and Afghanistan have demonstrated unequivocally the limits of conventional warfare. This is not bad news—for us as human beings, that is—but it does close off another Keynesian route out of the current crisis.

So—if traditional Keynesian monetary and fiscal policies can't end this recession, and if there's not going to be another major war to pull us out, what are we going to do? Frankly, it is not clear to me that there is anything we can do to get us out of the economic mess we are in—short a restructuring of our basic economic institutions that goes well beyond anything currently contemplated by even the most radical elements of "respectable" opinion.

Of course I may be wrong. Perhaps a combination of judicious policies and good luck will pull us out of this recession. But even if this should turn out to be the case, we are far from home free. For there is another major crisis waiting in the wings, one presciently foreseen by Habermas thirty-eight years ago.

III. Back to Habermas

As the present crisis makes clear, a healthy capitalism requires economic growth. When growth falters, we don't glide smoothly to a steady-state economy. We crash. So, when growth slows, we scramble madly to "stimulate" the economy, to get people buying again, consuming more. But this growth imperative presents us with a profound problem. Habermas called it the "ecological balance."

> The established mechanisms of growth . . . are faced with two important material limitations: on the one hand, the supply of finite resources—the area of cultivatable and inhabitable land, fresh water, . . . and non-regenerating raw materials . . . ; on the other hand, the capacities of irreplaceable ecological systems to absorb pollutants, such as radioactive byproducts, or *carbon dioxide.*
>
> Even on optimistic assumptions *one* absolute limitation on growth can be stated (if not for the time being, precisely determined): namely, the limit of the environment's ability to absorb heat from energy consumption. If economic growth is necessarily coupled to increasing consumption of energy, and if all natural energy that is transformed into economically useful energy is ultimately released as heat . . . then the increased consumption of energy must result, in the long run, in *a global rise in temperature.* (According to the present state of knowledge the critical interval is about 75–150 years.) (42–3, my emphases)

These words were written nearly forty years ago. I do not need to tell you that they are not dated. Of course, not all growth stresses the environment. If unemployed people are put to work installing solar panels on rooftops, the economy grows. But no one pretends that most of the growth will be of this sort.

My argument thus far is this: (a) The current tools available to the government are insufficient to bring us out of the current economic crisis and back to a social democratic "advanced capitalism" that appeared to have found a solution to such crises. (b) Should this claim prove to be false, we would soon be confronted with another, even less tractable, potentially more devastating, crisis. One the one hand Uncle Sam urges to "spend, spend, spend"—before it is too late. On the other hand, environmentalists scream that our over-consumption is killing the planet. To use Habermas's terminology, we in the midst of a full-scale rationality crisis. What follows?

Not revolution—at least not immediately or automatically. According to Habermas, a necessary precondition for systems change is for the rationality crisis to provoke a legitimation crisis. That has not yet happened. To be sure there is widespread distrust of the elites who govern us, more now than at any time in recent history. The general public has long been cynical about politicians. The travesty of the Bush Administration deepened this cynicism. Corporate CEOs, who have seen their pay skyrocket from 40 times the average worker in the 1970s to nearly 400 times now, are also in disrepute. (Witness the reception accorded the CEOs of Ford, Chrysler and GM when they appeared before Congress.) The "Masters of the Universe," those Wall Street wizards who made so much money because they were (presumably) so much smarter than the rest of us have also tumbled from their pedestals.

What follows? Conventional wisdom does not envisage fundamental change. Even so perceptive a thinker as Joseph Stiglitz, while predicting "most likely a long and extended downturn," is sure that "we will recover eventually. That's not a question."[20] But suppose conventional wisdom proves wrong. Suppose the current rescue efforts fail—as FDR's failed—and that no World War comes along to save capitalism. Suppose more and more people come to see the present system as inherently flawed, in need of *radical* restructuring. What if we do wind up with a full-blown legitimation crisis? What then?

According to Habermas, the next stage is a "motivation crisis." But what exactly is that? Habermas's discussion of this stage is intriguing in its details, but murkier than his discussion of the other crisis stages regarding outcome. His basic thesis is that the motivational patterns essential for the functioning of advanced capitalism—civil privatism and familial-vocational privatism—are being systematically eroded, while at the same time the emergence of functionally equivalent motivations are precluded by the developmental logic of normative structures. This developmental logic points to universal values derived from a communicative ethics, and—his key claim—these values are incompatible with capitalism.

Advanced capitalism is formally democratic, but it depends for its existence in the passive acquiescence of the citizenry to rule by those who will protect the interests of the capitalist class.[21] But there is a deep tension here, for "the political theories of the bourgeois revolutions demanded *active* civic participation in democratically organized will-formation" (76). According to Habermas, this tension has been contained by the authoritarian residues of pre-bourgeois culture. We have long been conditioned to accept elite rule, rule by "the fathers," who always know best. But patriarchal ideology, and with it the "authoritarian personality" that so worried first-generation critical theorists, is disappearing. The authoritarian father has largely vanished, in part because of the women's movement, in part because of more egalitarian patterns of child rearing, in part because fathers (and middle class parents generally) can no longer protect their children's economic future as they once could (a point made eloquently by Barbara Ehrenreich in her classic *Fear of Falling*[22]).

There are other motivational problems. Education no longer guarantees commensurate employment. More and more young people are receiving more and more education, but "the connection between formal schooling and occupational success [is becoming] looser" (81). Moreover, "fragmented and monotonous labor processes are increasingly penetrating even those sectors in which an identity could previously be formed through the occupational role. Intrinsic motivation to achieve is less and less supported by the structure of labor processes in spheres of labor dependent on the market" (82).

Suppose we do experience a profound "motivation crisis." How might the motivation crisis be resolved? Moral chaos and societal breakdown would seem to be the logical result, although Habermas does not say this explicitly. (That's what happened in the Soviet Union.) He worries about the replacement of the current system by "an administrative system shielded from parties and the public," one that no longer needs ethical legitimation, and hence is no longer threatened by a motivation crisis. But Habermas is not willing to accept the anti-democratic claim that this is the only choice for highly complex societies.[23]

Habermas's hope lies with the young—better and more highly educated than ever before, less susceptible to authoritarian (patriarchal) leaders, more imbued with universal values.

But what are the "young radicals" to do? They should not "retreat to a Marxistically embellished orthodoxy," for we must have "theoretical clarity about what we do *not* know." The orthodox left thinks it knows more than it does. The young are called upon instead to "expose the stress limits of advanced capitalism to conspicuous tests" and to take up the struggle against "the stabilization of a nature-like social system over the heads of its citizens," a system that would give up on a concept Habermas refuses to relinquish: "old European human dignity" (143).

And then? *Legitimation Crisis* stops cold at this point. We are left hanging. The book ends. We are left with critique, with protest, with struggle—but no indication whatsoever as to what positive program these "young radicals" might advocate, no guidance as to what their ultimate vision might be.

IV. Beyond Habermas, Back to the Present, On to the Future

I don't think we should fault Habermas for not providing us with a theoretical sketch of a better alternative. There was so much (as he realized) that we did not know then. Think for a moment of the economic "experiments" going strong in the mid-1970s: The Soviet Union's centrally-planned economy had not yet entered its terminal decline; the East German planning model appeared promising to some; Maoist China was promoting a distinctive "Chinese road to socialism;" there were experiments with markets under socialism underway in Hungary; there was an experiment with both markets and worker self-management in Yugoslavia. How was this all going to play out? No one knew at the time. No one could know.

That was then, 1973, and this is now, 2011. We know more now than we did back then—and we are in the midst of an economic slump more serious than anything heretofore experienced in the postwar West. What are the alternatives facing us now?

- A return to neoliberalism? For a quarter of a century, since the Reagan-Thatcher "Revolution," neoliberalism has reigned supreme—and it has brought us to the present catastrophe (and wreaked havoc throughout the global south). To be sure, there are idiots who never learn (most of the Republican Party), but, should they be successful at turning back the clock, "the worst will continue to worsen."

- Fascism, friendly or otherwise? Despite the perennial fears of many on the Left, this option would not seem likely either. Fascism as an economic model (authoritarian capitalism) has been tried, not only by Mussolini and Hitler, but also by a large number of anti-communist military and civilian dictatorships since WWII. None of these economies has flourished. None of instigating regimes has survived. I don't see fascism as a threat, at least not at this point in time.

- A return to social democracy? This was the Obama promise: a revitalization of the "welfare state," including universal health care, a return to an active fiscal policy, with tax cuts to stimulate consumption and a large federally-funded jobs program. It remains the program of most Left forces. I see these as important steps in the right direction, but, as I have argued, they don't address the underlying problem: massive indebtedness due to low wages. I have argued that there would seem to be no way to return to that "Golden Age" of ever rising real wages, certainly not in the Age of Globalization. Moreover, an economy that requires ever increasing consumption to stay healthy is ecologically unsustainable.

- A new form of socialism. Hmmmm. Let's think about that.

Mainstream opinion still finds this option incredible. In his *The Return of Depression Economics and the Crisis of 2008*, Paul Krugman asks,

> Who now can use the words of socialism with a straight face? As a member of the baby boomer generation, I can remember when the idea of revolution, of brave men pushing history forward, had a certain glamour. Now it is a sick joke. . . . The truth is that the heart has gone out of the opposition to capitalism.[24]

This is the mainstream view, to be sure, but then, surprisingly, Krugman strikes a different note, just a paragraph later:

> Capitalism is secure, not only because of its successes—which have been very real—but because no one has a plausible alternative. This situation will not last forever. Surely there will be other ideologies, other dreams, and they will emerge sooner rather than later if the Great Recession persists and deepens.[25]

Perhaps the time is right for dreams and dreamers. Perhaps philosophers can make a contribution here. We shouldn't forget our roots. Plato wasn't shy about dreaming of an ideal society, a just society—however daunting the transition question. John Rawls urged us to be "realistically utopian." "Political philosophy is realistically utopian," he says, "when it extends what are ordinarily thought of as the limits of practical political possibility." Such philosophy, following Rousseau, "takes men as they are, and laws as they might be" as the basis for constructing and defending an ideal that exists as yet "nowhere," but is in fact within our reach.[26]

It is important to realize that we could have a full-employment, democratic economy that is immune to financial speculation and the havoc such speculation can wreak, and—at least as significant—an economy that does not need to grow to remain healthy. This aspiration is a "dream"—but not an impossible dream.

Let us begin, not with an abstract model, but with what we now know in light of the economic experiments of the past century.

- We now know that competitive markets are essential to the functioning of a complex, developed economy. This is the *negative* lesson of the socialist experiments of the twentieth century. Markets cannot be replaced wholesale by planning.

- We now know that some sort of democratic regulation of investment flows is essential to rational, stable, sustainable development—for individual countries and for the world economy as a whole. This is the *negative* lesson of the neoliberal experiments of the last thirty years, now culminating in a global meltdown. Financial markets are not to be trusted. They are not benign. We need some sort of "investment democracy" to complement the "consumer democracy" of the goods and services market.

There is something else we know—at least those of us who study such things. Actually, most people do not know this important fact. It is not something talked about on television or in polite company. It is too embarrassing.

- We now know that productive enterprises can be run democratically with little or no loss of efficiency, often with a gain in efficiency, and almost always with considerable gain in employment security. This is the positive lesson of a great many recent experiments in alternative forms of workplace organization.

This fact is embarrassing, because it raises an awkward question. Why is it that in a country such as ours that celebrates, indeed almost deifies, democracy, that allows us to elect our mayors, our state and local legislators, the national leaders that can send us off to kill or be killed . . . why is it that in such a country we can't elect our bosses?

The obvious answer is that workplace democracy doesn't work, that ordinary workers don't have the competence or self-discipline to select good managers. The problem with this obvious answer is that it is empirically false. There are thousands of successful worker-run enterprises operating around the world. These have been extensively studied. To my knowledge there does not exist a single comparative study that finds the authoritarian (i.e., capitalist) model superior to the democratic one.[27]

For students of democracy this result is not surprising. To be sure, there are problems with democracy. Excessive debate can be time-consuming, hindering timely action. Good leadership can be stifled it doesn't have adequate autonomy.

Majorities can oppress minorities. These are standard problems in all democracies, for which there are standard solutions. Representative structures must be put in place; management must be given sufficient power and autonomy to make difficult decisions without being second-guessed at every turn; laws must protect minority rights.

With the right structures in place, workplace democracy works. Not perfectly. Bad managers are sometimes appointed. Bad decisions are sometimes made. Democratic firms sometimes fail. But Winston Churchill's dictum appears to hold: "Democracy is the worst form of government—except for all the others that have been tried from time to time."[28]

Given what we now know, how might we structure an economy such as our own to give us a Rawlian "realistic utopia"? Let me give you a picture of what I like to call "Economic Democracy. Let's start with the three basic institutions.

The first is the market. Economic Democracy is a competitive market economy. Incentives remain in place for firms to use their resources efficiently, to innovate and to respond effectively to consumer demand.

The second basic institution is workplace democracy. Most (but not all) enterprises are run democratically by workers, whose incomes are no longer wages, but shares (not necessarily equal) of profits. Workers elect a workers council, one worker, one vote, to fill the role currently filled by a corporation's Board of Directors, namely, to select upper management and to oversee major enterprise decisions.

The third basic institution is what I call "social control of investment." Private financial markets are replaced by a public investment banking. Investment funds come, not from private savers, but from a flat-rate capital-assets tax levied on all business enterprises. (It is important to break the link between private savings and investment funds if we are to gain democratic control over the latter.) All of these revenues are returned to state and local investment banks, each region receiving its per-capita share. All the collected taxes are reinvested in the economy. Loans are granted only to those projects that promise to be profitable, but priority is given to those that create the most employment.

To these three basic institutions (the market, workplace democracy and social control of investment), let us add three supplements:

- The government will serve as an employer of last resort. All able-bodied people who want to work will have a job.

- A network of private and cooperative Savings and Loan associations will exist to provide home mortgages and other consumer loans. (In Economic Democracy, the allocation of capital for business investment is kept sharply distinct from providing credit for consumer purchases.)

- Economic Democracy will retain a capitalist sector, comprised of small businesses and larger "entrepreneurial firms." (An "entrepreneurial firm" is one whose founder remains actively involved in its management. When the entrepreneur retires, or wishes to cash out, he sells the firm to the state, which then turns it over its employees to be run democratically.)

Let me ask you to take it on faith (or at least to suspend disbelief) that such a system is economically viable. I have argued the case at length in both *Against Capitalism* and *After Capitalism*.[29] The important point I wish to make here is that Economic Democracy is not vulnerable to the kind of economic crisis we are now experiencing.

The basic reason is quite simple. Apart from locally-based savings and loan associations, there are no private financial markets in Economic Democracy. Markets for goods and services remain, but there are no stock markets, bond markets, hedge funds, private equity firms, or investment banks concocting collateralized debt obligations, currency swaps and all the other sorts of derivatives. So there's no possibility of financial speculation, no possibility of "irrational exuberance."

The financial system is quite transparent. A capital assets tax is collected from businesses, then loaned out to enterprises wanting to expand, or to individuals wanting to start new businesses. Loan officers are public officials, whose salaries are tied to loan performances.

Consider the crisis we are now experiencing, the proximate cause of which was the bursting of the housing bubble. Such a housing bubble, fueled by the massive demand for mortgage-backed securities, couldn't happen under Economic Democracy, since there are no such securities. Home mortgages are still issued, but these stay with the Savings and Loan of origin, who have every reason to scrutinize potential loan recipients with care. They aren't sold off to be "securitized," (thus relieving the banks of all risk). Nor is there a vast pool of money, (wealthy investors, pension funds, etc.) out there looking for speculative opportunities, eager to make lots of money with their money. (It is interesting to note that Krugman, in spelling out his own plan for economic recovery projects that "it will come close to full temporary nationalization of a significant part of the financial system"—though he is quick to add, "this isn't a long term goal, a matter of seizing the economy's commanding heights: finance should be reprivatized as soon as it is safe to do so." He doesn't say why. Clearly, he wants to reassure everyone that he is not a closet socialist, "for nothing could be worse than failing to do what is necessary out of fear that acting to save the financial system is somehow 'socialism.'"[30])

Economic Democracy is vulnerable neither to speculative excesses nor to the deeper problem confronting a capitalist economy, namely, insufficient effective demand, due ultimately to the fact that wages are a cost of production. Wages are not a cost of production in a democratic firm. Workers get a specified share of the firm's profit, not a wage—so all productivity gains are captured by the firm's workforce. There are no excess profits seeking an investment outlet.

You will recall that capitalism faces two types of crisis: economic crises such as the one we are now facing, due to deficient effective demand, and ecological crises, derived from the fact that a capitalist economy must constantly grow to remain healthy. Economic Democracy is better positioned than capitalism to avoid ecological crises, for several structural reasons.

It is a fundamental fact about a democratic firm, long noted in the theoretical literature, that it lacks the expansionary dynamic of a capitalist firm.[31] Democratic firms tend to maximize profit per worker, not total profits. That is to say, doubling the size of a capitalist firm will double the owners' profits, whereas doubling the size of a democratic firm leaves everyone's per capita share the same. In short, democratic firms are not incentivized to grow. Unless there are serious economies of scale involved, bigger is not better.

Moreover—a second structural reason—since funds for investment in an Economic Democracy come from taxes (the capital assets tax), not from private investors, the economy is not hostage to "investor confidence." So it does not have to keep growing to remain healthy. Economic Democracy can be a stable, sustainable "no-growth economy," whereas, as I have argued elsewhere, "sustainable capitalism" is an oxymoron.[32]

Actually, "no-growth" is a misnomer. Productivity increases under Economic Democracy still occur, but they are more likely to translate into increased leisure than increased consumption. The economy will continue to experience "growth," but the growth will be mostly in free time, not consumption. Hence, we might be able, at long last, to slow down, spend more time with family and friends, read the books, listen to the music, see the films we've long wanted to read, listen to and see. We might even have time to smell the flowers.

Interestingly enough, Keynes himself speculated about the tenor of life in a society no longer plagued by material scarcity. In a remarkable essay written shortly after the onset of the Great Depression, he muses about the "Economic Possibilities for Our Grandchildren."

> We shall use the new-found bounty of nature quite differently than the way he rich use it today, and will map out for ourselves a plan of life quite otherwise than theirs. . . . What work there still remains to be done will be as widely shared as possible— three hour shifts, or a fifteen-hour week. . . . There will also be great changes in our morals. . . . I see us free to return to some of the most sure and certain principles of religion and traditional virtue—that avarice is a vice, that the extraction of usury is a misdemeanor, and the love of money is detestable, that those walk most truly in the paths of virtue and sane wisdom who take least thought for the morrow. . . . We shall honor those who can teach us how to pluck the hour and the day virtuously and well, the delightful people who are capable of taking direct enjoyment in things.[33]

Keynes wrote these words in 1930, at a time when "the prevailing world depression, the enormous anomaly of unemployment, the disastrous mistakes we have made, blind us to what is going on under the surface."[34] He was wrong, of course. The grandchildren of his generation may have lived in a post-war social democracy that looks good to us now, mired as we are in recession, but they were still far from the promised land.

Keynes was wrong—or was he? In fact, he was not referring literally to his grandchildren, but metaphorically. His projection was for "a hundred years hence," i.e., 2030. Might there be things "going on under the surface" right now that could bring us to sustainable, democratic, human world?

V. On Revolution, i.e., On Getting from Here to There

Can we even imagine a transition from the deeply irrational, ultimately unsustainable economic system we presently inhabit to a democratic, socialist economy, where enterprises are run democratically, and economic stability no longer requires keeping our capitalists happy?

I think we can. Let's try. Suppose we do get a financial meltdown on the scale of the Great Depression. (That's certainly not hard to imagine. It was a couple of years ago, but no longer.) And suppose we had a government newly elected, determined to effect this transition. What would our new administration have to do?

The first thing would be to assure everyone, à la Franklin Roosevelt, that there's nothing to fear but fear itself. Remind everyone that we are not facing an incurable plague or nuclear war. Pieces of paper have suddenly lost their value, but our resources are still intact; our skill base is still intact. There's no reason for ordinary people to lose their jobs or see their incomes plummet—no material reason, that is.

What next? Well, since the stock market has tanked, let the government step in and buy up those now near-worthless shares of the publicly-traded non-financial corporations. The government can print the money, if need be. (As we know, in a depression it is essential to stimulate the economy by pumping money into it.) Suddenly our government has controlling interest in all the major corporations. Notice, these assets have not been "expropriated" by the government. They have been paid for at full market value. Whatever "expropriation" there might have been was done by those free-wheeling financial markets. (Marx might be amused. The expropriators have not been expropriated by the working class, as he had projected. They've done it to themselves.)

Let's now turn these enterprises over to the employees, to be run democratically. The employees (now voting members of their enterprise) can keep the existing management—indeed, for six months or so, let's insist that they do, while worker councils are set up to replace the boards of directors that used to represent the shareholders and oversee management. After six months, they can keep their managers or replace them as they see fit.

Thus are the "commanding heights" of the economy democratized. The workers don't own the firm. As taxpayers, we'll keep title. But the employees, not government officials, will control it. The firm won't pay dividends to shareholders anymore, for there aren't any shareholders. Instead they'll pay a leasing fee (capital-assets tax) to the government.

What about the financial sector? To begin with, let's nationalize all those financial institutions that are "too big to fail." (Indeed, this has happened already with Fannie Mae, Freddie Mac, and AIG.) Let's go further. Let's nationalize all our banks and other financial institutions.

Let's restructure our banking system, making it into something that more closely resembles the system we had in place before deregulation set in some three decades ago. Let's have a network of Savings and Loan associations that will handle home mortgages and other consumer loans. Funds will be deposited by private savers, and loaned out to creditworthy customers.

Let's also have a system of investment banks. These are the institutions responsible for providing credit to the business sector. This is the economically crucial sector. But let's not generate the funds for these banks by trying to entice private individuals to save. Let's not rely on the "animal spirits" of the wealthy for the liquidity necessary to keep our economy going. Let's generate these funds from a capital-assets tax.

There's another thing we should do. A lot of people have seen their pensions disappear. Let's restore those pensions. We'll pick a date before the crash. Whatever value a person's holdings in a pension fund was at that date will be transferred to that person's social security account, to be paid out as an annuity supplement to that person's basic social security income, when s/he retires.

One final thing: let's make the government the employer-of-last-resort. Decent, if low-wage, jobs will be available to anyone who cannot find employment in the capitalist or cooperative or administrative sectors of the economy.

That's it. The basic structure of our new, democratic socialist economy is in place. We've had a peaceful, productive, non-violent Revolution—not so different, abstractly, from the relatively peaceful, non-violent revolutions of 1989–1991 that so radically transformed Eastern Europe and Russia. Not so different—and yet completely different.

Let me close on a more philosophical note. Let us think of the philosophical tradition embracing Kant, Hegel, Marx and extending through Habermas that regards the human species as engaged in the process of creating an ever more rational world, grounded in freedom. The process is slow, often opaque, often subject to reversals, and yet, ultimately, there is a direction to history, and it is a direction that should give us hope.

I think there are good grounds for endorsing this view. We are, after all, a deeply pragmatic species, with an astonishing capacity for creative development.

When confronted with problems, we try to solve them. We experiment. We learn from our mistakes. If a solution exists, sooner or later we hit upon it.

I submit that we are reaching the point where we it is becoming clear that the old order has exhausted itself and is incapable of solving the problems that it has created. This thought is as yet consciously acknowledged by relatively few, but it is intuitively felt by many more. We may not be far from seeing that there is a better way. We cannot say with certainty that democracy, freedom, and rationality will prevail, but there will almost surely be a struggle. If progressive forces are to prevail, it will involve the efforts of millions. The slogan has already been articulated by the global justice movement: ANOTHER WORLD IS POSSIBLE. The task now is to actualize that possibility.

Impossible? Let me end with a final quote:

Whoever still lives, should never say never!

The secure is not secure.

So, the way it is, it will not remain.

—Bertold Brecht

David Schweickart, Loyola University Chicago

Notes

1. "Macroeconomic Priorities," *The American Economic Review* 93.1 (March 2003): 1.

2. Paul Krugman, *The Return of Depression Economics and the Crisis of 2008* (New York: Norton, 2009), 10.

3. Quoted by Nick Paumbarten, "In For It," *The New Yorker*, November 11, 2008, 44.

4. He doesn't use that self-description in *Legitimation Crisis*, but in an interview published in the special issue of *Telos* honoring his fiftieth birthday, Habermas remarks, "For us, as Marxists, there is the problem of interpreting the experiences of these movements [for black liberation, women's liberation, nuclear disarmament]" (Spring 1979: 165). So far as I know, Habermas has never repudiated that identification.

5. Page numbers given in the text refer to the English translation (by Thomas McCarthy) of *Legitimation Crisis* (Boston: Beacon, 1975).

6. Paul Samuelson, *Economics* (New York: McGraw-Hill, 1973), 883. Samuelson offered other scenarios as well, but did not take sides, claiming the various projections "represent the spread of best expert opinion."

7. Krugman, *Return of Depression Economics*, 3.

8. Mortimer Zuckerman, "Nine Reasons the Economy is Not Getting Better," *U.S. News and World Reports*, July 13, 2009.

9.   Cf. the last chapter of *Return of Depression Economics,* which also appeared in the December 15, 2008 issue of the *New York Review of Books,* pp. 8–10, entitled "What to Do About the Financial Crisis." Specifically, he proposes that we (1) get credit flowing again (by getting more capital into the system, (2) engage in "good old fiscal stimulus [by] sustaining and expanding government spending—sustaining it by providing aid to state and local governments, expanding it with spending on roads, bridges and other forms of infrastructure," and (3) rescue developing countries. We should then turn our attention to reform, bringing all institutions that act like banks under regulatory supervision the same as banks. For an overview of Krugman's critique, see *Newsweek,* April 6, 2009, whose cover features Krugman with the caption, "Obama is Wrong."

10.   Paul Krugman, *The Conscience of a Liberal* (New York: Norton, 2007), 3.

11.   Ibid. 124–7.

12.   This figure is taken from a videotaped lecture delivered October 5, 2008, available at http:/tinyurl.com/3pthrx.

13.   Barry Cynamon and Steven Fazzari, "Household Debt in the Consumer Age: Source of Growth, Risk of Collapse," *Capitalism and Society* 3.2 (2008): 23.

14.   Luci Ellis, "The Housing Meltdown: Why Did It Happen in the United States?" *Bank for International Settlements Working Paper, No. 259* (September 2008), 3.

15.   Krugman, *Conscience,* 18

16.   Robert Frank, *Richistan: A Journey Through the American Wealth Boom and the Lives of the New Rich* (New York: Crown Publishers, 2007), 151.

17.   Cynamon and Fazzari, "Household Debt," 18, 8.

18.   Home equity loans became available in late 1980s. In 2005 mortgage equity withdrawals reached $800b, a full 9 percent of disposable income, up from 2 percent in 1995. (See Robert Brenner, *The Economics of Global Turbulance* [New York: Verso, 2006], 321.) Credit card debt is equally substantial, and has also mushroomed over the last several decades, from $55b in 1980 to $880b in 2006. Even when adjusted for inflation, the expansion is astonishing—up seven-fold from 1980. (See *2008 New York Times Almanac* [New York: Penguin, 2007], 334.) Student loans have also increased substantially. Some 8.5 million post-secondary students and their parents owe $87 billion. Today the typical graduate of a four-year college or university owes $20,000, more than double what the typical graduate owed a decade ago. (See Lynnette Khalfani, *Zero Debt College Grads* [New York: Kaplan Publishing, 2007], vii–viii.) Automobile loans dwarf student loans. An estimated $575 billion in new and used auto loans are written every year, large numbers of which (100 percent of those originating with the automaker financiers) are repackaged and sold as securities. The average amount financed was $30,738 in 2007, up 40 percent in the last decade. (See Ken Bensinger, "New Cars That Are Fully Loaded—With Debt," *Los Angeles Times,* December 30, 2007, A-1.)

19.   Paul Krugman, "Back to What Obama Must Do," *Rolling Stone* (January 14, 2009).

20.   Interview with Amy Goodman, following Obama's February 24, 2009 address to the nation. Cf. democracynow.org.

21.   This requirement was stated openly by Harvard's Samuel Huntington, in his report on the "democratic distemper" to the David Rockefeller's Trilateral Commission, back in the days

when political activism was beginning to scare political elites: "The effective operation of a democratic political system usually requires some measure of apathy and non-involvement." Michael Crozier, Samuel Huntingon, and Joji Watanuki, *The Crisis of Democracy: Report on the Governability of Democracies to the Trilateral Commission* (New York University Press, 1975), 114.

22. Barbara Ehrenreich, *Fear of Falling: The Inner Life of the Middle Class* (New York: Pantheon, 1989).

23. Niklas Luhmann, Germany's leading systems-theorist at the time, was an influential proponent of this thesis. Habermas engages Luhman's argument at length in the penultimate section of *Legitimation Crisis*.

24. Krugman, *Return of Depression Economics*, 14.

25. Ibid. He adds, "But for now capitalism rules the world unchallenged."

26. John Rawls, *The Law of Peoples* (Cambridge, MA: Havard University Press, 1999), 6–7.

27. For a sampling of the evidence see my *After Capitalism*, 2nd Edition (Lanham, MD: Rowman and Littlefield, 2011), 60–2.

28. *The Official Report*, House of Commons (5th Series), vol. 444, 11 November 1947, 206–7.

29. David Schweickart, *Against Capitalism* (Cambridge: Cambridge University Press, 1993), *After Capitalism*, (Lanham, MD: Rowman and Littlefield, 2002), and *After Capitalism*, Revised Edition (Lanham, MD: Rowman and Littlefield, 2011).

30. Krugman, *Return of Depression Economics*, 186.

31. Cf. Benjamin Ward, "Market Syndicalism," American Economic Review 48 (1958): 566–89.

32. David Schweickart, "Is Sustainable Capitalism an Oxymoron?" *Perspectives on Global Development and Technology* 8 (2009): 557–78.

33. John Maynard Keynes, "Economic Possibilities for Our Grandchildren," In *Essays in Persuasion* (New York: Norton, 1963), 368–72.

34. Ibid. 359.

Part II:
THE 2010 NASSP
PRESIDENTIAL ADDRESS

The Voluntary Transactions Principle and the Free Market Ideal

ALISTAIR M. MACLEOD

I. Introduction: Freedom, Markets, and Free Markets

Everyone is in favor of freedom. Everyone is in favor of markets. Yet not everyone is a fan of the free market ideal. Are those who favor freedom and who favor markets but who don't favor "free markets" being inconsistent?

The answer depends, unsurprisingly, on how "free markets" are conceived. According to one widely accepted view of the free market ideal—the view to which "neo-liberals" subscribe—the voluntariness of market transactions is a sufficient condition of their defensibility, and laws or regulations that restrict the options of market participants are consequently looked at askance. If this conception of the free market ideal is thought to be canonical, then the complex view that one can be in favor of both freedom and markets without being committed to the free market ideal cannot be dismissed as internally inconsistent. On the contrary, it arguably embodies an important truth, a truth that is often obscured by propagandists for a neo-liberal economic doctrine.

However, the three claims embedded in the view that one can be in favor of freedom and in favor of markets, yet not in favor of the free market ideal—claims that constitute an intriguing triad—need not be taken to be inconsistent. The reason is that the neo-liberal conception of the free market ideal cannot be regarded as canonical, either historically or philosophically.

It isn't canonical historically, for example, because the great Scottish moral philosopher, Adam Smith—often regarded as the father of modern economics—whose deployment of the metaphor of the "invisible hand" in his description of the workings of the market is erroneously invoked by neo-liberals as the progenitor of their version of the free market ideal, did not endorse the neo-liberal vision of free markets. Recent work by both economists and philosophers on what Adam Smith actually believed about the institution of the market has shown that neo-liberal admirers of Adam Smith—like Milton Friedman and Alan Greenspan—have as-cribed to him a conception of the free market ideal that he would have repudiated.[1]

The neo-liberal conception of the free market ideal is also no longer regarded as canonical philosophically, partly because Adam Smith's views have been snatched back from the clutches of his neo-liberal admirers, but also for a second, more important, reason. With the resurgence of interest in political philosophy sparked by the appearance of John Rawls's *A Theory of Justice* and by some of the social movements that got underway in the 1960's, the attention of philosophers has been focused on questions about the normative rationale for institutional arrangements in all the areas of social life (legal, political, economic, cultural, religious, etc.). It has become clear that there are more ways than one of conceiving of free markets and that the neo-liberal conception is at best only one of these.[2] A choice consequently has to be made among these alternative conceptions of the free market ideal—a choice that must reflect not only a wide range of empirical considerations but also, crucially, the relevant normative considerations, including (perhaps especially) considerations of justice and fairness.[3]

II. Free Markets and the Voluntary Transactions Principle

If the choice among conceptions of the free market is to be made judiciously, an initial point of agreement among sponsors of rival conceptions should be noted. On any plausible account of the principle that provides the normative underpinning for defensible free market arrangements, it is the principle that calls for market participants to interact voluntarily. It is the principle that calls for the deals they strike and the agreements they reach when goods and services are bought, sold, or exchanged to be fully voluntary.

It is tempting to suppose that this means that the voluntary transactions principle (as it might be dubbed) sanctions any market transaction that is voluntarily entered into by market participants, no matter what its content or its consequences happen to be. It is tempting to suppose, to put the same point somewhat differently, that the voluntariness of a marketplace transaction is a sufficient condition of its defensibility.

While this supposition is perhaps tempting, it must be rejected.[4] When anti-combines (or anti-trust) legislation prohibits voluntary transactions that lead to the merging of corporate enterprises if the mergers threaten to undermine market competition, no challenge is being issued to the free market ideal. When the freedom of market-participants is restricted in order to protect at least the most fundamental interests of potentially affected third-parties, there need be no breach of the free market ideal. And the free market ideal doesn't have to be jettisoned when the options available to the parties when they negotiate the terms on which they will do business have to be circumscribed in various ways—whether by rules that require the payment of transaction-related taxes, or by rules that outlaw goods and services of certain sorts (dangerous drugs and weapons, for example, or freelance "enforcement" services), or by rules that call for disclosure of adequate information about marketable goods and services, or by contract-related rules that prohibit unconscionable or exploitative terms, and so on. While there may be disagreement among defenders of particular versions of the free market ideal about the defensibility of some of the constraints to which market participants are subject—disagreement, accordingly, about the precise content and scope of the voluntary transactions principle—the important general point is that the mere existence of freedom-restricting rules and regulations cannot be cited as evidence that the free market ideal is being abandoned. There is no plausible interpretation of this ideal that would give market participants *carte blanche*—wholly unrestricted freedom—in setting the terms on which they interact.

The fact that markets that constrain economic transactions in a variety of ways can nevertheless be regarded as exemplifying (some version of) the free market ideal shows that the crucial normative issues have to do, not with affirmation of the desirability of having market participants interact voluntarily—that can be taken for granted—but with vindication of the constraints to which the voluntary transactions principle must be subject if it is to provide a defensible rationale for free market arrangements. What is fundamentally at stake in disputes about the best way to conceive of free market arrangements is determination of the content and scope of the voluntary transactions principle through identification of the kinds of constraints to which market participants ought to be subject when they seek to interact with one another on a voluntary basis. There is no necessary contradiction between holding, on the one hand, that market interaction must be subject to certain constraints and, on the other hand, that market transactions ought normally to be voluntary. To specify the content and scope of the voluntary transactions principle is precisely to identify the constraints to which recognition should be given by the individual members of society as they seek to interact on a voluntary basis with one another.

It's important to notice that when the voluntary transactions principle—on some appropriate account of its content and scope—is said to underpin defensible free market arrangements, a principle that has an application in a broad range of non-economic contexts is being applied in the economic domain. When, for example, we embrace the view that the members of a society ought to be free, in a wide variety of non-economic contexts—social, political, cultural, recreational, educational, etc.—to enter into relationships with others in the pursuit of shared goals and projects, we are effectively recognizing the role the voluntary transactions principle plays in providing the normative basis for large areas of individual and social life. Just as in the economic domain the principle must be subject to various constraints, so too in the many areas of life beyond the narrowly economic, it must be seen to be a principle whose scope is circumscribed by the constraints to which is subject.

III. Arguments for Free Markets

Recognition of the centrality to debates about how free markets are to be conceived of questions about the content and scope of the voluntary transactions principle is closely related to the interpretation of what is arguably the least contentious of the arguments that have been advanced for free markets. According to this argument—the "liberty" argument—what is at stake in acceptance or rejection of free markets is the ideal of individual liberty or autonomy.

Apart from the notoriously slippery "invisible hand" argument[5] for free markets, there are broadly three readily distinguishable arguments to which appeal is often made.

The first is the "efficiency" argument, according to which "free" markets ought to be instituted, or maintained, because they are conducive to the efficient operation of the economy. While this is a claim that has—clearly—a substantial empirical component, its assessment also hinges, crucially, on how "efficiency" is to be understood. And if, as seems likely, the "efficiency" of institutional strategies is a function of the role they play in the effective and economical pursuit of some broad social goal, a great deal of importance attaches to the precise specification of this goal.

The second is the "justice" argument: "free markets," it is said, have the great virtue of allocating the benefits of market interaction to market participants in proportion to their contribution to the economy: those who contribute much are rewarded more generously than those who contribute little. According to this view, the free market is a miraculously impersonal device for the bringing about of justice because it ensures that market participants receive the economic rewards they deserve. Most contemporary philosophers are skeptical of this argument, at least partly because they are skeptical of the way in which the slippery notion of desert is exploited in the argument. It is rejected outright by F. A. Hayek, one of the most celebrated defenders of the free market system, because of its confused understanding of the way in which a free market operates. In a striking passage in *The Mirage of Social Justice* (the central volume of his magnum opus *Law, Legislation, and Liberty*), he writes:

> It is probably a misfortune that, especially in the USA, popular writers like Samuel Smiles and Horatio Alger, and later the sociologist W. G. Sumner, have defended free enterprise on the ground that it regularly rewards the deserving, and it bodes ill for the future of the market order that this seems to have become the only defense of it which is understood by the general public. That it has largely become the basis of the self-esteem of the businessman often gives him an air of self-righteousness which does not make him more popular.[6]

The third of the familiar arguments for the free market ideal is the "liberty" argument: "free markets" make it possible for the members of a society to enjoy in the economic domain the kind of freedom in giving content and shape to their lives that commitment to the broader ideal of individual liberty (or autonomy) calls for.

It is this third argument that is closely related to the claim that the voluntary transactions principle provides the normative underpinning for the free market ideal. It is the argument that spells out most directly what it is about voluntary market interaction itself that we find so intuitively appealing when we cast about for an account of the normative rationale for free market arrangements: there seems to be something intrinsically valuable (it's plausible to think) about market institutions that protect the freedom of the members of a society to make their own economic decisions. Both the other arguments—the efficiency argument and the justice argument—seem by contrast to represent free market arrangements as having at best merely instrumental value, either because they contribute (allegedly) to the efficient operation of the economy or because they make it possible (allegedly) for a just or fair distribution of the fruits of the economy to be effected. Claims of these kinds about the instrumental value of free market arrangements are obviously vulnerable to the criticisms of those who agree that both economic efficiency (in some suitably specified sense) and economic justice (again, on some circumspect account of what it requires) are desiderata but who, at the same time, doubt whether available evidence supports either the view that free markets are maximally efficient or the view that they actually contribute to economic justice. No parallel critique of the liberty argument can be mounted. Why? Because anyone who sets store by the freedom of individuals to give shape to their lives is bound to be predisposed to favor economic arrangements that purport to protect their freedom in the economic domain—which is precisely what the liberty argument represents as the great virtue of free market arrangements.

While there's a strong case to be made for the view that the most fundamental reason for favoring free markets is that they reflect the importance we attach to individuals being free to make the economic decisions that help to give content and structure to their lives, how the liberty argument is to be understood is a matter of considerable controversy.

IV. Three Myths about the Liberty Ideal

There are, for example, several myths about the liberty ideal that serve to obscure what is most appealing in the view that free markets should be endorsed because they contribute to the protection of the freedom of individuals to make their own economic decisions.

(1) First, there is the myth that "freedom is one and indivisible"—a myth that helps sustain the idea that any attempt to restrict this or that particular freedom (any attempt, for example, to restrict the market options of market participants) is bound to have a deleterious impact on the protection of other freedoms. Thus, it

may be claimed that anyone who values freedom of speech or freedom of religion has reason to oppose regulatory intervention in the economy.

(2) Second, there's the myth that freedom as such—freedom in all the forms it can assume—is something we should value. Despite its surface plausibility, this view is exposed to a number of fatal objections.

The idea that there's always a case for valuing particular freedoms, even the freedoms we end up having to restrict, and that consequently it's only on the basis of "balance of reasons" considerations that any freedom can be defensibly limited has some strongly counter-intuitive consequences. It would require, for example, that when the criminal law forbids the deliberate taking of human life or when it prohibits physical assault, this is not because no value attaches to the freedom to kill people or to the freedom to bash them up but rather because, when we balance the case for protecting the freedom to kill people or to assault them against the case for forbidding killing and assault, the case for forbidding killing and assault is so much weightier that we have to conclude that on balance these particular freedoms must be disallowed. However, the criminal code's prohibitions of murder and assault are not grounded in any such "balancing" judgment. No such judgment is needed because no value attaches to the freedom to kill people or to bash people up. There's consequently not even an "other things being equal" reason for regarding these freedoms as at least in principle worthy of protection.

A second objection to the claim that freedom as such is something we should value is that it discourages serious investigation of the arguments for wanting to support this or that particular freedom. These often quite specific arguments merit careful consideration for two reasons.

First, insufficient curiosity about the reasons we have for the value we attach to particular freedoms—those freedoms that we undoubtedly do value, and value a great deal, like freedom of speech—is that it can contribute to too broad an account of the particular freedoms in question. In the case of free speech, for example, it has lent support to sponsorship of the view that the only defensible free speech doctrine is one that protects freedom of speech in absolutely all contexts, regardless of the content or the consequences of the particular speech-act in question.

A second reason for the importance that attaches to exploration of the reasons for the value we attach to particular freedoms is that otherwise we may be at a loss to explain why it's more important to protect these freedoms in certain circumstances than in others. Thus—to stick to the case of freedom of speech—it becomes difficult to explain why freedom of speech for some purposes and in some contexts is more worthy of protection than freedom of speech for certain other purposes in certain other contexts. Even if we thought that hate speech or the freedom to make false reputation-undermining statements about other people should be protected under a free speech doctrine—and both are highly contentious claims—it would be absurd to suppose that protection of these particular freedoms is as important as protection of freedom of political expression and freedom of the press.

(3) A third myth—though in this case one that has sometimes been fostered by philosophers—is that we can give effective practical recognition to the freedoms we have reason to value simply by protecting them from interferences of various sorts—whether the interferences are in the public domain (as is the case when the interference is legal or political) or whether it originates in the private sector in threats issued by individuals, groups, churches, corporations, clubs, unions, or any one of a number of voluntary associations or organizations. The most influential proselytizers of this myth have been the philosophical sponsors of the doctrine of "negative liberty." According to this doctrine, defense of freedom must always take the form of warding off attempts to restrict or limit or constrain or otherwise "interfere with" the exercise of freedom.

This myth contributes to an unduly narrow view of the conditions a society must seek to establish if the ideal of individual liberty is to be effectively implemented. In the political domain, for example, the freedom of citizens to participate on terms of equality in collective decision-making processes can be undermined not only by direct interference with the freedom to vote but also by failure to provide citizens with the opportunity to be heard—which is precisely what happens when the rich use their wealth in political campaigns to get their message out to the electorate in ways that drown out the voices of less affluent citizens. Again, appropriate measures to foster opportunities for effective citizen participation may not be adopted or funded adequately. This is the case, for example, when education for citizenship is either neglected altogether or allowed to take the form of subtle indoctrination, or when virtually all the news media are allowed to be beholden to special economic or religious or political interest-groups, or when there is politically-motivated resistance to reform of the electoral system of the kind that would enable legislatures and governments to more fairly represent the views and the interests of members of the electorate. In all these ways, the political freedom of the members of a society can be under threat in ways not envisaged (or captured) by the doctrine of "negative liberty."

V. Myths about Liberty and the Free Market Ideal

It's not difficult to illustrate the ways in which these myths about the liberty ideal can contribute to distortions in the deployment of the liberty argument for the free market.

(1) The myth that "freedom is one and indivisible" can lend color to the specious claim that any attempt to curtail the freedom of market participants should be resisted not only by those who value economic freedom but also by those who

think it important to protect freedom in areas of human life other than the narrowly economic—by those who value political freedom, or freedom of speech, or freedom of religion, for example. While there are, of course, many complex ways in which particular freedoms may be interconnected, it's false that the linkages are so close and tight that limiting any one of these freedoms in any way whatsoever constitutes a threat to effective protection of all the others.

(2) The myth that freedom as such is something we should value underlies the specious claim that to value individual liberty is to be committed to resisting any restriction on freedom in any area of human life and that consequently, in the economic domain, there's a standing presumption in favor of permitting market participants to interact in any way they please, with restrictions always having to be justified by demonstrating that the interests safeguarded by the restrictions are sufficiently compelling to outweigh the importance that attaches to untrammeled freedom for market participants. Since there isn't any good reason to think that freedom in all the forms it can take is presumptively valuable—indeed there's excellent reason to think that freedoms of certain kinds shouldn't be given any protection whatsoever and should indeed, in some cases, be entirely disallowed under threat of severe punishment—it's a disservice to clear thinking about freedom-related normative questions to suppose that the onus is always on those who favor laws, rules, or regulations that restrict some activity to rebut a standing presumption in favor of freedom to engage in that activity.

(3) The myth (associated with the philosophical doctrine of "negative liberty") that all it takes to ensure the enjoyment of individual liberty is avoidance (and prevention) of interference with the exercise of freedom has also had an adverse impact on judicious articulation of the free market ideal. It has encouraged adoption of the view that ideally a free market is one in which market participants are allowed to interact voluntarily without being subject to state-sponsored laws or regulations that restrict their options. On this view, even rules that require those who market goods and services to avoid potentially misleading advertising or to provide adequate public disclosure of relevant information about what they are selling can be regarded as prima facie breaches of the free market ideal, simply because they restrict the freedom of those who market goods and services to adopt promotional strategies of their own choosing. Because freedom—conceived as "negative" freedom—is restricted by such requirements, their imposition by the state is a prima facie violation of the free market ideal.

VI. Individual Liberty and the Voluntary Transactions Principle

While the individual liberty ideal is indeed relevant to the defense of (both economic and non-economic) institutional arrangements that protect the freedom of the members of society, it can be justifiably invoked only if familiar myths about the liberty ideal are roundly rejected and if a satisfactory alternative account is offered of the content and contours of the ideal.

I clearly can't hope to provide in this paper even an outline of the alternative account that is needed. Instead, I propose to return to the narrower question[7] I was posing earlier about the voluntary transactions principle—viz. whether this principle must be understood to provide only qualified endorsement of the idea that voluntary interaction is a desideratum in the good society. Even this narrower question is too large for me to take on here since it cannot be answered properly without specification and justification of the many qualifications that have to be built into a defensible version of the voluntary transactions principle. Consequently, no effort will be made in this paper to specify—or to explore the rationale for—the various constraints that serve to delimit the scope of this principle. My limited aim in what follows is to lend support to the view that only a constrained version of the principle is defensible by drawing attention to some of the contexts—non-economic as well as economic—in which application of an unqualified version of the principle yields plainly unacceptable results.

VII. Counterexamples to an Unqualified Version of the Voluntary Transactions Principle

Just before the dawn of the Reagan era—in 1979—Milton Friedman, in a collaborative work with his wife Rose Friedman, published a book, *Free to Choose*, in which they set out, in language aimed at the public at large, the case for what they took to be Adam Smith's vision of a free market. According to this Smithian vision—or rather, according to the Friedmans' account of the Smithian vision—all the members of a society stand to benefit when market participants are allowed to interact in a fully voluntary manner. The book was based on fifteen lectures presented a couple of years earlier by Milton Friedman in a television series that was the longest commercial ever aired for the neo-liberal version of the free market ideal. According to this view, the free market system is one that is allowed to operate independently of restrictive government legislation, and without regulation or even monitoring[8] of economic activity. Moreover, it embodies miraculously self-correcting mechanisms that reward the economic contributions of individual market participants in ways that simultaneously promote the public interest.

As has been brilliantly demonstrated by Joseph Stiglitz,[9] it was this conception of the free market that provided the inspiration for many of the policies that led to the economic meltdown in 2008, the policies set, for example, by Alan Greenspan at the Federal Reserve, and by a host of officials and politicians who supported deregulation of the financial sector of the economy. By presenting a series of counterexamples to the view that the mere voluntariness of market interaction can help to usher in a free society in which justice prevails, I hope to illustrate—and perhaps also to lend support in a small way to—the principal thesis of this paper, which is that only a heavily qualified version of the voluntary transactions principle can provide the normative underpinning for a defensible form of the free market ideal. Implicit in this thesis, of course, is the claim not only that there are many possible versions of this ideal (which is often denied by defenders of neo-liberal free market arrangements) but also that at least one of these versions *can* be defended (which is often denied by critics of the neo-liberal ideal). Since free market rhetoric, despite its seductive ambiguities, continues to have positive resonance in debates about the structure and scope of market arrangements, adoption of a resolutely anti-free-market stance diminishes significantly the likelihood of success in the ongoing battle for progressive market reforms. Fortunately, the availability of normatively powerful arguments for free market arrangements that are consistent with these reforms makes it quite unnecessary—and therefore counter-productive—to cede to defenders of the neo-liberal market model a proprietary claim to use of the language of "free markets."

The counterexamples I present are all situations in which voluntary transactions of various kinds take place—sometimes in market-related contexts, sometimes in non-market settings—but in which the mere voluntariness of the transactions does not suffice to generate any rights or duties for the parties. What these cases show is that it's a mistake to think that it's immaterial to the rights and duties ostensibly generated by voluntary transactions what the content is of the actions performed by the parties to these transactions. The duties and rights generated by an agent's voluntary actions are not independent of the normative content of those actions. Indeed, the actions in question must be permissible—that is, they must be actions the agent has a right to perform—if their voluntary performance is to generate further rights and duties.

Since the voluntary transactions principle has an application both in market and in non-market contexts, and since it is certain general similarities between these applications that I want to highlight, only some of the cases are market-related. I begin with a couple of non-market cases.

(A) Situations in which Promises Are Made

Take the case, first, of a promise made by a party hack (let's call him Slime) to the fellow-members of a Dirty Tricks Campaign Committee. He promises to disseminate, subtly but effectively, false reputation-undermining stories about the private life and business practices of a popular but feared political opponent. Is he under an obligation to spread these rumors, and do the other members of the committee have a right that he keep his promise? Despite the voluntariness of the promise he has made, the answer seems clearly to be "no"—and the reason, equally clearly, is that what the dirty trickster is promising to do is uncontroversially wrong.

The obvious moral (I suggest) is that promissory obligations (and the rights that can be correlated with these obligations) are generated by voluntary promises only if what the person making the promise undertakes to do is itself permissible—that is, only if what the promisor is undertaking to do is something he or she has a right to do. If the action the promisor is undertaking to perform is clearly wrong, even a voluntary promise is powerless to make it obligatory. Promising to perform some permissible action serves to secure its transfer from the category of the permissible to the category of the obligatory. But it would be magic worthy of a medieval alchemist if an action that is clearly wrong could be rendered obligatory simply by the making of a promise to perform it.

While contemporary moral philosophers would like to see themselves as united in the rejection of anything that smacks of medieval magic, some of them still cling to what they seem to regard as a usable remnant of the view of promissory obligation I'm here rejecting. They continue to think that the making of a promise, no matter what its content, really does generate an obligation to do what has been promised, although they concede that the obligation is merely an "other things being equal" or "*prima facie*" obligation, not a "come hell or high water" obligation. A promissory obligation can consequently be overridden if it turns out to be in conflict with some weightier obligation, in which event the person who made the promise will be justified in concluding that there's an "all things considered" obligation to break the promise. On this view Slime's promise to his co-conspirators on the campaign committee really does generate an obligation on his part to spread scurrilous rumors about the feared political opponent, but only if "other things are equal." If he decides in the event that it would be wrong for him to keep the promise, it will be on the basis of an "all things considered" judgment, a judgment balancing the case for keeping the promise against the case for breaking it.

It will be clear that I reject this view. It still embodies the claim—even if in a somewhat milder version—that the power we are exercising when we promise to perform some action X converts X from an action it would be wrong to do in the absence of the promise into an action there's an obligation to do—though now it is conceded that the obligation is merely *prima facie* and can thus be overridden. This claim should in my view be rejected as a still-disreputable holdover from the view that to make a promise is to perform an act of moral magic, an act that can transform an otherwise disreputable act into one there's a *prima facie* obligation to perform. The claim can be refuted, I suggest, by noting one of its strongly counterintuitive implications. Thus, in the Dirty Trickster case, Slime's conduct, if he keeps his promise would have to be thought to be slightly less reprehensible than it would have been had he simply set about spreading the rumors without having promised to do so. It has, after all, one redeeming feature: in spreading these rumors Slime is keeping a promise. If it's conceded that solemnly promising to do something that is clearly wrong and then doing it is, if anything, worse (and certainly no better) than simply doing it, then it must also be conceded that we have here a *reductio* of even the toned-down version of the view of promissory obligation that I argue should be summarily rejected.

(B) Situations in which Consent Is Granted

A second counter-example highlights a situation in which consent to some arrangement has been given voluntarily.

Sam has fled the scene of a serious accident for which he was principally responsible, and he asks Steve, an old friend, to consent to his concocting an alibi that places him in Steve's home at the time of the accident. If Steve consents to back up Sam's alibi and tells the police that Sam was visiting him at the time of the accident, is he simply discharging an obligation he has incurred, courtesy the fact that he freely consented to support Sam's account of events? And does Sam have a right—a right grounded in the fact that Steve consented to the concoction of the alibi—to expect Steve's support?

It seems clear that the fact that Steve has consented—and consented (let it be supposed) in a fully voluntary manner—to back up Sam's concocted alibi provides no basis for thinking that Steve has a duty to stand by Sam in this particular way or that Sam has a right to this sort of support from Steve. And the explanation too is obvious. What Steve has consented to in agreeing to support Sam's concocted alibi is clearly wrong. While voluntary consent is a necessary condition of the existence of consent-generated rights and duties, a second crucial condition is the permissibility of what is being consented to. Like promissory duties (and the associated rights), consent-generated duties and rights are not content-independent.

(C) Voluntary Transactions In Market Settings

I turn now to a number of contexts in which the voluntary transactions to which market participants are parties do not generate the rights and duties they might be thought to generate.

There are, for example, voluntary market transactions between factory owners and their employees that expose employees to hazardous working conditions, or that provide them with exploitatively low levels of remuneration, or that deny them reasonable security of tenure, or that afford them inadequate opportunities to build up pension-entitlements, and so on.

Again, there are voluntary market transactions—for example, those involved in corporate takeovers—that enable companies to make "restructuring" personnel decisions without adequately compensating long-term employees for the loss of their jobs, or to operate newly-acquired manufacturing enterprises in ways that do serious, more or less irreversible, damage to the environment, or to relocate enterprises to low-wage regions or countries without regard to the disruptive impact of such decisions on local communities, and so on.

And there are voluntary market transactions between corporations and public relations companies that involve the purchase of promotional strategies that withhold crucial information about market products and services or that package advertising messages in ways designed to bamboozle unwary consumers.

In all these cases, and myriad others like them, marketplace transactions cannot plausibly be faulted on the ground that they are not fully voluntary. If they are open to objection, it is because of their content and consequences.

VIII. Implications for the Voluntary Transactions Principle

How, then, is the voluntary transactions principle to be conceived if it is to serve as a principle for the vetting of a broad swath of the interactions that are thought to generate duties and rights for those who are parties to them? What the cases I have briefly reviewed all point to, I suggest, is the need to reject any version of the principle for which the mere voluntariness of a transaction is taken to generate duties and rights for the parties, and to endorse instead only a version for which the principle is recognized to be subject to (a potentially large number of) constraints or qualifications, constraints or qualifications that restrict its scope (perhaps considerably). Instead of its being thought of as a principle that can be appealed to in support of any voluntary transaction, no matter what its content or consequences, it should be viewed as a principle that facilitates endorsement of institutional arrangements (including market arrangements) that encourage voluntary interaction only when that interaction doesn't itself violate important principles (including principles of justice and fairness).

IX. The Voluntary Transactions Principle and the Free Market Ideal

If the free market ideal points to the justifiability of market arrangements that satisfy only a qualified version of the voluntary transactions principle—and if consequently the free market arrangements for which this principle provides a basis are arrangements that promote and protect the voluntary interaction of market participants only when the content (and the consequences) of the transactions to which they are parties are not at odds with other principles for the assessment of institutional arrangements (not at odds especially, perhaps, with principles of justice and fairness)—then the fear that the free market ideal is at odds in some systematic way with the principles that determine the fairness of market transactions is a gratuitous fear. There is no obstacle to market arrangements being both free and fair. Advocates of fairness in the structuring of markets and advocates of free markets need not be at loggerheads. Moreover, if a judicious understanding of the content and scope of the voluntary transactions principle shows how and why there need be no conflict, then both of two warring philosophies for the assessment of market arrangements are arguably put out of court. On the one hand, we can rule out the views of philosophers like Hayek whose free market enthusiasms induce them to reject altogether the applicability of principles of justice to market relationships and activities. On the other, we can reject the views of those philosophers whose desire to accommodate both liberty and justice as principles relevant to the evaluation of markets prompts them to think that freedom and fairness are values subject to trade-off and that consequently the best we can hope for is judiciousness in the making of the inescapable trade-off judgments.

X. A Concluding Note on the Implementation of the Free Market Ideal

On the question how the free market ideal, on this account of its content and rationale, is to be best implemented, it should be noted that there's no need to suppose, either that laws prohibiting unacceptable forms of market interaction provide the whole answer, or that the rest of the answer must take the form of modifying a society's institutions—its economic, social, or political institutions. G. A. Cohen, who for a quarter of a century was one of Isaiah Berlin's successors in the political theory chair at Oxford, spent the final years of his distinguished career as a philosopher battling what he took to be the false view that justice in society can be fully achieved by purely institutional means. While he took for granted that the reform of institutional arrangements has the importance liberal egalitarians like John Rawls take it to have, he held that the personal choices people make also have an indispensable contribution to make. As he put it in the Preface to his Gifford Lectures, "egalitarian justice is not only, as Rawlsian liberalism teaches, a matter of rules that define the structure of society, but also a matter of personal attitude and choice."[10]

Almost half a century earlier, Bertrand Russell (in his "Reflections on my Eightieth Birthday") nicely anticipated Cohen's view. Russell wrote:

> There are those who hold that everything depends on institutions, and that good institutions will inevitably bring the millennium. And, on the other hand, there are those who believe that what is needed is a change of heart, and that, in comparison, institutions are of little account. I cannot accept either view. Institutions mould character, and character transforms institutions. Reforms in both must march hand in hand.[11]

The free market ideal needs for its implementation the reform of many of the rules that govern market interaction, but it cannot be fully realized unless market participants are prepared to make decisions that even ideally formulated market rules can't be expected to require.

Alistair M. Macleod, Queen's University

Notes

1.   See, for example, Amartya Sen's general introduction to Adam Smith's *The Theory of Moral Sentiments* (New York, New York: Penguin Classics, 2009).

2.   See, for example, Alistair M. Macleod, "Globalization, Markets and the Ideal of Economic Freedom," *The Journal of Social Philosophy* 36.2 (2005): 143–58, and "Free Markets and Democracy: Clashing Ideals in a Globalizing World?," *The Journal of Social Philosophy* 37.1 (2006): 139–62.

3.   There are of course practical as well as theoretical reasons for opposing the neo-liberal orthodoxy that has all too often shaped the thinking of policy-makers in their approach to both domestic and global economic issues. The 2008 financial crisis that has engulfed many domestic economies and still threatens global economic arrangements was in large measure brought about by the assumption that market forces yield benefits for society as a whole most impressively when they are allowed to operate without much or any government regulation or monitoring, let alone intervention. While there seems to be an impressive consensus among economic observers that the animus against regulation of financial markets and lax discharge by officials of their regulatory responsibilities played a major role in precipitating the recent crisis—and while one of the casualties of the crisis was consequently the neo-liberal conception of the free market—it's perhaps too soon to tell whether the required changes in market structures will be brought about, given the sadly effective lobbying efforts that are being made by powerful financial institutions to maintain neo-liberal economic arrangements.

4.   It is part of the purpose of this paper to explain why the supposition that the mere voluntariness of market transactions is all it takes to vindicate free market arrangements must be rejected. Here I simply note, summarily, how implausible it is to take this supposition for granted.

5.   The argument is "slippery" because it can be variously interpreted. There is good reason to think, for example, not only that Adam Smith—in the two passages in his writings in which the metaphor of the "invisible hand" is deployed—did not have a single, determinately-structured argument in mind, but also that modern economists like Milton Friedman interpret the argument in yet another way. See, for example, Alistair M. Macleod, "Invisible Hand Arguments: Milton Friedman and Adam Smith," *The Journal of Scottish Philosophy* 5.2 (2007): 103–17.

6.   F. A. Hayek, *The Mirage of Social Justice* (Chicago, Illinois: University of Chicago Press, 1976), 74.

7.   The question is narrower because whereas specification of the content and contours of the ideal of individual liberty requires attention to be given to the freedoms that play an important role in the lives of individuals both when they are interacting with others and when they are not, the voluntary transactions principle has an application only to their social interactions.

8.   That is, "monitoring" of the sort that calls for mandatory disclosure to government agencies of many otherwise "private" features of economic activity.

9.   Joseph E. Stiglitz, *Free Fall: America, Free Markets and the Sinking of the World Economy* (New York, NY: W.W. Norton, 2010).

10. G. A. Cohen, *If You're an Egalitarian, How Come You're So Rich?* (Cambridge, MA: Harvard University Press, 2000).

11. Bertrand Russell, *Portraits from Memory, and Other Essays* (London: Allen and Unwin, 1956).

Part III:
Explorations in Social Justice

Does the Human Right to Health Lack Content?

MARTIN GUNDERSON

Abstract: The human right to health is crucial in the fight against global poverty. Health and an adequate standard of living are intimately connected. Poor health can make it difficult to overcome poverty, and poverty can make it difficult to attain good health. For the human right to health to be effective, however, it must have sufficient content to do the important normative work of rights. In the first part of this paper I give plausible arguments against the very existence of a human right to health based on its lack of content and extend this to other social rights such as the right to adequate income, housing and education. In the second part of the paper I provide a defense of human social rights, including the human right to health, by arguing that these human rights, though abstract, have enough content to function as rights.

I. Introduction

The human right to health is a lynch pin in the fight against global poverty, since health and standard of living are intimately connected.[1] Poor health can make it difficult for a person to overcome poverty, and poverty can make it difficult to attain good health. This is reflected in various human rights declarations and covenants. Article 25(1) of the *Universal Declaration of Human Rights*, for example, clearly ties health with an adequate standard of living when it states, "Everyone has the right to a standard of living adequate for the health and well-being of himself and of his family, including food, clothing, housing and medical care and necessary social services."[2] In addition, health is of such obvious importance in the lives of persons and communities that it seems to merit the protection afforded by a right to health care.

This assumes, of course, that the human rights to health and an adequate standard of living have sufficient content to do the normative work expected of human rights. As Ronald Dworkin notes, "there is no more serious complaint against a government than that it has violated human rights."[3] Human rights enacted in international covenants can be used as reasons for demanding legal action, and some have argued that governments that violate human rights are, to that extent, not even legitimate.[4] Human rights are also used to provide reasons for determining which nations receive loans from international organizations such as the World Bank and the International Monetary Fund, which nations are admitted to NATO or the European Union, and for domestic critiques of all sorts.[5] In short, human rights are high priority norms that justify state and sometimes international action.[6] Unfortunately it is not clear whether the human rights to health and an adequate standard of living have enough content to do this work.

I will focus on the right to health because the content problems are near the surface and because Norman Daniels's recent book, *Just Health: Meeting Health Needs Fairly*, provides the resources for skeptical arguments against a human right to health.[7] I will speak primarily of a right to health, which should be understood as covering claims to health-related needs such as access to health information, a safe workplace and a clean environment as well medical services and treatments. It does not, of course, mean that the state has a duty to make us healthy regardless of our condition, since in many cases that will be impossible.[8] Although I focus on the right to health, the concerns about a human right to health can be extended to other social rights. In the first part of this paper I give plausible arguments against the very existence of a human right to health based on its lack of content and extend this to other social rights such as the right to adequate income, housing and education.[9] In the second part of the paper I provide a defense of human social rights, including the human right to health, by arguing that these human rights, though abstract, have enough content to function as rights. My concern is to defend the putative human right to health against two skeptical arguments based on lack of content, rather than to offer a philosophical justification of the human right to health.

II. A Skeptical Argument at the Level of Theory

One skeptical argument regarding the right to health can be put quite simply as follows: (1) The identity and existence of any human right is determined by its content. (2) The content of the right to health is given in terms of the specific entitlements to health-related goods, services and protections that the right-holder can claim. (3) At least in the case of the right to health, the entitlements are determined by conditions and cultural norms that vary from nation to nation. (4) Therefore, the right to health varies from nation to nation. (5) Human rights are universal in that they apply globally. (6) Therefore, there is no human right to health. The argument could also be summed up in a dilemma. If the right to health is universal, then it lacks uniform content and cannot do the serious work of human rights. If, however, the right to health is given sufficient content to function as a right, then it will vary by nation and not be universal in which case it will not be a human right.

Each of these premises is plausible. The first premise, in fact, appears to be so obvious as to not need defending. Human rights have normative force by specifying duties.[10] Unless we know the content of a human right we will be unable to determine what duties the right specifies, and some have argued that rights that do not entail duties are not genuine rights.[11] We also need to know how to separate human rights from other norms and values and how to individuate one human right from another. All of this requires being able to specify the content of human rights.

The second premise is also plausible, though by no means as obvious as the first premise. As James Nickel notes, the object of a right will be "some freedom, power, immunity, or benefit."[12] There is, in short, something to which the right entitles us. It is important to specify these entitlements because they determine what duties correspond to the right. The entitlements must also be specified in order to determine the scope of the right and how it is to be weighed against competing rights and values.

The object of the human right to health and its corresponding duties are quite complex. The Committee on Economic, Social and Cultural Rights reasonably holds that social rights such as the right to health pose three sorts of duties on states. There is a duty not to violate rights. Here the object of the right to health is freedom from actions of the state that are detrimental to health. There is also a duty to protect rights from violations by third parties, where the object is obvious protection from third party harms to health. Third, there is a duty to fulfill rights, which is interpreted as the duty to progressively realize the right to health.[13]

The object of the first two sorts of duties is fairly clear—an entitlement to protection from actions of the state and others that undermine health. But how are we to understand what it means to speak of the duty of progressive realization of health? The state is in no position simply to create a healthy citizenry, since health is obviously affected by many factors that are out of the state's control. The best the state can do is to provide such things as health care services, health education, and public health measures to ensure, for example, safe drinking water and quick response to epidemics.[14] As these are specified, the duties of states to right-holders become clearer.

The third premise, that health entitlements are relative to particular nations, is also plausible, though the argument for it needs elaboration. Norman Daniels is correct that the right to specific health related entitlements must be determined locally. He proceeds by arguing that principles of justice provide content for the right to health, but that these principles will provide different content in different societies.[15] What we are entitled to claim depends on our fair share of the goods and services available, and this requires principles of distributive justice.[16] Hence the right to health depends on principles of distributive justice for its content. In a world where there is a shortage of organs for transplant, for example, not everyone who needs an organ will have a right to one.[17] Who receives the scarce organs will be determined in part by principles of distributive justice. Even where medical resources are not scarce, whether one has a right to a particular medical service or good depends on the priority of that good in relation to other goods needed by society such as education and defense, and that priority is determined in part by principles of distributive justice.

After establishing that a theory of justice is needed to provide substance to the right to health, Daniels gives two reasons for thinking that the moral right to health is relative to particular societies. The first reason rests on Daniels's view of the special value of health and health care. Daniels believes that each society has a normal opportunity range of options that are open to people if they have sufficient talent. Poor health can prevent someone from access to the normal opportunity range, and health care can help to mitigate this. Different societies, however, with different traditions and different levels of wealth will have different opportunity ranges. Since what makes health care special, according to Daniels, is that it protects the normal opportunity range for a given society, the right to health is relative to the different normal opportunity ranges present in different societies.[18] Even if one does not accept Daniels's view of the special value of health, however, there are other reasons for thinking that health-related entitlements that provide the content of the right to health are determined locally.

Daniels's second reason for thinking that the right to health is relative to society concerns the need for deliberation in applying principles of distributive justice and rights.[19] Although a theory of justice can provide part of the substance needed for specific health related entitlements, it does not completely determine what we are entitled to. On Daniels's view, the process of fair deliberation, which he calls accountability for reasonableness, requires that policies be adopted on the basis of rationales that are publicly accessible and reasonable in the sense that they appeal to "evidence, reasons and principles that are accepted as relevant by ('fair minded') people who are disposed to finding mutually justifiable terms of cooperation."[20] In addition, the policies adopted must be open to revision, and the process must be governed by public regulation.[21] But, these deliberations will play out differently in different societies and therefore produce different entitlements.

We are driven into deliberation, according to Daniels, because principles of justice are not able to take account of complexities that vary with individual societies. For example we need to resolve baseline problems concerning the extent to which the health policies we adopt should deal with resources so as to make up for past injustices that have resulted in an unfair distribution of health benefits and burdens.[22] In addition, rationing problems raise such issues as whether to pursue modest benefits for many people or greater benefits for fewer people in the context of particular health issues.[23] What counts as a resolution of these complexities cannot be determined a priori, and the distribution policies that are adopted must result from fair deliberation in order to have legitimacy.[24]

We are also driven into deliberation by our inability to anticipate future needs and resources. Whatever principles of distribution we start with, new developments in health care and new health needs will require deliberation to interpret and apply existing principles. We cannot simply proceed in these new areas by mapping out what current rights and principles of justice entail. Rather the right to health and related principles of justice needs to be sufficiently abstract to allow for a variety of interpretations.[25] For example, expensive drugs or techniques may be developed that make only modest improvements in health or that enhance health without treating a specific malady. Whether society should invest in these at the expense of other social goals will require renewed deliberation. In addition, deliberation will be required to deal with emerging health needs that arise with newly discovered environmental risks. Whether society should concentrate on reducing a particular environmental risk or developing medical treatments to deal with the ensuing health problems, for example, depends on deliberation in particular contexts.

There is an additional reason for thinking that Daniels is correct that the right to specific health services is relative to society. As previously noted, rights correlate with duties that provide for the normative force of rights. The right to have specific health needs met must correlate with duties of persons or institutions to supply those needs. Rights are claims, and claims make sense insofar as there is a person or institution to which the claim is to be addressed. As Christan Reus-Smit has argued in expanding on the work of Henry Shue, the assignment of such duties requires the mediation of institutions (sets of rules, norms and principles).[26] In the absence of institutions that assign duties it is not clear just who has a duty to supply a particular person with, for example, needed anti-retroviral drugs. Hence, as Reus-Smit notes, institutional rules, norms and principles give meaning to rights and make them intelligible.[27] Different nations will, of course, have different values, traditions, and economic systems that warrant the design of different institutions to enforce human rights and hence different assignments of duties. This means that the right to health will have a different content in different nations.

All of this poses an obvious problem for the view that there is a human right to health. If human rights are rights held by individual humans in virtue of being human then they apply universally, and it is reasonable to suppose that the claims and entitlements embodied in those rights will apply universally regardless of the right holder's society or nation. If Daniels's argument that the right to health care entitlements is relative to particular societies is correct, however, then it appears that there is no human right to health.

Daniels's arguments for the relativity of the moral right to health can be extended to other social rights. Deliberation is required to determine the fair share of food, shelter, education and other necessities just as it is required to determine specific health-related entitlements. Differences in availability, social needs, and cultural history will shape deliberations regarding all of these goods so that rights are given content that reflects the particular society in which the deliberation occurs. As a result it is not possible to set a definite scope and weight for social rights that will apply globally.[28]

III. A Skeptical Argument at the Level of Practice

There is a related skeptical argument that applies primarily to the view that there can be a meaningful human right to health in international law. (1) An effective international human rights covenant providing for a human right to health is possible only if it is accepted by the majority of nations. (2) Nations will not, however, agree on the justification for a human right to health. (3) Therefore, a human rights covenant specifying a right to health needs to be incompletely theorized in the sense that it does not require a particular justification and allows for a variety of justifications.[29] (4) However, the content of a right is determined by its justification. (5) Therefore, an incompletely theorized right to health lacks content. (6) The identity and existence of any right is determined by its content. (7) Therefore, the agreed upon human right to health is not a genuine human right at all.

The argument can also be stated as a dilemma. If a human right to health is to gain wide acceptance among nations in the form of an article in an effective human rights covenant, then it must be incompletely theorized, but then it will lack content and not be a genuine right. If, however, a human right to health is to be given adequate content, it will need to be given a coherent justification, but then it will not be widely accepted and not effective internationally. Either way, an effective international covenant guaranteeing a human right to health will not be possible.

The first two premises are fairly obvious and do not require argument. The sixth premise, which was part of the skeptical argument at the level of theory, has already been discussed. The fourth premise, however, is not so obvious. As Alistair M. Macleod briefly argues in his essay, "The Structure of Arguments for Human Rights," the content of human rights is shaped by the justification of those rights, and it follows that if incompatible justifications are given for a particular right, its content will not be coherent.[30] At least the content will not be sufficiently coherent for the right to perform its function of enabling high priority claims. It is worthwhile arguing for this in more detail. The content of a right is determined in part by the scope of a right—the objects to which it applies and the persons who have the right. We need to know what the justification of a right is in order to settle disputes regarding these issues of scope. Does the right to health, for example, cover the right to an abortion or to assisted reproduction in the form of *in vitro* fertilization? A society that is dominated by prolife religious views might believe strongly in a right to health, while denying that it covers abortion and in vitro fertilization. On the other hand, a liberal secular society might have no problem with a right to abortion while arguing that the cost of *in vitro* fertilization is a matter of choice, extremely expensive, and simply beyond the scope of what should be covered by a right to health. Of course, a wealthy society that places a high value on individual choice might claim that both abortion and *in vitro* fertilization are included in the right to health. Even if there is agreement on scope, different justifications may assign different weight to a human right in competition with other rights and the demands of social wellbeing. Hence, different justifications of the right to health will entail different entitlements to health-related services and goods and have different content.

There is also a conceptual reason why we cannot separate the content of a right from its justification. As law students soon learn, one does not know the law simply by memorizing the language of statutes. One needs to know how the courts apply the statutes. The same is true for human rights norms. To know what a particular human right really means, we need to know how it is applied—what entitlements it provides. Since the justification of a right will determine its application, the justification will thereby determine its meaning. Hence, nations that offer different justifications of the right to health and thereby apply it in different ways will, in effect, be dealing with different rights even through the same name is used.

IV. The Importance of Abstract Rights

The way to respond to both skeptical arguments is to show that an abstract human right to health that is incompletely theorized and does not fully specify entitlements to particular services and goods can nonetheless have enough content to do the serious work of a human right. In the case of the theoretically skeptical argument, this requires rejecting the second premise, that the content of the human right to health is determined by specific health-related entitlements to particular goods and services. In the case of the skeptical argument regarding practice, this requires showing that from premise three (a human right to health must be incompletely theorized) and premise four (the content of rights is determined by their justification) it does not follow that a human right to health lacks sufficient content to be a genuine right. Different foundational justifications may overlap sufficiently to entail the same abstract human right, while providing for different applications of that right. What needs to be shown in the case of both arguments is that the abstract human right to health has sufficient content to be considered a genuine right.

Rights lie along a continuum of abstraction and concreteness.[31] According to Ronald Dworkin, abstract rights state a general political aim without indicating the weight or scope of the rights. As a result, abstract rights do not indicate just how they are to be balanced against other rights or competing social goals.[32] Concrete rights, by contrast are specified more precisely so that they indicate more clearly how they are to be balanced against other political aims on particular occasions.[33] Dworkin states that the rights to dignity, equality and free speech are abstract rights.[34] Freedom of speech can be interpreted in different ways, for example, and give rise to various specific rights in concrete applications. In *Justice for Hedgehogs*, Dworkin argues that our concept of rights, including human rights, is an "interpretive concept" that needs to be interpreted in light of other values and principles to yield conceptions of human rights that can be applied.[35] The human right to health is no less abstract than the right to freedom of speech. The right to health can be interpreted in different ways and implemented with different specific regulations depending on the context in which the rights are claimed. Health-related regulations implementing workplace safety, for example, will obviously be quite different for librarians and steelworkers. An example of a concrete right to health care, by contrast, would be the right of a person who has a certain medical history to receive a pancreas transplant, to use one of Daniels's examples.[36]

Jack Donnelly captures these levels of abstraction nicely with his three-tier approach that distinguishes concepts, conceptions and implementations of human rights.[37] At the level of concepts, human rights are universal, though abstract. Conceptions are interpretations of concepts and take account of the differing values of various cultures. Human rights increasingly gain substance as we move through the levels of conception and implementation. At the levels of conception and implementation, different cultures will embrace different versions of rights, and talk of a form of relativism makes sense, according to Donnelly. Donnelly calls this "relative universality."[38] More work is needed, however, to spell out the sort of substance that concepts of human rights have. In particular it needs to be shown how abstract rights can entail duties, give rise to claims, and carry significant normative weight. How are we to do this with the supposed human right to health?

The object of the abstract human right to health can be stated as an abstract concept of health on which diverse justifications can overlap and which can be interpreted in different ways. This notion of health includes at least an absence of disabilities, injuries, diseases and disorders. At least in paradigm cases such as malaria and paraplegia it is clear what counts as a disease or disability, though there are, of course, debatable cases such as some mental disorders. The object of the right to health also includes conditions, such as workplace safety and a clean environment, that are necessary to maintain health, though these too can be interpreted in different ways and are compatible with various justifications. It is important for the purpose of a human right that the concept of health not be given a precise definition. Overlapping justifications are necessary to get an agreement on a human rights covenant, and this requires that the rights agreed to be abstract.[39]

It also needs to be shown that such an abstract concept of health can be stated as a human right that is capable of doing the work of a right. As was noted in discussing Daniels's argument, rights embody certain features. Rights are entitlements.[40] They are also high priority norms that typically override social concerns that are not themselves rights, and rights entail duties. Unless this can be shown, it could be argued that abstract human rights, such as the right to health, are mere manifesto rights and do not do any significant work other than setting vague goals.[41] It is certainly true that abstract rights set goals.[42] But these are such morally significant goals that citizens and others affected by national policies can demand that nations pursue them as something to which they are entitled, though the entitlements are themselves abstract. As previously noted, the right to health requires nations to work for the progressive realization of the right to health. A citizen is therefore entitled under the right to health to have his or her government work progressively towards more effective public health policies, even though it is not specified just what the policies should be.[43] In effect, citizens are entitled to have their governments adopt health policies and work to implement them. Citizens can also demand a minimum level of health care in the sense of demanding that the government adopt policies that determine what a reasonable minimum of health care is, given available resources, and that the government seek to ensure at least that minimum.

If it is not clear who has a duty to provide health care services or to protect health in general, citizens are entitled to demand that governments create institutions that assign such duties. Moreover, this can be justifiably demanded as something to which people are entitled even though the specifics of such institutions have not been worked out. When a nation refuses or is unable to take any action to maintain the health of its citizens, those citizens can justifiably demand that a different level of government work to provide effective health care institutions. If this is still of no avail, these citizens can demand international action in the form of aid and diplomatic pressure.

In addition, the human right to health, though abstract, still carries significant normative weight. The right to health typically outweighs competing social considerations that are not based on rights even when the entitlements it enables are abstract and we cannot specify the precise weight of the right to health in comparison with other rights.[44] For example, a government is morally obligated to pursue the project of improving health rather than exploring space when funds are not adequate for both. The abstract human right to health also affects the weight of claims that are made for concrete health care services. In order to produce a concrete claim, the abstract right needs to be given a justification and combined with principles of fair distribution and conclusions based on a fair deliberative process as well as empirical facts regarding health, health care and resource availability. But these considerations are under the umbrella of a human right to health, and the eventual concrete legal rights that are created carry the full weight of a human right. A violation of the principles derived under this umbrella is not merely an instance of unfortunate treatment by a nation; it is a violation of a human right.

Abstract human rights also manifest content in several other ways. Human rights, though abstract, can help to focus policy discussion and shape debate.[45] As Charles Beitz notes, human rights contain significant information such as specifying the nature and importance of benefits and harms as well as goals to which appropriate agents should direct their actions.[46] In addition, even highly abstract rights indicate paradigm cases.[47] The human right to health, for example, clearly provides that people have a right to public efforts to combat epidemics and decrease the incidence of maternal and infant mortality. These paradigm cases focus discussion because they are widely accepted fixed points from which we can reason by analogy.

In the case of skepticism at the theoretical level these considerations show that the human right to health has content, including abstract entitlements, even though it does not entail a wide range of concrete entitlements to particular goods and services. In short, the skeptical argument incorrectly states in the second premise that a human right to health gets its meaningful content entirely from the specific goods and services to which people are entitled under the right. The skeptical argument at the level of practice also incorrectly assumes this. The conclusion that an incompletely theorized human right to health lacks content does not follow from the premise that a human right to health must be incompletely theorized to achieve international agreement and the premise that the content of a right to health is determined by its justification. The incompatible justifications for human rights, which fuel skeptical worries, occur when human rights are applied within various societies to produce different concrete entitlements to specific goods and services. This degree of detailed justification is needed for human rights covenants, however, only if it is assumed that human rights get their entire content from these concrete entitlements that result from the application of human rights. When that assumption is abandoned, the argument no longer goes through. At the level of abstract human rights justifications can overlap, and human rights covenants can be agreed upon. In particular, the right to health, as has been argued, can be abstract and still have sufficient content to do the normative work of a right.

In the end, both skeptical arguments mistakenly identify the content of the right to health wholly with entitlements to specific health-related goods and services at the level of application. For the purposes of both philosophical analysis and international human rights practice, abstraction enables agreement on sufficient content to secure the main features of a right to health, though the different justifications accepted by various societies entail different applications regarding specific health-related goods and services.

V. Conclusion

Norman Daniels is correct that the human right to health cannot be applied without principles of justice and a process of fair deliberation. He is also correct that the right to health does not simply entail entitlements to specific health-related services and goods. Moreover, as Daniels shows, these specific entitlements will differ in different societies. His analysis can also be extended to social rights generally.

While it is tempting to draw skeptical conclusions from Daniels's insights, they do not, in fact, provide reason to deny that there are social human rights including a human right to health. A human right to health needs to be abstract in order to be universal, but it can still have enough content to generate claims and carry significant normative weight.

Martin Gunderson, Macalester College

Notes

1.   Norman Daniels, *Just Health: Meeting Health Needs Fairly* (Cambridge: Cambridge University Press, 2008), chap. 3. See also Michael Marmot, *The Status Syndrome: How Social Standing Affects Our Health and Longevity* (New York: Henry Holdt, Times Books, 2004).

2.   *Universal Declaration of Human Rights*, 1948, accessible at http://www.un.org/Overview /rights.html.

3.   Ronald Dworkin, *Is Democracy Possible Here?* (Princeton and Oxford: Princeton University Press, 2006), 28.

4.   Allen Buchanan, "Recognitional Legitimacy and the State System," *Philosophy and Public Affairs* 28 (1999): 52–6.

5.   Allen Buchanan, "Taking the Human Out of Human Rights," in *Rawls's Law of Peoples: A Realistic Utopia?*, ed. Rex Martin and David A. Reidy (Malden, MA and Oxford: Blackwell Publishing, 2006), 165–6.

6.   For a discussion of rights as high priority, mandatory norms, see James Nickel, *Making Sense of Human Rights*, 2nd edition (Malden, MA and Oxford: Blackwell Publishing, 2007), 41. Ronald Dworkin famously went so far as to call rights "trumps." Ronald Dworkin, *Taking Rights Seriously* (Cambridge, MA: Harvard University Press, 1977), xi. Dworkin sees human rights, as well as political rights, as trumps. See his *Justice for Hedgehogs* (Cambridge, MA: Harvard University Press, 2011), 329 and 332.

7.   Although Daniels provides some of the resources from which a skeptical argument can be assembled, it is not clear how skeptical Daniels himself is about a human right to health or health care. He states that we cannot derive specific entitlements from a human right to health and notes how health-related entitlements are relative to society, but he also argues that the human rights approach to health embodied in international law has several strengths. See Daniels, *Just Health*, 14–6, 313, and chap. 12 generally.

8.   For a discussion of the distinction between a right to health and a right to health care, see Kristen Hessler and Allen Buchanan, "Specifying the Content of the Human Right to Health Care," in *Justice and Health Care: Selected Essays*, ed. Allen Buchanan (Oxford and New York: Oxford University Press, 1999), 205–6; Allen Buchanan, "The Right to a Decent Minimum of Health Care," *Philosophy and Public Affairs* 13 (1984): 55–6; Daniels, *Just Health*, 145; and James Griffin, *On Human Rights* (Oxford and New York: Oxford University Press, 2008), 99.

9.   I follow James Nickel in referring to such rights as social rights rather than welfare rights to avoid the implication that these are necessarily rights to receive welfare and to avoid the connotations of "being on welfare." See Nickel, *Making Sense of Human Rights*, 137. I call them social, rather than economic, rights to distinguish them from economic liberties such as the right to buy and sell property or enter into contracts.

10.   Nickel, *Making Sense of Human Rights*, 38–41. For a discussion of how social rights entail duties, see Andrew Fagan, *Human Rights: Confronting Myths and Misunderstandings* (Cheldenham, UK and Northampton, MA: Edward Elgar, 2009), 27–8, and chap. 6, especially 128–40. See also Elizabeth Ashford, "The Duties Imposed by the Human Right to Basic Necessities," in *Freedom from Poverty as a Human Right: Who Owes What to the Very Poor?*, ed. Thomas Pogge (New York: Oxford University Press, 2007): 183–218.

11.   Onora O'Neill uses the correlation between rights and duties to develop a critique of social rights. See O'Neill, "The Dark Side of Human Rights," *International Affairs* 81 (2005): 427–39 at 433. See also Bernard Williams, "Human Rights and Relativism," in *In the Beginning Was the Deed*, ed. Bernard Williams (Princeton and Oxford: Princeton University Press, 2005), 64.

12.   Nickel, *Making Sense of Human Rights*, 23.

13.   Committee on Economic, Social, and Cultural Rights, "General Comment No. 14: The Right to the Highest Attainable Standard of Health (Article 12 of the International Covenant on Economic, Social, and Cultural Rights)," UN doc. E/C, July 4, 2000.

14.   Hesler and Buchanan, "Specifying the Content of the Human Right to Healthcare," 205–6; Buchanan, "The Right to a Decent Minimum of Health Care," 55–6; and Daniels, *Just Health*, 145.

15.   Daniels, *Just Health*, 14–6, 146 and 117–39. John Skorupski also argues that the right to health care must be determined locally, although he does not give as detailed an argument as Daniels does. See John Skorupski, "Human Rights," in *The Philosophy of International Law*, ed. Samantha Besson and John Tasioulas (Oxford and New York: Oxford University Press, 2010), 367–8.

16.   Daniels, *Just Health*, 15.

17.   Ibid., 317.

18.   Ibid., 146.

19.   Ibid., 117–39. For a somewhat different argument that health care entitlements will need to vary locally because of the role of democratic choice, see Hessler and Buchanan, "Specifying the Content of the Human Right to Health Care," 216–7.

20.   Daniels, *Just Health*, 118.

21.   Ibid.

22.   Ibid., 304–5.

23.   Ibid., 308–11.

24.   Ibid., 312.

25.   This type of argument is commonly made regarding constitutional law where it is claimed that constitutional rights need to be abstract so that they can be flexible and applied to changing conditions that could not have been anticipated. See, for instance, Cass R.

Sunstein, *Legal Reasoning and Political Conflict* (New York and Oxford: Oxford University Press, 1996), 40–1.

26. Christan Reus-Smit, "On Rights and Institutions," in *Global Basic Rights*, ed. Charles R. Beitz and Robert E. Goodin (Oxford: Oxford University Press, 2009): 25–48, especially 29–37. Reus-Smit is concerned with all rights, especially social rights, and not just the right to health. See also Charles Beitz, *The Idea of Human Rights* (Oxford: Oxford University Press, 2009), 121.

27. Reus-Smit, "On Rights and Institutions," 29–30.

28. This is reflected in international human rights covenants and documents that speak simply of the progressive realization of rights. For example, Article 11(1) of the *International Covenant on Economic, Social and Cultural Rights* states,

> The States Parties to the present Covenant recognize the right of everyone to an adequate standard of living for himself and his family, including adequate food, clothing and housing, and to the continuous improvement of living conditions. The States Parties will take appropriate steps to ensure the realization of this right. Article 11(1), *International Covenant on Economic, Social and Cultural Rights* (1966)

See also Article 2(1) of the *International Covenant on Economic, Social and Cultural Rights* and United Nations Committee on Economic, Social and Cultural Rights, "The Right to the Highest Attainable Standard of Health," General Comment 14, 22nd Session, UN Document E/C 12/2000/4.

29. Cass R. Sunstein has extolled the virtues of incompletely theorized agreements in several publications using virtually the same arguments. See "Incompletely Theorized Agreements," *Harvard Law Review* 108 (1995): 1733–72; Sunstein, *Legal Reasoning and Political Conflict*, especially chap. 2; and Sunstein, "Constitutional Agreements without Constitutional Theories," *Ratio Juris* 13 (2000): 117–30. For an application of incompletely theorized agreements to the right to health, see Jennifer Prah Ruger, *Health and Social Justice* (Oxford: Oxford University Press, 2010), chap. 3; and Ruger, "Toward a Theory of a Right to Health: Capability and Incompletely Theorized Agreements," *Yale Journal of Law and Humanities* (2006): 273–326.

30. Alistair M. Macleod, "The Structure of Arguments for Human Rights" in *Universal Human Rights: Moral Order in a Divided World*, ed. David A. Reidy and Mortimer N. S. Sellers (Lanham: Rowman & Littlefield Publishers, Inc., 2005), 21–2.

31. Ronald Dworkin, *Taking Rights Seriously*, 93. Dworkin notes that the distinction between abstract and concrete rights is a matter of degree, although he treats it as a matter of kind for the purposes of the points he wants to make.

32. Dworkin, *Taking Rights Seriously*, 93.

33. Ibid.

34. Ibid. Dworkin is concerned with civil and political rights rather than social rights.

35. Dworkin, *Justice for Hedgehogs*, chaps. 8 and 15.

36. Daniels, *Just Health*, 317. Dworkin gives as an example the right of a newspaper to publish defense plans classified as secret provided it would not put soldiers in immediate physical danger. See Dworkin, *Taking Rights Seriously*, 93.

37. Jack Donnelly, "The Relative Universality of Human Rights," *Human Rights Quarterly* 29 (2007): 281–306 at Section 12, 298–301. See also Jack Donnelly, *Universal Human Rights in Theory and Practice*, Section 6.4, 93–8.

38. Donnelly, "The Relative Universality of Human Rights," 299.

39. This has led some to adopt an overlapping consensus model of human rights, though it is important to note that this is not a philosophical justification of human rights, since only one justification might turn out to be philosophically correct. See Amy Gutman, "Introduction," in *Human Rights as Politics and Idolatry*, ed. Michael Ingnatieff (Princeton and Oxford: Princeton University Press, 2001), xviii–xix; Charles Taylor, "Conditions of an Unforced Consensus on Human Rights," in *The East Asian Challenge for Human Rights*, ed. Joanne Bauer and Daniel Bell (Cambridge University Press, 1999), 124–44; and Charles Taylor, "A World Consensus on Human Rights?," *Dissent* (Summer, 1996): 15–21, reprinted in *The Philosophy of Human Rights*, ed. Patrick Hayden (St. Paul, Paragon House, 2001), 409–22. John Gardner also defends what is basically an overlapping consensus model, although he does not refer to it by that name. See John Gardner, "Simply in Virtue of Being Human: The Whos and Whys of Human Rights," *Journal of Ethics and Social Philosophy* 2 (February 2008): 21–2.

40. See also, for example, Jack Donnelly, *Universal Human Rights in Theory and Practice*, 2nd edition (Ithaca, Cornell University Press, 2003), 8.

41. Joel Feinberg, "The Nature and Value of Rights," in *Rights, Justice and the Bounds of Liberty*, ed. Joel Feinberg (Princeton, NJ: Princeton University Press, 1980), 153, reprinted from *Journal of Value Inquiry* 4 (1970): 243–57.

42. Beitz, *The Idea of Human Rights*, 117–21. Beitz defends manifesto rights, and in dealing with this issue I rely on some of Beitz's insights.

43. Committee on Economic, Social, and Cultural Rights, "General Comment No. 14: The Right to the Highest Attainable Standard of Health (Article 12 of the International Covenant on Economic, Social, and Cultural Rights)," UN doc. E/C, July 4, 2000. See also Pablo Gilabert, "The Feasibility of Basic Socioeconomic Human Rights: A Conceptual Exploration," *The Philosophical Quarterly* 59 (2009): 659–681 at 673–4 for an argument similar to the one I develop here

44. In discussing international human rights documents, Steven D. Jamar notes that the right to health "includes at least the power of the people to demand that the state address the relevant issues and that it treat the health of people as a human right, as a claim and interest of the first order." Steven D. Jamar, "The International Human Right to Health," *Southern University Law Review* 22 (1994): 1–68 at 35.

45. According to Michael Ignatieff, "At best, rights create a common framework, a common set of reference points that can assist parties in conflict to deliberate together." Michael Ignatieff, *Human Rights as Politics and Idolatry*, ed. Amy Gutmann (Princeton and Oxford: Princeton University Press, 2001), 20. See also Beitz, *The Idea of Human Rights*, 9.

46. Beitz, *The Idea of Human Rights*, 119.

47. This point is also made by Ronald Dworkin. To paraphrase one of Dworkin's examples, someone who claims that the thumbscrew and rack are not torture is not defending a different conception of torture so much as failing to talk about the concept of torture at all. Dworkin, *Taking Rights Seriously*, 134.

John Stuart Mill on Health Care Reform

SEAN DONAGHUE JOHNSTON

Abstract: In this essay, I explore John Stuart Mill's theory of government and its application to the issue of health care reform. In particular, I ask whether Mill's theory of government would justify or condemn the creation of a public health-insurance option. Although Mill's deep distrust of governmental authority would seem to align him with Republicans, Tea Partiers, libertarians, and others, who cast the public option as a "government takeover" of "our" health care system, I argue that Mill offers good reasons for seriously considering some form of government-operated health insurance. For Mill theorizes government as having a positive as well as a negative role to play in people's lives, and he explicitly endorses "public options" in different areas of life. According to his theory of government, a public health-insurance option would be just as long as it would meet the following two conditions: (1) it would not invade the "reserved territory" of individual liberty; and (2) "the case of expediency is strong." I argue that a public option would in fact meet both of these conditions, and that Mill would have likely endorsed it as an effective solution to the current health care crisis in the United States.

I

This essay poses the following question: Where would John Stuart Mill have stood on the issue of health care reform in the United States? In particular, would Mill have supported or opposed the current administration's proposal for a public health-insurance option? Although the public option was eventually dropped from the reform bill, the debate that it sparked raises a number of questions concerning the legitimate relationship between the individual and the state. These questions include: Should the state take positive action to promote the general welfare (and health) of its citizens, or should it take up the role of the "night-watchman," protecting citizens from outright harm but leaving them alone to pursue their own good in their own ways? Does society have a right to tax the wealthy for the sake of those who are less well-off, or, more specifically, to tax those who can afford private health insurance for the sake of those who cannot? Does government involvement in health care interfere with individual liberty, and, if so, does society have a *right*, or perhaps even a *duty*, to restrict individual liberty in order to promote other, conflicting values, such as equality, desert, or the public welfare? In short, would a public option be *just*? Nowhere does Mill actually discuss the specific case of government-operated health insurance; nevertheless, as this essay will show, his thoughts on the relationship between the individual and the state, or between liberty and authority, are instructive and will help us to answer questions about the justice of government involvement in health care.[1] Also, applying Mill's thought to the concrete political issue of health care reform will help us to develop a better understanding of his theory of government and the specific value that it has for us today.

In the second section of the essay, I will use textual evidence to show that Mill sees government as having a positive role to play in promoting the public welfare. I will then argue, in sections three and four, that government involvement in health care would promote rather than diminish individual liberty and that it would maximize utility. In section five I will address the concern that some people have that a public option might "drift" toward a single-payer health-insurance system and thus toward some form of "socialism." I will conclude that there is nothing in Mill's works to suggest that government-operated health insurance would be necessarily unjust, and that Mill would very likely have endorsed the public option as an effective solution to the American health care crisis.

II

Mill's commitment to individual liberty, along with his apparent distrust of governmental authority, would seem to align him with opponents of the public option who maintain that "more government" is not the solution to our problems; and his warning, in *On Liberty*, that any unnecessary enlargement of government power is a "great evil," is more or less echoed by Republicans, libertarians, and Tea Partiers, who warn us about the dangers of "big government" and about a "government takeover" of "our" health care system.[2] This apparent connection between Mill and opponents of the public option is strengthened by the fact that some scholars have interpreted Mill as a libertarian. Isaiah Berlin, for example, considers Mill to be a champion of "negative" liberty, claiming that Mill "reduced [the state] to what Lasalle contemptuously described as the functions of a night-watchman or traffic policeman."[3] Similarly, Nicholas Capaldi claims that Mill's idea of good government is "minimal government," meaning that the state's only function is to protect liberty and not to promote the public welfare.[4] As Capaldi puts it: "Nowhere does Mill maintain that the state has a positive function to improve or to aid the progress, fulfillment, and self-realization of its citizens."[5] "The justification for intervention," he explains, "is not positive but negative. It is not to promote the maximization of welfare but only to protect freedom."[6] Clearly, on this libertarian reading of Mill, it would be extremely difficult to justify the creation of a public option in health care.

If the state's only function is to protect liberty, then it would seem to follow that it has no positive duty to provide health insurance to its citizens. However, as I will argue, Mill is not a libertarian. On the contrary, Mill argues explicitly *against* the libertarian position and presents us with a more positive conception of government agency that would in fact justify the creation of a public health-insurance option.

In his essay on Samuel Taylor Coleridge, Mill endorses an apparently libertarian conception of government, which he refers to as "the *let alone* doctrine." "Beyond suppressing force and fraud," he asserts, "governments can seldom, without doing more harm than good, attempt to chain up the free agency of individuals."[7] At first glance, this comment would appear to confirm the libertarian reading of Mill discussed above. However, it turns out that Mill is also critical of the "let alone" doctrine, claiming that "one half of it is true, and the other half false." Thus, he goes on to qualify his endorsement by asking rhetorically:

> But does it follow from this that government cannot exercise *a free agency of its own*?—that it cannot beneficially employ its powers, its means of information, and its pecuniary resources (so far surpassing those of any other association or of any individual), in *promoting the public welfare* by a thousand means which individuals would never think of, would have no sufficient motives to attempt, or no sufficient powers to accomplish?[8]

Mill agrees with proponents of the "let alone" doctrine (i.e., libertarians) insofar as he believes that government should not "chain up the free agency of individuals." However, Mill also suggests that government ought to be able to promote the public welfare via "a free agency of its own." Thus, for Mill, the "free agency" of the state does not necessarily conflict with that of individuals. On the contrary, it is a necessary complement to it, for the state is capable of promoting the public welfare in ways which private individuals (and the free market) are not. It can provide a public health-insurance option, for example, to the tens of millions of Americans who cannot afford private insurance. It can also take positive measures to insure that everyone receives a basic education, that roads and highways are paved, that destructive fires are put out, that the economy does not fail, and that countless other essential needs are met. Thus, as Mill suggests, government has a positive rather than a purely negative role to play in people's lives; that is, it does (and should do) a great deal more than protect liberty.

Mill's assessment of the "let alone" doctrine in the "Coleridge" essay is consistent with his argument for the toleration of minority opinions in *On Liberty*. After arguing for toleration in cases where the more popular opinion is either entirely true or entirely false, Mill goes on to consider a third possibility:

> But there is a commoner case than either of these; when the conflicting doctrines, instead of being one true and the other false, share the truth between them; and the nonconforming opinion is needed to supply the remainder of the truth, of which the received doctrine embodies only a part.[9]

Mill clearly considers the "let alone" doctrine to be an instance of this third case. He states explicitly that "one half of it is true, and the other half false." Also, in the *Autobiography*, Mill reveals that when he was writing the "Coleridge" essay, he "was writing for Radicals and Liberals" of his day and that "it was [his] business to dwell most on that in writers of a different school, *from the knowledge of which they might derive most improvement.*"[10] What this means is that Mill wrote the "Coleridge" essay as a deliberate attempt "to supply the remainder of the truth, of which the received doctrine embodies only a part;" and that, in this case, "the remainder of the truth" is supplied by arguments in favor of the positive promotion of the public welfare.

Thus, to those who oppose the public option on the grounds that "more government" is not the solution to our problems, Mill would likely say that they are only half right. They are right to believe, with Mill, that any *unnecessary* enlargement of government power is a "great evil." However, they are wrong to believe that *any* enlargement of government power is a "great evil," for government does in fact have a positive role to play in people's lives. The private sector has failed to provide for the medical needs of all Americans: nearly fifty million Americans are uninsured, either because they are unemployed or because their employers do not provide them with benefits and they cannot afford to pay for insurance on their own; many other Americans who *do* have insurance are denied coverage because of "pre-existing conditions"[11] or for other reasons, and are thus left with a choice between suffering unnecessarily and going into crippling debt. Why should government not exercise "a free agency of its own" in this particular instance? Why should it not "beneficially employ its powers, its means of information, and its pecuniary resources" in order to provide a public health-insurance option to those who cannot afford private insurance? Opponents of health care reform ought to take Mill's advice and be a bit more receptive to the "other half" of the truth, which is that government is equipped to provide for the medical needs of Americans in ways that the private sector is not.

III

In *Principles of Political Economy*, Mill discusses the "multifarious character" of the functions of government, listing what he believes to be some uncontroversial examples of government functions that extend beyond the protection of liberty, including the administration of property, the regulation of contracts, and the care of individuals who cannot take care of themselves (i.e., children, the insane, and the mentally handicapped). He concludes:

> Examples might be indefinitely multiplied without intruding on any disputed ground. But enough has been said to show that the admitted functions of government embrace *a much wider field than can easily be included within the ring-fence of any restrictive*

definition, and that it is hardly possible to find any ground of justification common to them all, except the comprehensive one of *general expediency*; nor to limit the interference of government by any universal rule, *save the simple and vague one, that it should never be admitted but when the case of expediency is strong.*[12]

Clearly, libertarian limitations on the functions of government would be far too "restrictive" for Mill. The only universal rule that can be appealed to is "the simple and vague one" that government interference should be avoided unless "the case of expediency is strong." This appears to be more of a rule of thumb than a universal principle, and one may be reasonably concerned that it could be used to justify excessive state control. Nevertheless, one may be just as reasonably concerned that a too-restrictive definition of government functions would prevent the state from acting in cases where it *ought* to act. As Mill puts it in *On Liberty*, "The interference of government is, with about equal frequency, improperly invoked and improperly condemned."[13]

Mill's solution to this problem is the Liberty Principle, which receives its fullest and most familiar treatment in *On Liberty*.[14] However, in *Principles of Political Economy*, Mill formulates an early version of this principle: "There is a circle around every individual human being, which no government . . . ought to be permitted to overstep" unless it is to prevent harm to others; this "reserved territory," Mill continues, "ought to include all that part which concerns only the life, whether inward or outward, of the individual, and does not affect the interests of others."[15] Thus, according to Mill, government agency ought to be limited by the following two principles:

1. It should never be admitted but when the case of expediency is strong. Call this the Expediency Principle (EP).
2. It must not invade the "reserved territory" of individual liberty, unless it is to prevent harm to others. This is commonly known as the Liberty Principle (LP).[16]

In this and the following sections of the paper, I will discuss these two principles, starting with the second, and I will argue that a public health-insurance option would in fact meet their conditions.

Would a public option violate the second principle (LP)? Mill does not seem to think so. Only a short paragraph after formulating his early version of LP, Mill explains that there are positive functions of government "which do not restrain individual free agency." He says:

When a government provides means for fulfilling a certain end, leaving individuals free to avail themselves of different means if in their opinion preferable, there is no infringement of liberty, no irksome or degrading restraint. One of the principal objections to government interference is then absent.[17]

A government may provide services, or "means for fulfilling a certain end," to its citizens, then, without interfering with anyone's liberty. In other words, a government may provide a *public option* to its citizens without violating LP. Even more to the point, Mill states:

> There is [a] kind of intervention which is not authoritative: . . . when, leaving individuals free to use their own means of pursuing any object of general interest, the government, not meddling with them, *but not trusting the object solely to their care*, establishes, side by side with their arrangements, *an agency of its own for a like purpose*. Thus, it is one thing to maintain a Church Establishment, and another to refuse toleration to other religions, or to persons professing no religion. It is one thing to provide schools or colleges, and another to require that no person shall act as an instructor of youth without a government licence. There might be a national bank, or a government manufactory, without any monopoly against private banks and manufactories. . . . There may be public hospitals, without any restriction upon private medical or surgical practice.[18]

And, one might add, there may be a public health-insurance option without any monopoly against private insurance companies. Why should the government leave such an important public good entirely in the hands of private companies, whose primary goal is to make a profit, and who therefore have a direct interest in denying people the coverage that they need? Why should the government not establish "an agency of its own," "side by side with their arrangements," for the simple purpose of providing citizens with basic coverage? Such an "agency," according to Mill, would not interfere with individual liberty; it would merely offer individuals an *option* which they may *choose* to either accept or decline.

Mill acknowledges that some people might object to the compulsory taxes that a public option would entail. After all, the people who would be taxed for a public option in health care are the ones who can already afford health insurance; that is, they would be forced to pay for a benefit that *others* would receive. Would this not interfere with their *freedom* to use their income as they see fit? Would it not, therefore, violate LP? First of all, it is not actually true that a public health-insurance option would be paid for by taxpayers. It would have to finance itself in the same way that private insurance companies do: through consumer premiums. What would make it different from private insurance options, however, is that it would be not-for-profit and that it would be accountable to government rather than to corporate shareholders. Thus, the public option would be one of those "rare cases" in which government agency "pays its own expenses" and therefore "involves nothing of a compulsory nature."[19]

Nevertheless, even if the public option *were* financed by taxpayers, it would still not violate LP. In *On Liberty*, Mill divides the "reserved territory" of individual liberty into the following three "domains": (1) the "inward domain of consciousness," which includes freedom of belief and opinion as well as freedom of the press; (2) liberty of "tastes and pursuits" and the freedom to live according to one's own "plan of life"; and (3) freedom of association.[20] Taxation, when it is in the service of the public welfare (and, presumably, when it is kept within reasonable limits), does not interfere with these "domains" of liberty: that is, taxation does not prevent individuals from practicing whatever religion they want, from forming and professing their own opinions, from developing their own "tastes and pursuits," from living according to their own "plan of life," or from associating with whomever they like. Thus, in *Principles of Political Economy*, Mill devotes several lengthy chapters to the subject of taxation, and nowhere does he suggest that an individual should not be taxed for a public good that he or she chooses not to make use of. As long as the individual is free to develop and pursue his or her own conception of the good—that is, as long as society does not tell the individual what to believe, how to live, or whom to associate with—there is no violation of LP.[21]

Thus, a public health-insurance option would not interfere with individual liberty. In fact, it would actually *promote* liberty in positive ways. For one cannot really develop and pursue one's own conception of the good if one is suffering unnecessarily from a debilitating disease; nor can one really live according to one's own "plan of life" if one is forced to spend one's life paying off debt. By providing affordable coverage to those who cannot afford private insurance, a public option would *free* people from unnecessary suffering and debt, thus helping them to realize their potential as free beings. A public option would therefore *exceed* the conditions of LP, since it would actually promote rather than diminish individual liberty.

IV

Would a public health-insurance option meet the conditions of the Expediency Principle (EP)? The term "expediency" can be understood in either a moral or a non-moral sense. In the *non-moral* sense, expediency simply means usefulness. A public option in health care would be "useful" to the extent that it would promote the public welfare, e.g., by making the population healthier and more productive, and by reducing poverty caused by exorbitant health care costs. In the *moral* sense, expediency is equivalent to the principle of utility, which holds that an action or policy is good if it maximizes happiness or pleasure and minimizes unhappiness or pain. A public option would provide us with the opportunity to minimize many of the evils that exist in the United States today, including unnecessary suffering and death, bankruptcy, debt and poverty, and the fear and anxiety that are caused by these evils. Moreover, when individuals are freed from these overwhelming concerns, they become more capable of pursuing their own happiness in their own way. Thus, a public option would fulfill the utilitarian goal of promoting the greatest happiness for the greatest number of people.

One might appeal, however, to an objection that is often raised against utilitarianism in general: that the "greatest happiness" is promoted only by sacrificing the happiness of some for the sake of others. According to this objection, the people who would be taxed for the public option are the ones who can already afford health insurance; that is, they would be obligated to pay for a benefit that *others* would receive. Would this not have a detrimental effect on *their* happiness? Again, it is not actually true that a public option would be paid for by taxpayers. However, even if it were, it seems obvious enough that the negative consequences of having a public option would pale in comparison to the negative consequences of not having one. Having to pay taxes is a relatively small sacrifice to make (as long as these taxes are kept within reasonable bounds) if it means alleviating the distress of those tens of millions of Americans who cannot afford private insurance. This is especially true if the actual taxpayers could be limited to the extremely wealthy, i.e., to those who are capable of making this sacrifice at very little cost to their own happiness and comfort.

Nevertheless, even if one grants that paying taxes is the lesser of two evils, one may object that these utilitarian "calculations" miss the bigger picture. For it may turn out that, all things considered, people are happiest when the "free agency" of government is *minimized*. Thus, according to Jan Narveson, "it is not logically impossible" to maintain that Mill's utilitarianism actually commits him to the libertarian position. Narveson explains:

> [T]o argue that Libertarianism is actually supported by utilitarianism, one must in effect argue that *it is in the public interest to have everything private*: that the sum of human happiness (or whatever one takes utility to be) will be maximized if with respect to every particular thing there is some particular person or voluntary acting group of persons such that what is done with that thing, within the limits of the rights of others, is determined entirely by the will of *that* person or group.[22]

Certainly, Narveson is right to point out that such conclusions are not logically impossible. But does libertarianism really promote utility? Is it really "in the public interest to have everything private"? More specifically, are Americans really better off *not* having a public health-insurance option? Is utility maximized if the dispensation of health insurance is "determined entirely by the will" of private companies? To argue that libertarianism is *actually* supported by utilitarianism, one would have to show that it *actually* promotes utility.

In fact, health insurance is a good case study because, at least in the United States, it is already (almost) entirely in the hands of private companies. These companies are motivated solely by profit, and so it is clearly not always in their interest to provide people with the coverage that they need. This is precisely what led to the health care crisis in the United States: nearly fifty million Americans are completely uninsured, while many of those who *do* have insurance are denied coverage because of "pre-existing conditions" or for other reasons, and are thus left with a choice between suffering unnecessarily and going into crippling debt. Recent legislation has addressed this problem by making it illegal for insurance companies to discriminate on the basis of "pre-existing conditions" and by making it mandatory for people to buy health insurance.[23] These measures are designed to promote the public good by *limiting* the extent to which health care is "determined by the will" of private companies, since the will of these companies has shown itself to be in direct conflict with the public interest. It seems to me, then, that the best way to promote utility in this case is not to "have everything private," for this would only exacerbate the problem. The solution is in fact *more* rather than less government involvement—and the next logical step would be a public option.

It may certainly be true that it is in the public interest to have *some* or even *most* things private. But why rule out public agency altogether? To maintain that *all* things should be private, without exception, is to block government from acting in cases where it ought to act. Yet Mill does not make this mistake, for he explicitly allows for the possibility of exceptions to the "general practice" of laissez-faire. In *Principles of Political Economy*, Mill explains that, "if the commodity [e.g., health insurance] be one, *in the quality of which society has much at stake*, the balance of advantages may be in favour of some mode and degree of intervention, by the authorized representatives of the collective interest of the state."[24] Does society not have "much at stake" in health care? What "commodity" could be of greater importance to the public interest? Indeed, if government intervention may be justified anywhere, it is in the domain of health care.

V

Even if one is not in principle opposed to the creation of a public option, one may be concerned about its long-term consequences. In particular, one may be concerned that a public option would drive premiums down and consequently put private insurance companies out of business; that this would result in even more government control of health care; and that it would eventually lead to the creation of a "single-payer" system, much like the one in Canada, where government-operated, publicly-funded health insurance is the *only* option. In short, one may be concerned that a public option would "drift" toward "socialism." This possibility is extremely unlikely, since private insurance companies could (and no doubt would) remain competitive by offering, to those who could afford it, more comprehensive coverage than that which would be provided by the public option. Nevertheless, it does raise important questions about the justice of "socialized medicine." Would a "single-payer" system promote the greatest happiness for the greatest number of people? Would it respect the "reserved territory" of individual liberty? In short, would it meet the conditions of EP and LP?

A single-payer system would be "expedient" for many of the same reasons that a public option would: that is, it would insure that all citizens receive medical coverage, thereby making the population healthier and more productive; it would reduce the occurrence of unnecessary suffering and death; it would alleviate debt due to exorbitant medical expenses; it would free people from the fear and anxiety caused by being uninsured or by the possibility of being denied coverage; and it would make people in general healthier and therefore happier. It would also promote individual liberty by literally *freeing* people from their concerns over health care: for a person who has all of his or her medical needs taken care of, without having to worry about the financial consequences of getting sick, is more capable of developing and pursuing his or her own conception of the good than one who does not. Health insurance is therefore a *precondition* for liberty, and it ought to be guaranteed to everyone, whether in the form of a single-payer system, a public option, or, failing these, an individual mandate.

Yet one might object that a single-payer system would diminish individual liberty by eliminating people's *options*. The advantage of a public option, according to this objection, is that it would be one option among many, while a single-payer system would not allow any choice whatsoever in the matter of health insurance. It is doubtful, however, that a system of private health insurance (with or without a public option) actually provides any more *tangible* options than a single-payer system. In the United States, for instance, health insurance is employment-based, which means that an individual's health insurance is typically already chosen for him or her by his or her employer. He or she may be provided with some choice of policy, but this choice is limited to what he or she can afford. Meanwhile, those who cannot afford any insurance at all are currently left without *any* options. The only class to whom private health insurance provides any real freedom of choice is the wealthy. A single-payer system would therefore create more freedom than it would destroy, since it would enable people of *all classes* to direct more of their energy toward pursuing their own happiness in their own way.

VI

State power is indeed limited by individual liberty to the extent that it cannot be used to force people to adopt any particular religion or opinion or way of life. However, it does not follow from this that government is limited to the *sole* function of protecting liberty. For Mill, state power can be used in a number of positive ways to promote the public welfare, and this may include providing basic health insurance to all citizens. A public health-insurance option would be just to the extent that it would meet the following conditions: (1) it would not invade the "reserved territory" of individual liberty; and (2) "the case of expediency is strong." I have suggested that a public option would meet these conditions, and that Mill would therefore have endorsed it as a viable solution to the current health care crisis in the United States.

Sean Donaghue Johnston, Binghamton University

Notes

Thanks to all of the following people: my anonymous reviewers at *Social Philosophy Today*; Wendy Donner, Alistair Macleod, Jan Narveson, Stephen Nathanson, and all others who contributed to the discussion that followed the presentation of this paper at Ryerson University; Bat-Ami Bar On; and my wife and family.

1. John Stuart Mill, *On Liberty*, in *Utilitarianism, On Liberty, Considerations on Representative Government, Remarks on Bentham's Philosophy*, ed. Geraint Williams (London: J. M. Dent, 1993), 70.

2. Ibid., 180.

3. Isaiah Berlin, "Two Concepts of Liberty," in *Social and Political Philosophy: Contemporary Readings*, ed. Baruch A. Brody and George Sher (Fort Worth, Texas: Harcourt Brace College Publishers, 1999), 628.

4. Nicholas Capaldi, "The Libertarian Philosophy of John Stuart Mill" *Reason Papers* 9 (1983): 15.

5. Ibid., 8.

6. Ibid., 7.

7. John Stuart Mill, "Coleridge," in *Mill's Essays on Literature and Society*, ed. J. B. Schneewind (New York: The Macmillan Company, 1965), 336.

8. Ibid., 336–7.

9. Mill, *On Liberty*, 113.

10. John Stuart Mill, *Autobiography of John Stuart Mill* (New York: Columbia University Press, 1924), 153; italics mine.

11. Fortunately, the reform bill has made it illegal for insurance companies to discriminate on the basis of "pre-existing conditions." However, opponents are now actually fighting to *repeal* the bill in its entirety!

12. John Stuart Mill, *Principles of Political Economy, with Some of Their Applications to Social Philosophy*, in *Collected Works of John Stuart Mill*, Volumes II and III, ed. J. M. Robson (Toronto: University of Toronto Press, 1965), 803–4.

13. Mill, *On Liberty* , 78.

14. Ibid., see 78–81.

15. Mill, *Principles of Political Economy*, 938.

16. It is perhaps even more commonly known as the Harm Principle because of its proviso. However, I prefer to call it the Liberty Principle, since, as I understand it, it does not state that government cannot act *at all* unless it is to prevent harm to others. Rather, the principle states that government can act *as long as* it does not invade the "reserved territory" of individual liberty, but that, *if it does* invade this "reserved territory," it can only be for the sake of preventing harm to others. This distinction makes sense when it is remembered that the "free agency" of the state does not necessarily conflict with that of individuals. That is, there is "room" for government to act, "outside" of the "reserved territory" of individual liberty. I will clarify and elaborate upon this point in the following discussion.

17. Mill, *Principles of Political Economy*, 938–9.

18. Ibid., 937; italics mine.

19. Ibid., 939 fn.

20. Mill, *On Liberty*, 80–1.

21. Mill, *Principles of Political Economy*, 5: 2–6.

22. Jan Narveson, "Rights and Utilitarianism," in *New Essays on John Stuart Mill and Utilitarianism*, ed. Wesley E. Cooper, Kai Nielsen, and Steven C. Patten (Guelph, Ontario: Canadian Association for Publishing in Philosophy, 1979), 150; italics in original.

23. Legislators are now debating the justice of this individual mandate. Many believe that a mandate forcing individuals to buy health insurance is coercive and that it is therefore a clear violation of individual liberty. I disagree, since I consider health insurance to be a *precondition* for liberty. A person who has (reliable) health insurance is *freer*, in my opinion, than one who has to constantly worry about the financial consequences of getting sick. Nevertheless, even if the mandate *does* interfere with individual liberty, it may still be justified on the basis of the Liberty Principle's proviso. Robert E. Moffit makes the case that the individual mandate would protect those who have health insurance from "free riders." For those who have health insurance are the ones who end up having to pay for the emergency care of those who do not, through their own insurance premiums and through taxes. Thus, according to Moffit: "An individual mandate for insurance . . . is not simply to assure other people protection from the ravages of a serious illness, however socially desirable that may be; it is also to protect ourselves. Such self-protection is justified within the context of individual freedom; the precedent for this view can be traced to none other than John Stuart Mill" (p. 103). Thus, although the individual mandate is not the most desirable solution to our health care problems, it is perhaps the next best thing to a public option. See Robert E. Moffit, "Personal Freedom, Responsibility, and Mandates," *Health Affairs* 13.2 (1994): 101–4.

24. Mill, *Principles of Political Economy*, 947; italics mine.

You've Earned It!: A Criticism of Sher's Account of Desert in Wages

RYAN JENKINS

Abstract: Desert is a notion ubiquitous in our moral discourse, and the importance of its dictates is perhaps clearest when dealing with the distribution of material resources. George Sher has provided one account of desert in wages, answering the question, "How do workers deserve their wage?" Sher relies on the violation of preexisting "independent standards" that dictate how much of a certain good we think people are entitled to in general. When these standards are violated, they call for an offsetting response at a later point in time in order to restore the moral equilibrium. I argue that this formalization of desert is flawed at the theoretical level and that it has further difficulties when applied to wages in particular. Lastly, I offer some brief remarks about what I think are the criteria for establishing desert in wages.

I. Introduction

Desert is a notion that is ubiquitous in our moral and political discourse. We say that athletes deserve awards, virtuous people deserve to be happy, skillful paintings deserve admiration, and landmarks deserve to be appreciated. We also talk about people getting what they've earned, or getting their due, whether it is a gold medal or a life sentence. These kinds of desert claims have powerful normative implications and they inform our opinions of right and wrong in important ways.[1]

Few desert claims can be said to have such important material consequences as those dealing with the distribution of goods, including wealth, within a society. People often think it a great moral outrage when someone is unable to claim what she deserves, and this response can be especially strong when the desert is in the realm of employment. Because of the importance distributive justice, I will explore the role of desert therein: what about a worker makes her deserve a wage?[2]

George Sher has provided an answer to this question, but I will attempt to show that his theory is unsatisfactory. First, the theory has conceptual problems that I will draw out regarding temporality and agent responsibility. Second, regarding wages in particular, Sher's treatment of deserved differentials in pay is suspect.

II. A Primer on Desert

Desert is usually agreed to be a three-place relationship. To make a desert claim is usually to make a statement of the form "Agent A deserves good G in virtue of basis B."[3] The basis B must be a certain kind of fact about agent A. For example, the fact that someone else has worked hard cannot be a basis for *my* deserving a paycheck. Additionally, the bases of desert and the deserved treatment are linked in a relation of fit: some fact like my having brown hair is not a legitimate basis for my deserving to be awarded a medal for winning a foot race.

Desert judgments involve appraising attitudes of the features of a person.[4] This means that the judgment "Alice deserves to succeed" is imbued with moral character and expresses a stance toward Alice. Our adopting evaluative attitudes toward a person's features or actions is intertwined with our feeling that she deserves something. Desert judgments also have some normative force: if we believe that agent A deserves to receive good G, then we believe it would be morally better for A to receive G and that this desert is a *pro tanto* reason that A receive G.

Philosophers disagree, however, over which desert bases are appropriate for wages. Ability, effort, and utility have all been proposed as the sole basis for deserving a wage.[5] However, compelling criticisms have been leveled against each, and it seems unlikely that there is a plausible monist account of desert in wages. Any satisfactory account will have to be more complex.

There are also disagreements over whether desert necessarily responds to responsibility. In keeping with the responsibility literature, I will call this the voluntarist-nonvoluntarist disagreement. I support a voluntarist conception of desert and have three reasons for doing so. First, I have a strong intuition that nonvoluntarist desert claims are simply misapplying the term *desert*. We sometimes say that victims deserve compensation, that the soldier in the most pain deserves the last shot of morphine, or that human beings deserve respect. These are nonvoluntarist claims, since they claim that an agent can deserve something in virtue of a basis for which she is not responsible. But these are not true cases of desert, so I prefer to test potential desert claims by substituting "deserves" for "has earned." Is it the case that a victim has earned compensation? She has not: she has simply been in the wrong place at the wrong time. Has a human being earned respect by being born of a certain species? Again, she has not done anything special to deserve that treatment. More evidence for voluntarism about desert comes from Scheffler's argument that the reactive attitudes, which are paradigmatic examples of deserved treatment, necessarily respond to responsibility.[6] To feel indignant toward someone while believing that she did not deserve to be the object of that attitude would be to hold an inappropriate or unjustified attitude.

It seems to me that when people use 'desert' to refer to nonvoluntarist bases, they are using the term loosely, and really mean to refer to reasons deriving from entitlements, needs, utilities, etc. This use of 'desert' threatens to rob desert claims of their characteristic force. "These views run the risk of utilizing the notion [of desert] in too loose a sense, so that to claim that someone deserves something just means that it would be good if that person got that thing."[7] Of course, we want to prevent this from happening, and should support a voluntarist position.

Second, even if all desert claims must not be voluntarist, we can certainly agree that desert in wages must be a kind of desert that responds solely to responsibility. To propose a basis for desert in wages—the purpose of this project—that allowed an agent to deserve a wage without expending effort would not be acceptable. It is contained within the concept of a wage itself that work has been done—i.e., that the wage is earned.

Third, we should note that we suffer no loss in the range of claims we can make about economic distributions even if we narrow our use of the term 'desert.' In the cases I mention above, there clearly remain very compelling reasons that the agents in question ought to receive the respective treatment. Victims are entitled to compensation and human beings to respect. In the case of the soldier, utility is plausibly maximized if the soldier in the most pain gets the last shot of morphine, and many would think that provides a good reason that she receive it. We lose nothing and gain clarity by restricting our desert claims to only voluntarist claims. For all of the above reasons, a voluntarist conception of desert will guide me in this paper.

III. Sher on Diachronic Fairness

George Sher puts forth a theory of desert meant to explain a subset of desert claims, including claims about wages. Sher first observes that some desert claims "allow an imbalance that exists at one time to be rectified at another."[8] For example, those who have committed crimes deserve punishment at a later date to "offset" their crimes. In an attempt to capture the intuition that some benefits and burdens should be balanced across time, Sher creates a principle of diachronic fairness (DF). In its third and final incarnation, DF3, Sher's principle is this:

> (DF3) For every good G, every person M, and every period of time P, if M has less (more) of G than he should during P, then M should have correspondingly more (less) of G or some related good than he otherwise should during some later period P."[9]

DF3 seeks to balance benefits and burdens over time. But DF3 "cannot be triggered by just any benefit or burden. Rather, the trigger must be some feature that benefits and burdens sometimes possess."[10] To explain when benefits and burdens fall under the purview of DF3, Sher relies on what he calls "independent standards." Some benefits and burdens are governed by independent standards or norms that "demand that persons enjoy benefits or suffer burdens at particular times, or during particular periods."[11] When these standards are violated, an offsetting is required. To use one of Sher's examples, it is plausible to suppose there exists an independent standard such as "no one should have to endure a certain amount of bad luck."[12] When that standard is violated—when things don't go as that standard would require—we feel that the world would be a better place if that lack of luck were rectified through some sort of compensatory occurrence, say, if that same agent were to experience a run of good luck some time later. Then, a kind of moral balance has been restored.

Sher also argues that DF3 helps to explain typical beliefs about punishment. Since DF3 calls for a lack or excess of a certain good G to be compensated by a corresponding lack or excess of that good (or a related good) at a later time, Sher has to identify some good that is at issue in both the commission of a crime and the suffering of imprisonment. Sher proposes "freedom from moral restraint" as the good at issue in both of these cases.[13] A criminal, he says, has experienced an excess of freedom from restraint that is corrected when she is deprived of that same good at a later date by being sent to prison. Again, the moral equilibrium is restored.

Sher also uses his principle of diachronic fairness to explain the widely held intuition that people deserve wages. He says,

> It is uncontroversial that labor is generally considered a burden, and that wages are never deserved until work is actually done. Thus, deserved wages, like other deserved benefits, may be construed as offsetting prior deviations from independent standards.[14]

What Sher has to show is that a certain kind of work violates—i.e., deviates from—an independent standard. In addition, in order to explain desert in wages, it must be plausible that the violation of that standard requires a compensatory payment of a wage. Is there such a standard? Sher says Miller has offered three possible bases for desert in wages: (1) the danger, difficulty, or unpleasantness of a job, (2) effort expended, and (3) contribution to a company's productivity.[15] Sher is interested in seeing if any of these bases offered by Miller could be thought of as independent standards that are violated by working.

So, does work violate standards (1) by being overly dangerous, difficult, or unpleasant, (2) by involving effort, or (3) by contributing to someone else's productivity? First, we think that some jobs violate independent standards in the sense that they are too dangerous, difficult, or unpleasant to be required of workers, but certainly work does not systematically violate one of these standards.[16] Therefore, we could not use appeals to the first kind of standards to justify desert for wages in general. Sher also observes that (2) putting forth an effort and (3) contributing to productivity do not in themselves violate any standards. That is, neither putting forth an effort nor helping others reach their goals *per se* always give rise to desert claims about wages. Clearly, I can put forth effort on projects of my own without thereby deserving a wage and I can help my neighbor paint her fence without deserving a wage from her.

Instead, as Sher points out, "in the context of a typical work situation," it is the combination of a person's effort and the fact that it contributes to another's ends that makes the worker deserving of a wage. Sher's combination of effort and contribution to another's ends he calls the "subordination of labor."[17]

Sher's full argument, then, looks like this:

1. There exists an independent standard that no person should have his labor subordinated to another's ends.

2. When a person does have his labor subordinated to another's ends, this violation of an independent standard appropriately falls under the purview of DF3.

3. DF3 dictates that, when this standard has been violated, the agent ought to be compensated with the same, or an appropriately similar, good to offset his previous lack.

4. Because a worker has declined to pursue his own goals by working for someone else, "DF3 calls for a response that furthers the worker's [own] purposes in turn."[18] Though we can't literally further the worker's purposes, we can provide him with the means to do that: "A wage," says Sher, "which an employee can convert to goods and services of his own choosing, is singularly well suited to serve this function."[19]

5. The agent who subordinated his labor to another's ends therefore ought to receive a wage so that he may further his own purposes in turn.

This is how Sher explains desert for wages with an appeal to diachronic balancing. But, in addition to thinking that workers deserve wages in general, we also think that some differentials in pay are deserved—we think some workers deserve more than others. Sher presumably makes room for differentials in pay based on the amount of effort that workers expend, and he also tells us that appealing to violations of standards regarding danger, difficulty, and unpleasantness could account for deserved differentials in pay. So, then, the degree to which our primary standard—the subjugation of labor—is violated, combined with additional violations of standards barring dangerous, difficult or unpleasant work, determines the desert of a worker because they all affect the degree to which a worker has subordinated her labor.

IV. Problems in Sher's Theory

I find that Sher's approach to diachronic of desert—the kind that he believes governs wages—has problems that should give us pause. First, his use of independent standards broadens his conception of desert to include bases for which the agent is not responsible. I find this unacceptable for dealing with wages. Second, Sher's theory has an insensitivity to time when dealing with punishment, which is its motivating case. Finally, Sher's analysis of deserved differentials in pay is suspect as well.

The first two of these are problems for Sher's theory of desert in general. We might think that as long as Sher's theory acceptably handles wages we should pass over the first two criticisms. But Sher's approach to diachronic desert is inextricably bound to his explanation of desert and wages. If Sher's theory in the abstract is marred by difficulty, then we should not be content to hold our noses during its application to wages. If anything, these problems indicate that Sher is erring on the side of parsimony by hoping to account for the desert of different goods with a single theory. If the problems I lay out below are serious, though, they give us reason to think that we would do better to focus on desert in wages itself rather than trying to provide an account that captures wages, punishment, and other goods that are seemingly unrelated.

A. Voluntarist and Nonvoluntarist Desert Bases

Sher's independent standards yield a range of recommendations for a variety of reasons. Here is one way to draw that out. We might assent to two separate independent standards that, upon their violation, would yield the same recommendations for compensation, but for very different reasons. Here are two such plausible standards: (1) a person should only have to endure a certain amount of bad luck; (2) a person who has trained should enjoy success in the appropriate endeavor. Now let's imagine two amateur golfers that have taken to the links, Jones and Smith. Jones has done poorly his last several games, due to unpredictable changes in the wind just after his tee shots. Smith, on the other hand, has trained for months in preparation, but is still having difficulty lowering his score. We can see that a violation of one of the above independent standards has taken place in each case: Jones has endured more bad luck than we think appropriate, and Smith has trained intensively to no avail. According to the independent standards we recognize and DF3, both Smith and Jones deserve to succeed in this (or a future) game. But, certainly, these are two very different reasons for attributing their deserts. As we can see, the standard at issue in Smith's case is voluntarist—it is tied to his responsibility for past actions—while the standard in Jones's case is not. If a voluntarist view of desert is correct, as I argued above, then Jones ought to do well, but doesn't deserve to. And even if desert turns out to include nonvoluntarist reasons, explanations that differ in their reliance on responsibility ought to be clearly distinguishable.

Sher's embrace of nonvoluntarist desert bases is clearest when he discusses compensation for victims, which I referred to above as a paradigmatic case of the improper use of 'desert.' Sher argues that compensation can be deserved because there are independent standards governing the ways people may be treated and the suffering that people should have to undergo. When violated, the former standards demand punishment while the latter demand compensation.[20] But what about people who suffer harm through no one's fault? We often believe that certain lives simply contain too much hardship. This is perhaps the ultimate case of nonvoluntarist reasons: not only is the agent a victim (they have not themselves given an appraisable performance), but they are not even a victim of anyone's, they are a victim of circumstances. It becomes more difficult to assert against fate this kind of free-floating independent standard, and Sher seems to appreciate the difficulty. When any connection to responsibility is removed from the equation, Sher says that he is sympathetic to the view that such hardships demand compensation, but "I have no compelling arguments for it."[21] He is content to leave that question open. The problem is that I see no important distinction between cases of terrible fate and cases of genuine victimhood: if the basis for some agent's deserving a good must be a performance of theirs, then in neither case does the agent deserve compensation.

B. Temporality and Independent Standards

I have a reason for thinking that DF3, combined with the violations of independent standards, might also fail to capture a temporal sensitivity that is very important in desert claims. Think about the following example, taken from Sher:

1. We feel that people are entitled to a certain amount of freedom from moral restraint.
2. When a person commits a crime, she has enjoyed an excess of this freedom.
3. We compensate for this one-time excess by imprisoning her, depriving her of some freedom.[22]

This is Sher's archetypical example that motivates his conception of desert as a diachronic balancing act. But Sher's principle does not specify any particular temporal direction in which it is working: DF3 is designed to compensate for a lack or an excess of the good G. That means that DF3 ought to be applicable if we reverse the way in which the standard is violated. Let's take a look at what would happen, though, in Sher's paradigmatic example of diachronic desert:

1. We feel that people are entitled to a certain amount of freedom from moral restraint.
2. When a person has been wrongly convicted of a crime and imprisoned, she has been deprived of that freedom.
3. To compensate, we gift her with an offsetting excess of freedom, permitting her to commit a crime under a carefully chosen set of circumstances.

This, of course, is ridiculous.[23] The wrongfully imprisoned, after being exonerated, are most often given money, if they are given anything at all. While this does not completely eradicate the wrong wrought by the state, it is not inappropriate, either. Monetary compensation is a fitting repayment for lost income during time spent in prison, but there are other losses that don't seem to merit a simple financial payment. In particular, wrongful incarceration often results in lifelong psychological trauma that requires extensive counseling and rehabilitation.

So, then, why doesn't Sher's DF3 account for this kind of violation of a standard? Perhaps it is because the simple language of the standards he provides ignores some vital complexity in our thinking. It might also be the fault of DF3, which is not sensitive to the unidirectional temporal manner in which some standards are characteristically violated. We might try to avoid this problem by tweaking our independent standards. Instead of phrasing them as, "People are entitled to some certain amount of freedom from moral restraint," perhaps they would be better phrased as, "People are entitled to some certain amount of freedom from moral restraint and no more." Now, we have a standard that is sensitive to violation only by criminals, and is not violated when someone is wrongfully imprisoned. The problem, of course, is that we would have to come up with a separate standard that does govern wrongful imprisonment, and it would bear a striking resemblance to our previous standard (with the only difference being "no more" reading "no less"). This second standard would also have to be formulated in such a way so as to recommend financial recompense upon violation if this is taken to be the proper mode of compensation in this case. Let's make our standards explicit for the sake of clarity:

Punishment$_1$: People are entitled to some certain amount of freedom from moral restraint and no more.

Punishment$_2$: People are entitled to some certain amount of freedom from moral restraint and no less.

Both of these standards govern the amount of freedom from moral restraint that people are allowed to have, but they differ with regard to the rectifications that they require. The commission of a crime violates Punishment$_1$. DF3 would simply demand that we take some of the agent's freedom from moral restraint away to restore the equilibrium. The imprisonment of an innocent person would violate Punishment$_2$, and that violation would require that we compensate the agent with money. This "splitting" of the independent standard regarding freedom from moral restraint, though, feels *ad hoc*, and the fact that these new standards recommend different rectificatory action based on the way in which the standard was violated should make us uneasy. DF3 says that there is some good G or an analogous good that should be repaid to rectify the injustice, but what that good is should not depend on how the standard was violated.

Perhaps this is only a problem for Sher's theory when it is applied to punishment. But the same problem arises in the case of wages, though in a more subtle form. Sher's theory requires the subjugation of labor to be offset by a monetary payment. Suppose we reverse the order in this case as well, and imagine that Smith's employer has paid him in advance for work he plans to do. In this case, it is strange to say that Smith's employer deserves to have Smith's labor subordinated to him. It is natural, instead, to say that Smith's employer is entitled to the work through some implicit agreement. Here, reversing the violation of the independent standard at issue in wages takes us out of the realm of deserts altogether.

C. Danger, Difficulty and Unpleasantness

One requirement of an account of desert in wages is that it explain deserved differentials in pay. When asked why, between two workers who deserve their wage, one deserves more than the other, a natural response is to appeal to some unpleasant facts about the one worker's job. These additional burdens, which are often cashed out in terms of "danger, difficulty and unpleasantness," stand in need of offsetting. Sher includes a discussion of these factors as well, but it is somewhat unclear how to explain deserved differentials in terms of Sher's independent standards.

The connection between the subjugation of labor and the desert of a wage is made clear: a worker is sacrificing her own interests to further her employer's. Therefore, she ought to be given the means to pursue her own interests, and a wage is "uniquely suited" for this purpose. It is not clear, however, exactly why those enduring danger, difficulty, or unpleasantness deserve a higher wage. That is, why does enduring danger make a person more deserving of financial recompense? If we were using a theory relying on the shouldering of burdens to explain desert, as some theorists do, we could say that danger, difficulty, and unpleasantness are simply further burdens that demand further monetary compensation. But Sher is appealing to the violation of a standard that calls for a lack of certain goods to be compensated later by the same, or a related, good. So, we can ask: under Sher's conception, if a person risks danger in her work, why doesn't she deserve, instead, a period of safety? That is the most natural way to restore the balance, since this worker has plausibly lacked safety for a period. Likewise for those completing a difficult task, or those enduring unpleasant jobs: why don't they deserve, say, a period of leisure?

I suspect Sher would answer that money is, again, uniquely suited to provide these workers with safety or leisure. The former claim is suspect—guaranteeing a person safety through monetary payment seems unlikely—and the latter could be more easily accomplished with the simple reward of more vacation time.[24] Sher does not rigorously analyze appeals to violations of these standards as reasons for a higher wage, but it is not clear how these considerations, on Sher's theory, give reasons for a higher wage.

For these reasons, I find Sher's explanation of desert in wages a difficult one to support. Now, I will offer some preliminary remarks about what I think are the conditions for deserving a wage. First of all, work has to have been done. This will not come as a surprise for two reasons: (1) I have so far leaned heavily on my belief that desert in general requires an action or performance, and (2) wages are by their nature given in exchange for work having been done. Second, the work has to have been subordinated to another's ends. This criterion I have in common with Sher, but it should also be obvious from an analysis of what a wage is. Wages are not paid out from an agent to herself, they are paid from the employer to the employee, where the latter has done some work for the former. So far this conception is rather thin. It would justify paying wages for assassinations as well as counting blades of grass. In order to keep out those cases, the work done must be socially valuable. This criterion is most controversial and most difficult to elaborate, but it also flows naturally from an investigation of desert and wages. Desert is an appraising attitude, whereby we take a moral stance toward some action. We ought not give wages for pointless actions nor for harmful ones. The former are undeserving actions; the latter are deserving of resentment, not a wage. It is admittedly difficult to articulate what it means for an action to be socially valuable, and it would certainly have to wait for another paper. But the inclusion of a criterion of value is necessary to round out a conception of desert and wages. These conditions are independently necessary and jointly sufficient: if a worker has subordinated their labor to another's ends, and their work has been socially valuable, then they deserve a payment from their employer for their work.

V. Conclusion

Our strong intuitions about desert guide us in our judgments about the distribution of goods, and so we should look for a theoretical explanation of exactly how deserts come about. George Sher has supplied one explanation that relies on the diachronic balancing of some benefits and burdens, and has applied his theory to desert in wages. In this paper, I have exposed some of the problems of that theory. I showed that Sher fails to discriminate between desert bases that do and do not depend on responsibility, that the temporal balancing act of his theory can lead to strange recommendations, and that his theory of deserved differentials in wages is also suspect. I think a more promising approach than Sher's would be to examine particular deserved goods and try to establish their necessary and sufficient conditions, rather than providing a theory of desert in the abstract and trying to make particular deserts compatible with that theory. Finally, I sketched the outlines of such a theory of desert in wages that I think has strong intuitive attractiveness.

Ryan Jenkins, University of Colorado Boulder

Notes

This paper has benefitted greatly from audience comments at the 27th International Social Philosophy Conference. I am also grateful for comments on earlier drafts from Randolph Clarke, M. Victoria Costa, Patrick Mason, David McNaughton, and Kelly Vincent.

1.   For a detailed discussion of the relationship between theories of justice and empirical evidence of beliefs about desert, see David Miller, "Distributive Justice, What People Think," *Ethics* 102.3 (April 1992): 555–93.

2.   It seems likely that desert alone does not exhaust the list of moral reasons that could be given to support a distribution of wages. I agree that reasons such as need, entitlement, and social utility probably also play an important role in determining the justice of a wage.

3.   Sometimes, a fourth place is added to the relationship: from X. In this paper, I will not discuss the fourth place in the relationship, as I take it to be uninteresting that, insofar as an agent deserves a wage, she deserves it from her employer.

4.   *Desert and Justice*, ed. Serena Olsaretti (New York: Oxford University Press, 2003), 4.

5.   Jeffrey Moriarty, "Do CEOs Get Paid Too Much?" *Business Ethics Quarterly* 15.2 (April 2005): 257–81.

6.   Samuel Scheffler, "Distributive Justice and Economic Desert," in Olsaretti, *Desert and Justice*, 71ff.

7.   Olsaretti, *Desert and Justice*, 6.

8.   George Sher, *Desert* (New York: Princeton University Press, 1987), 91.

9.   Ibid., 94.

10.   Ibid.

11.   Ibid.

12.   Ibid., 91.

13.   Ibid., 82–3.

14.   Ibid., 99. Sher is not concerned with the kind of work we do for ourselves or for others *pro bono*. He is concerned with work done for another and at the direction of another in order to make a living. This is not work done for fun, enrichment, altruism, or reasons besides its being one's capitalist employ.

15.   Sher, *Desert*, 100. Sher is referencing David Miller, *Principles of Social Justice* (New York: Harvard University Press, 2001).

16.   Nonetheless, violations of standards regarding danger, difficulty and unpleasantness help Sher to justify differentials in pay. This is discussed below.

17.   Sher treats the concepts of productivity, contribution and subordination as very closely related—so much so that I will treat them as interchangeable. To Sher, the more a worker produces, the more she is contributing to her employer's ends, and the more of her labor is subordinated. See Sher, *Desert*, 101–2.

18.   Ibid.,102.

19.   Ibid.

20.   Ibid., 97.

21.   Ibid., 99.

22.   Ibid., 82–3.

23.   Sher does anticipate a similar problem with his explanation of punishment (ibid.). That problem is that it might award "free crimes" to people who have simply had to bear some

hardship in their life. But that is not the particular objection I am making. I am not making a claim about any kind of previous hardships, but wrongful imprisonment in particular.

24. It is also plausible that certain jobs have an amount of social stigma that is endured by their workers. Perhaps a higher salary is meant to offset this stigma by imparting an ostensible recognition by society of an employee's worth. See Michael Walzer, *Spheres of Justice: A Defense of Pluralism and Equality* (New York: Basic Books, 1984) for more on this idea.

The Incompleteness of Luck Egalitarianism

RYAN LONG

I. Introduction

Luck egalitarianism makes a fundamental distinction between inequalities for which agents are responsible and inequalities stemming entirely from luck. The aim of the view is, other things being equal, to ignore the former and rectify the latter. The ideal situation is that each person exerts an equal amount of control over her place in the distribution, and that deviations from distributive equality caused solely by luck are minimized. The essential thought behind luck egalitarianism is agnostic on the metric of equality. You can have a luck egalitarian theory about welfare, or resources, or several other metrics. We need only keep in view that these theories aim to make the distribution (of whichever metric) shaped primarily by things for which the agent is responsible, such as informed and free choices, and to compensate for inequalities stemming solely from luck. Paradigm forms of luck that generate unjust inequalities are the wealth or class of the family to which one is born, discrimination based on one's sex or race, and the market value of one's native endowments (the portion of one's talents that are purely innate rather than intentionally cultivated). The view is compatible with great levels of distributive inequality, so long as those inequalities have the proper sorts of causes. When a bearer of an inequality is responsible for her condition, that inequality can be just.

The egalitarian theories of G. A. Cohen, Ronald Dworkin, Larry Temkin, John Roemer, and Richard Arneson are prime examples of luck egalitarian views. Arneson claims this group is united in thinking that "the essence of social justice is the imperative to improve the condition of people who suffer from simple bad luck."[1] Temkin argues that "it is bad—unjust and unfair—for some to be worse off than others through no fault [or choice] of their own."[2] Dworkin argues for a view that is "ambition sensitive" and "endowment insensitive," in other words, sensitive to choices and efforts, insensitive to arbitrary circumstances and native endowments. Cohen claims that "genuine choice excuses otherwise unacceptable inequalities."[3] These theorists all view deviations from distributive equality through the lens of responsibility. Whether it is unjust for someone to be worse off than others depends on whether that person is responsible for being worse off than others. Whether it is unjust for someone to be better off than others depends on whether she has done anything to make herself better off, or whether she is merely lucky (e.g., born into a privileged position). Inequalities stemming from choice are treated differently from inequalities stemming from luck.

The only conditions under which these theories allow luck to generate just inequalities are when we make free choices whose outcomes are shaped by luck. This is what Dworkin calls option luck, as opposed to the mere brute luck of, say, your starting place in society or your innate talents. If a person makes a free choice to take a risk, under ideal conditions they can be responsible for that choice. A resulting inequality can therefore be just, even though it is partially generated by forces outside that person's control. Therefore luck egalitarianism does not attempt to neutralize all luck. It rather wants to make the distribution of benefits and burdens in society maximally sensitive to choice, even if those choices have outcomes that are partially determined by forces outside the agent's control. Luck egalitarianism primarily wants to neutralize inequalities that stem from brute luck.

In this paper I will motivate luck egalitarianism as a compelling theory, argue that it is incomplete and lacks the normative resources to achieve its stated ends, and then briefly outline my strategy for rehabilitating the theory. My goal is to develop a new criticism of luck egalitarianism and to argue that the same concerns that push one to accept the view also lead one to conclude that it is an incomplete theory of equality. The positive remarks at the end attempt to briefly outline a strategy for solving this problem without rejecting luck egalitarianism entirely.

II. Motivating Luck Egalitarianism

II.1. The Value of Choice

There is a *prima facie* plausibility to a morally and politically salient distinction between choice and luck. The distinction shapes ethical judgment. We evaluate what an agent chose or did, not what happened to or befell the agent. That which is outside the domain of choice seems outside the domain of responsibility. In the context of egalitarianism, this distinction indicates that our lives should be sensitive to our choices—distributive justice should not make lives insensitive to choice, or do away with the option of taking substantive risks. Choice sensitivity is of intrinsic and instrumental value.

The intrinsic value is illuminated when we consider that the alternative, undermining choice-sensitivity, is incompatible with our conception of ourselves as free and autonomous agents. Consider what Scanlon calls the symbolic value of choice—if we are free to choose then we are seen and treated as someone qualified to choose. If we are not allowed to make a choice, this is demeaning.[4] Typically we abridge the power of choice for children or those who are deemed deficient in some way, or we abridge the power of choice based on a patriarchal rationale. The egalitarian upshot is that our lives should not be unduly shaped by that which is not the product of our choices. Our welfare, resources, social status, and opportunities should not fundamentally be determined by forces outside our control.

The instrumental value of choice-sensitivity has to do with theories of productivity and efficiency. For familiar *laissez faire* reasons, it is thought that conditions of unconstrained choice lead to greater productivity. Under such conditions we will have a larger amount of goods to distribute than if choices were regulated and constrained, and thus we will be in a stronger position to aid those who are worse off than others through no fault of their own. Choice sensitivity also encourages efficiency in the following way. If agents know that they must bear the benefits and burdens of their choices, this incentivizes prudent choices.[5]

We see then that this value of choice is ecumenical. It can be supported by leftist concerns for autonomy, rightist concerns for negative liberty, or economic concerns about efficiency and productivity. All of these favor choice-sensitivity, and insofar as luck egalitarianism emphasizes choice-sensitivity, it is justified by the value of choice. Luck egalitarianism gives us a way to pursue a form of equality without letting the imprudent exploit the prudent and without subsidizing bad choices. It follows that luck egalitarianism can be endorsed by those who otherwise would not be egalitarians. As Cohen says, luck egalitarianism can co-opt "the most powerful idea in the arsenal of the anti-egalitarian right: the idea of choice and responsibility."[6] The things anti-egalitarians typically find objectionable about a commitment to equality, such as an impulse to have strict distributive equality for its own sake (which strikes them as based in envy), or the possibility that we ought to level down everyone's condition in order to reach equality, or that we need to subsidize bad choices, are not in view here.

II.2. Resolving Troublesome Distributive Cases

If our metric of equality has anything to do with welfare, that is, with the happiness or pleasure one gets out of life, then we have the problem of expensive tastes. To obtain the same level of welfare, people with different tastes may require radically different amounts of resources. But it hardly seems fair to redistribute more resources to someone simply because they have expensive tastes. What if I need champagne to obtain a given level of welfare, but you can obtain it with the champagne of beers? Is it fair to subsidize my expensive taste? Even more worrisome, suppose that I have knowledge of the egalitarian scheme that is operative and then intentionally exploit the system by developing expensive tastes just to procure more resources.

Egalitarian theories that do not fundamentally appeal to the luck/choice distinction either have to move away from any concern for welfare, or they must subsidize too many cases of expensive tastes. Neither of these alternatives is very attractive. On the other hand, luck egalitarianism can make a distinction between tastes for which the person is responsible and tastes for which they are not. If we make a distinction between tastes that are chosen or intentionally cultivated versus tastes that are the product of environment, or are not identified with, or that the agent chooses to struggle against or revise, then we can get the right outcome in these cases. Only tastes that are strictly beyond the control of the agent, and hence cannot be considered the agent's responsibility, pose a problem of justice. Of course taking one of these strategies requires a lot of hard work in terms of spelling out how tastes are acquired and what sort of control we can exert over tastes. But luck egalitarianism has the resources to allow such work to be done, and that is a substantial improvement over alternate responses to expensive tastes. When we understand equality in terms of choice and responsibility, we are only concerned with expensive tastes in cases where their bearers absolutely cannot help having them and cannot change them.

Luck egalitarianism can give a similar response to the problem of free riders, those who would reap the benefits of a redistributive scheme without doing their fair share. We can differentiate those who cannot work and are not responsible for that fact from those who choose not to work, and we can subsidize only the former. This is another way that luck egalitarianism co-opts the values of anti-egalitarians and can attract adherents from across the political spectrum.

Another puzzling case has to do with how we prioritize aid under conditions of scarcity. If we can only aid a subset of candidates, it coheres with our understanding of fairness to first address those least responsible for their predicament, and then last (if at all) those who made choices that caused their predicament. Consider an example that Arneson uses to present the "basic idea" of luck egalitarianism. Suppose three groups of hikers are stranded on a mountain in a blizzard: experienced climbers who took a calculated risk and entered dangerous terrain marked with warning signs, children on a tour who are trapped in unmarked and typically safe terrain, and reckless tourists who ignored the warning signs and entered dangerous terrain.[7]

Further suppose we can only rescue one group. We are to pick which group based on the intrinsic merit of the decision—not based on what instrumental value the choice has in shaping future behavior. (Suppose the park is closing permanently.) It seems our intuition is that the children are most deserving of being saved. The climbers chose to take an informed risk and under the circumstances it is not unfair to make them bear the cost of that risk. The tourists were negligent, so again, it is not unfair to make them bear the consequences of their negligence. They violated a normative standard when they chose to ignore a warning that they ought to have heeded. The children are clearly the least responsible for their predicament. Arneson argues that the basic idea of luck egalitarianism is that the children deserve saving because their predicament is not due to choice.[8]

This is the procedure luck egalitarianism uses to resolve cases in which, due to some scarcity, we cannot aid all candidates. We rank situations by the extent to which they were generated by choice, which is to say, the extent to which the relevant agents are responsible for their predicaments. We prioritize aid to those least responsible for their predicament, and only then, if at all, give aid to those who are responsible. This gives a fair outcome in terms of expensive tastes, free riders, and aiding people under conditions of scarcity. Arneson's rescue example is artificial, but the reasoning can apply to many forms of scarcity. It can be used to argue that we ought to prioritize liver transplants in light of individual behavior, so that we aid last those who can be held responsible for damaging their livers through drinking. (I do not intend to defend such a policy here, but merely present it as an example of how this basic idea can be applied to a wide range of problems.)

This should be sufficient to show why one might be attracted to the basic idea of luck egalitarianism. I now turn to my criticism. I argue that any tenable form of luck egalitarianism, that is, any theory that puts defeasibility conditions on when individual choices have the right character to generate just inequalities, must not define equality solely in terms of choice, luck, and responsibility. Luck egalitarians are forced to become pluralists because their theory is inadequate to achieve their stated ends. They must incorporate other egalitarian values.

III. The Incompleteness of Luck Egalitarianism

Luck egalitarianism is not a full theory of equality. The theory's aim is to specify the justice (or injustice) of particular deviations from distributive equality in terms of the distinction between choice and luck. If the bearer of an inequality is genuinely responsible for her condition, then (absent other considerations) that inequality is not unjust. However, the resources internal to luck egalitarianism are inadequate to complete this project.

A given luck egalitarian theory is tenable only if it puts some defeasibility conditions on how individual choices can generate just inequalities. Tracing a given inequality back to an act of will does not alone show that it is just—what if the agent was coerced or had a severely constrained set of choices? What if the agent was privileged and had the option to take many favorable gambles unavailable to others?

In response to this problem Dworkin makes a compelling and natural, but flawed, move. He claims that "the argument in favor of allowing differences in option luck to affect income and wealth assumes that everyone has in principle the same gambles available to him. Someone who never had the opportunity to run a similar risk, and would have taken the opportunity had it been available, will still envy some of those who did have it."[9] My objection is that this gives us a picture of just inequalities that either sets an unattainable standard or is indeterminate.

One the one hand, we could have a resolute reading of the requirement that everyone have the same set of available gambles. However, actual gambles are in fact (almost) never in principle available to everyone, in which case Dworkin's theory judges few (or no) inequalities to be just. Thus the strong initial commitment to the value of choice would undermine itself, since it turns out that no choices actually meet the standard required for a resulting inequality to be just. This is unacceptable, since the theory was supposed to explain the difference between just and unjust inequalities, but it turns out that nothing meets the standard of being a just inequality.

On the other hand, we could specify the meaning of "in principle" sameness in a weaker sense. However, this cannot be done merely in the luck egalitarian language of choice alone. In the first prong of the dilemma, his theory undermines itself, given its strong initial commitment to choice and responsibility. The second prong shows that his theory is incomplete, and that if we want to remain luck egalitarians, we must move toward a pluralist understanding of equality. I present the argument against Dworkin, but this is a general problem facing any luck egalitarian theory that wants to employ defeasibility conditions on choice.

In order to gloss what "in principle" sameness means, we have to find a standard on a continuum from fine-grained to coarse-grained. At the fine-grained extreme, having the same opportunities to take gambles would mean having the exact same gambles available. At the coarse-grained extreme we would specify gambles in a maximally abstract sense—perhaps 'to take a gamble on owning a business.' It is not entirely clear where this end would terminate, but the idea is clear enough for our purposes. At the fine-grained extreme you and I must have options to take the exact same gambles. At the coarse-grained extreme these gambles become abstract and fungible, so that two persons can have the same options in principle, even though they are not strictly equivalent options.

The fine-grained extreme is clearly not Dworkin's view, nor is it a tenable view. It is simply the resolute reading given above. Dworkin's use of the phrase "in principle," is a way to move away from the fine-grained extreme. If he endorsed the resolute reading, Dworkin would have said all persons must have available the exact same gambles, not "in principle" the same gambles. In any case, the fine-grained extreme is not a tenable view because even the most invasive totalitarianism could never achieve exact parity of opportunities among a substantial set of citizens. Even in a highly egalitarian state, the options available to a given person will vary according to numerous factors, including their family and upbringing. We could never meet the condition that all people have the same options to take the same gambles. On this reading, the theory sets choice-based conditions on just inequalities that could never be met.

Thus we need to move on the continuum away from that extreme. To determine where we stop on the continuum, we must appeal to some further value or concern outside of luck egalitarianism. To say that two sets of available gambles are in principle the same is to say they are equivalent by some standard outside that continuum, to say that they are non-identical yet equal enough. There is nothing intrinsic to the concepts of choice, responsibility, or luck that will determine where we should be on this continuum. Those concepts are insufficient to tell us whether sets of options A and B are in principle the same. We need some further egalitarian value to tell us when two sets of options are in principle the same, because this is precisely a question about equality itself—what is it for two agents to be situated in circumstances that are not exactly the same, but equivalent enough such that the choices that they make can matter to distributive justice?

In order to determine whether two sets of gambles are equal enough, we need some normative standard. But luck egalitarianism's only norm is the value of choice, and that value is of no use here. Luck egalitarianism starts with a normative claim that individual choices have some value, and that the distribution should be highly choice-sensitive. Beyond that, luck egalitarianism is primarily a theory of causal origins: to evaluate a given inequality, we look at what caused it. This is of no help whatsoever in determining whether two sets of options are in principle the same. We need something beyond the value of choice to answer that question.

Therefore luck egalitarianism is incomplete. I make this point against Dworkin, but it is utterly general. If you want instead a defeasibility condition that states everyone simply needs some minimal set of opportunities, then you have the same problem. Luck egalitarianism cannot determine a just and sufficient minimum floor. It does not have the normative resources.

IV. A Brief Sketch of a Solution

I see two possible strategies for reforming luck egalitarianism. One is to incorporate further egalitarian values to help determine when two sets of options are equivalent enough. The other is to incorporate further egalitarian values to determine when persons have a sufficient set of available options. If we can successfully pursue either strategy then we will have the normative resources to resolve the defeasibility problem, and thus luck egalitarianism will be able to set clear, attainable conditions on when individual choices generate just deviations from distributive equality.

The most promising strategy is to define a sufficient set of options. I suspect that any attempt to determine a workable standard for specifying when two sets of options are equivalent enough will have to be so coarse-grained that it essentially collapses into the strategy of defining a sufficient set of options. The mere existence of the traditional family is sufficient to ensure that there will be substantial differences in the opportunities that different citizens have. Citizens will always have qualitatively different options available to them. Some citizens will also simply have more options than others, so there is no way to put the options available to different citizens in one-to-one correspondence. These are facts we simply must accept, since even totalitarian intervention cannot change them. I am also skeptical that we ought to be concerned with everyone having an equivalent set of opportunities, because this is close to valuing strict equality for its own sake and thus again raises the specter of envy. In some cases, it simply does not matter whether two persons had the same opportunities. Consider two extremely privileged individuals, one slightly more privileged than the other. If the slightly more privileged individual takes a risk unavailable to the slightly less privileged individual, and this leads to greater inequality between them, that does not concern me. Both of them had a wide range of opportunities and a fair chance to flourish in their society.

My preferred method for resolving this problem is a transition from Dworkin's concern over the equality of sets of available gambles to a concern over the social equality of persons. By social equality I have in mind something similar to Elizabeth Anderson's conception of democratic equality.[10] (This means I am co-opting one of the most powerful ideas in the arsenal of the anti-luck-egalitarian left.) A conception of social equality could appeal to what one needs to fully function as a citizen in a particular society, and what one needs to stand in social relationships to other citizens that are characterized by equal respect. If social equality requires that everyone has some minimal set of available options and some minimal amount of resources, then the question will not be whether everyone has in principle the same set of available gambles, but whether everyone has a sufficient set. This makes the defeasibility problem tractable. Going back to the language of "fine grained" and "coarse grained," we will give a relatively coarse-grained description of what sorts of options must be available to everyone to guarantee social equality.

Once we articulate a particular conception of the citizen and what is required for citizens to stand in social relations of equality, we can generate a benchmark for judging a set of available gambles sufficient. If a citizen chooses from among a sufficient set of available gambles, then her choices can create just deviations from strict distributive equality. We can go on to define types of gambles in terms of various goods and ends that are crucial to social equality. These key domains of choice would include opportunities for employment, income, education, mobility, recreation, self-expression, self-respect, and so on. As long as everyone has what they need to fully function as a citizen (such as access to education, the ability to move throughout the public sphere, a minimum level of material well being and security, access to information so they can be an informed voter, etc.), and as long as everyone has some sufficient set of opportunities available in each key domain of choice, then we have a genuine equality of position among persons. Luck egalitarianism needs this prior form of equality to obtain in order for the value of choice to carry any weight. Only when those conditions obtain can individual choices generate just deviations from strict distributive equality. When these conditions do not obtain, citizens make their choices from radically unequal starting positions, and thus there is no reason to think individual choice can generate just deviations from distributive equality. This minimum sufficient standard of material well being and available opportunities should be understood as society-specific, and as something that will change over time. It is a political question that must be worked out in light of the opportunities a given society makes available, that society's productive capacity, its resources, and so on.

This is how to resolve the incompleteness of luck egalitarianism. My argument establishing the incompleteness of the view was completely internal to luck egalitarianism, that is, it did not involve objections based in any competing view of equality. My solution to the problem, the appeal to a minimum set of opportunities and resources that each citizen must have to fully function as an equal citizen, also lets us answer many of the strongest external criticisms of luck egalitarianism. I will give one example. Elizabeth Anderson argues that luck egalitarianism abandons those citizens whose choices lead to catastrophic outcomes, and that the theory expresses no concern for the well-being of such persons. She discusses several cases of the following sort. Suppose a driver chose to forgo all forms of insurance and then negligently makes an illegal turn that causes an accident. This negligent driver suffers terrible injuries. He now requires extensive medical care and will need ongoing aid to deal with his permanent disabilities. Anderson worries that luck egalitarianism leads us to abandon this person entirely, because this person is responsible for their predicament and the theory sets no minimum floor of well-being and material security.[11] The problem can be generalized beyond this to include individuals whose choices lead to crushing poverty, either because they made imprudent choices or because they made reasonably prudent choices but nonetheless suffered terrible option luck in the marketplace.

My resolution of the internal incompleteness problem also solves this external objection. My variant of luck egalitarianism requires that everyone has a sufficient set of opportunities. For those opportunities to be meaningful, and for each person to be able to fully function as a citizen, there must be a minimum level of material well-being guaranteed for all. That minimum level is not forsaken even when individuals make choices that would otherwise put them in a desperate situation. Choice-sensitivity no longer requires us to abandon anyone. Everyone needs a minimum set of opportunities and a minimum level of material well-being for luck egalitarianism to be a compelling theory. When this condition does not obtain, then we ought not think that individual choices can generate just deviations from equality, because many choices will simply perpetuate prior unjust inequalities. Luck egalitarianism's emphasis on choice only makes sense when everyone is making their choices from a position of relative material security, and when they are choosing among a sufficient menu of real options. Further development of this strategy will allow us to preserve the deep truth in luck egalitarianism while resolving its incompleteness and improving its response to those people whose choices threaten their basic ability function as citizens.

Ryan Long, University of Chicago

Notes

1.   Richard J. Arneson, "Luck Egalitarianism Interpreted and Defended," *Philosophical Topics* 32.1/2 (2004): 1.

2.   Larry Temkin, *Inequality* (Oxford University Press, 1993), 13n21.

3.   G. A. Cohen, "On The Currency of Egalitarian Justice," *Ethics* 99 (1989): 931.

4.   T. M. Scanlon, *What We Owe To Each Other* (The Belknap Press, 1998), 251–255.

4.   Scanlon discusses other aspects of this instrumental value. If I am allowed to make a choice that impacts my life, this is more likely to satisfy my preferences and increase my level of welfare than if someone else makes the choice. See *What We Owe Each Other* page 252

6.   Cohen, "On The Currency of Egalitarian Justice," 933.

7.   Richard J. Arneson, "Luck Egalitarianism and Prioritarianism," *Ethics* 110.2 (2000): 4.

8.   Note that any attempt to explain away this case due to special obligations to children will not refute Arneson's conclusions. The example works as well if all parties are adults. Arneson's use of children in this example unfortunately clouds the issue.

9.   Ronald Dworkin, "What is Equality? Part 2: Equality of Resources," *Philosophy and Public Affairs* 10.4 (1981): 296.

10.   Elizabeth Anderson, "What is the Point of Equality?," *Ethics* 109.2 (1999): 313.

11.   Ibid., 295.

Domestic Violence as a Violation of Autonomy and Agency: The Required Response of the Kantian State

MARILEA BRAMER

Abstract: Contrary to what we might initially think, domestic violence is not simply a violation of respect. This characterization of domestic violence misses two key points. First, the issue of respect in connection with domestic violence is not as straightforward as it appears. Second, domestic violence is also a violation of care. These key points explain how domestic violence negatively affects a victim's autonomy and agency—the ability to choose and pursue her own goals and life plan.

We have a moral responsibility to respond to the problem of domestic violence as individuals. But the state also has a responsibility to respond. According to Kant in the *Doctrine of Right*, one of the purposes of the state is to secure just treatment for everyone. I argue that this includes an obligation to put in place policies and services that will promote the autonomy and agency of victims of domestic violence.

I. Introduction: Defining 'Domestic Violence'

Our personal relationships with partners or spouses can be unparalleled sources of great support and care. Unfortunately, the same characteristics of these relationships that make them sources of support and care also leave us vulnerable to abuse, including domestic violence. The latest economic recession has had a staggering double effect on domestic violence in the United States (and likely elsewhere): at the same time that government services are being cut because of budget constraints, incidences of domestic violence are on the rise because of the added stresses of individual job loss and income loss due to the recession.[1] Because of this, the need to examine the moral issue of domestic violence and to consider our obligations to victims, both as individuals and as citizens, is especially important at the present time.

The term 'domestic violence' can be understood in different ways. Typically, we think of domestic violence as violent behavior between two individuals who are spouses or partners. Sociologists refer to violent behavior between partners as intimate partner violence (IPV). Michael Johnson and Kathleen Ferraro have outlined at least four different kinds of IPV, including intimate terrorism (IT).[2] Intimate terrorism seems to encompass the behaviors we usually associate with the phrase "domestic violence": "the distinguishing feature of IT is a pattern of violence and nonviolent behaviors that indicates a general motive to control."[3] The nonviolent behaviors or control tactics include "emotional abuse, using children, using male privilege, economic abuse, threats, intimidation, and blaming."[4] Because intimate terrorism is the type of IPV that most closely corresponds to the common definition of "domestic violence," the discussion that follows will focus on intimate terrorism (IT).

Whether we refer to this kind of behavior as domestic violence or as intimate terrorism, it takes a terrible toll on the autonomy of the victim.[5] As individuals who operate in the world, we have autonomy and agency. Our autonomy is our ability to choose the principles by which we will live and our decisions to shape our actions by these principles. We exercise our agency when we act on these principles and on our decisions. Our possession of autonomy and agency are part of what make us human beings able to take part in the daily activities of life, including being involved in partnered relationships and being citizens of the state. In cases of intimate terrorism, though, the intimate terrorist works to effectively strip his partner of agency and autonomy. He does this through two main means: first, by working to undermine her autonomy and agency and thus showing that she is not worthy of respect; and second, by violating his obligation to give her the care that she rightly deserves as member of a partnered relationship.

In order to adequately address the problem of intimate terrorism and to help victims, we need to understand the two important moral components of personal relationships that are violated: respect and care. Understanding the violations of respect and care and the resulting consequences for the victim's autonomy and agency enables us to better understand the problem of domestic violence and what our response to it should be, both as individuals and as citizens of the state. After describing domestic violence as a violation of respect and care and the consequences of these violations for the autonomy and agency of the victim, I argue that, according to Kant, this threat requires the state to respond to the problem of intimate terrorism.

II. IT as a Violation of Respect

Our initial thoughts about intimate terrorism most likely point to it as a simple violation of respect: individuals who are violent towards their partners lack respect for them. Some might also be tempted to say that a person with self-respect would leave a relationship where violence occurred. The problem with both of these understandings of respect in connection with intimate terrorism is that they do not fully reflect the seriousness and the depth of the violation of respect that takes place and its effect on the victim's autonomy and agency. Here, I will argue that the first part of this assumption—that those who are violent towards their partners lack respect for their partners—is true, but that it does not adequately capture the denial of dignity and thus the worthiness for respect that is characteristic of intimate terrorism. We violate our duty to respect strangers when we are violent towards them. But the violation of respect that occurs in intimate terrorism is not the same kind of violation. Rather, it is a violation of the recognition that the victim is even worthy of respect at all. Similarly, the second part of the assumption is problematic because of the characteristics of intimate terrorism and the practical impediments to leaving which victims face. Because of this, the moral response towards victims of intimate terrorism must at a minimum involve removing these practical impediments.

The violation of respect that the abuser shows his partner in the form of abuse is one of the most obvious moral wrongs involved in IT.[6] As human beings with moral worth, we are right to expect that others should recognize this worth and show respect for us in part by not physically harming us. Respect requires more than this, but the basic expectation that others not harm us physically seems reasonable. If we simply stop our analysis of intimate terrorism here, we miss the important fact that the intimate terrorist is denying that his partner is even worthy of such respect in the first place.

For Kant, the reason we deserve respect from ourselves and others is because we are all beings with what Kant refers to as "autonomy of the will."[7] This is our capacity as rational agents to choose the principles by which we live and to shape our lives according to them.[8] It is the grounds for our dignity, or our value without price. Our dignity gives rise to our duty to respect each other, according to Kant: "The *respect* I have for others or that another can require from me . . . is therefore a recognition of *dignity* . . . in other human beings, that is, of a worth that has no price, no equivalent for which the object evaluated . . . could be exchanged."[9] Part of showing respect for others is showing respect for their autonomy and their agency—for their ability to choose their principles and goals and to act on them.[10] If someone poses a constant threat to an agent's agency over time, this threat will most likely begin to affect her autonomy itself.

This is especially true in cases of IT where the abuser is using violent and non-violent behaviors as a way to control his partner. He is trying to control her actions, and at some point, the victim of the abuse will begin to make choices about her life and her actions in response to this control. She will, for example, begin to shape her actions in a way to try and avoid more violence. Additionally, the control that her partner exercises over her will limit both what she can do (her agency) and her choices (her autonomy). Acting in ways that limit someone's agency or autonomy is more insidious than just the simple act of failing to show respect through a violent act. When the intimate terrorist acts in ways to limit his partner's agency and autonomy, he is in essence denying that she is the kind of being who should have agency and autonomy, which is a denial of her dignity as a human being.[11] After all, for Kant, we deserve respect because we have dignity. By attempting to control his partner, the intimate terrorist denies that his partner has the "worth without price" that all human beings have simply by virtue of being human.[12] This is because, consciously or unconsciously, he sees her as something that can be controlled or that he has a right to control. To him, she is something to be used, to be shaped into what he wants or to use as he desires. He treats her in the way we treat objects, as a means to some other end that we have. For Kant, ends are the goals or projects we have,[13] and means are what we use to achieve them. Human beings are ends in themselves: that is, because they have dignity, they can never be used merely as a means to some other goal.[14] By trying to control his partner, the intimate terrorist denies that she is an end in herself who has dignity.

The attempts of the intimate terrorist to subvert his partner's autonomy relate to the second assumption about self-respect some make about victims of IT: an individual with self-respect will not stay in a situation where she is abused. There are two problems with this assumption. First, the danger of making this assumption is that it leads to the conclusion that the victim is somehow morally responsible for her situation if she does not leave. We do not want to blame the victim for her situation, and it is especially problematic in cases of intimate terrorism where there are so many practical impediments to leaving. Second, it ignores the psychological effects of the intimate terrorist's actions aimed at subverting his victim's autonomy and agency.

In order to better consider the situation in which many victims of IT find themselves, we can look at the story of Fran Benedetto from Anna Quindlen's novel, *Black and Blue*.[15] Quindlen tells the story of Fran Benedetto. Fran, a nurse, is married to Bobby Benedetto, a police officer who is physically and emotionally abusive. Bobby's abuse and attempts to control Fran are examples of the behaviors characteristic of IT. Fran talks about the assumption that self-respect would lead a woman to leave an abusive partner:

> People can talk about self-respect all they want, and people do plenty, usually when they're talking about someone else's business. But whenever I thought about leaving, sometimes as much as leaving Bobby I thought about leaving my house. Balloon shades and miniblinds [sic] and the way I felt at night sleeping on my extra-firm mattress under my own roof that we'd hot-tarred the year after Robert was born—all of it helped keep me there. . . . Small things: routine, order. That's what kept me there for the longest time. That, and love. That, and fear. Not fear of Bobby, fear of winding up in some low-rent apartment subdivision with a window that looked out on a wall.

> . . . It took me a dozen years of house pride and seventeen years of marriage before
> I realized there were worse things than a cramped kitchen and grubby carpeting.[16]

Fran's description captures some of the other considerations that women face when they are considering leaving an abusive partner. They are not just leaving the person: they are leaving behind a life, a routine, a certain amount of predictability, and possibly their support network if they are forced to give up or have to leave behind friends and family. The intimate terrorist's actions, which subvert the autonomy and the agency of his partner, affect his partner's ability to leave the relationship. Victims of IT may lack the self-confidence to leave an abusive partner who has tried to reinforce feelings of inadequacy and dependency. Furthermore, victims of IT may fear that leaving will actually result in an increase in the frequency or severity of abuse, a fear that is not unfounded. Research has shown that women who leave abusive relationships are actually at greater risk for being killed by their partners than those women who do not leave.[17]

Yet, understanding the role of self-respect in relation to victims of domestic violence is also complicated. An understanding and sense of self-respect may play a large role in helping women to leave their abusive partners and in helping the women to regain a sense of control over their own lives. Although we do not want to blame women who have difficulty leaving because of the practical issues for a lack of self-respect, self-respect can still play a large role in helping the victims of intimate terrorism to regain their autonomy and agency. Indeed, Fran's description of why she stayed with Bobby seems to point to the fact that she was missing a sense of self-respect. If we are to understand how we can help victims of intimate terrorism, part of what we should do is to recognize and foster their sense of autonomy and agency, which is related to their sense of self-respect.

III. IT as a Violation of Care

Treating intimate terrorism only as a violation of respect, no matter how fundamental that violation, misses out on the other important violation—the violation of care. As individuals who join together in partnered relationships, we expect a certain level of care to come from those relationships. The exact components of that care may vary from relationship to relationship, but we do think that those in close relationships have a duty or an obligation to care about and for each other.[18] This care is contextual to the relationship; caring actions are based on the desire to care for another individual and show a responsiveness and engagement with the one being cared for.[19] Though the typical example of the caring relationship often described is one of a mother or a father to a child, caring occurs in all personal relationships, including partner relationships between adults.

When we enter into partner relationships, we have some expectations of our partners in terms of the care they will give us. We expect love and support, for example. The care that partners provide to each other allows each partner to exercise her or his autonomy and agency. Sometimes, this care comes in the form of psychological support. When I have doubts or fears about my ability to achieve a certain goal or end (for example, my ability to construct all the materials for a new course within a particular time frame, or my ability to obtain tenure), my partner is there to offer reassurance. At other times, the care is more practical: when I am sick, my partner makes sure that I eat, rest, and see the doctor, so that I can get well and resume my daily activities. In both cases, the care plays a role in my ability to be an autonomous agent. It's true that most times this care is not strictly necessary—I could accomplish these tasks and would eventually get well on my own. But, as someone in a partnered relationship, I expect my partner to care about me and for me, no matter how that care is shown. This expectation is reasonable for individuals in partnered relationships.

As care ethicist Rita Manning points out, if one focuses just on the physical harm involved in IT, one misses the failure of the abuser to provide the kind of care partners deserve:

> An ethic of care deepens the critique [of domestic abuse]. It's not just that the abuser has violated the rights of the victim of the abuse; the victim of abuse is deprived of the care that it was reasonable to expect in such a relationship. The jealousy of the abuser and the subsequent isolation of the victim of abuse compounds the abuse; the victim is deprived of care that is typically available only in partnering relationships in our society, and at the same time is unable to develop a partnership relationship that would satisfy the need for care, intimacy, and acceptance.[20]

Manning's analysis emphasizes that IT is both physically harmful and it deprives the victim of the care she has a right to expect as an individual in a partnered relationship. The failure to care is a violation of care that is especially problematic because of the nature of a partner relationship and the behaviors the intimate terrorist exhibits. The intimate terrorist not only fails to show appropriate care but acts in ways that are antithetical to moral caring. In a partner relationship which leaves us vulnerable because of the nature of the relationship, we should be able to expect our partner to care for us. Though this does not eliminate our vulnerability in these relationships, it mitigates it to some extent. But in the case of intimate terrorism, the intimate terrorist exploits the vulnerability inherent in the relationship in order to exercise control over his partner rather than responding to the vulnerability with caring. Looking at IT only as a violation of respect misses this important aspect of IT.

In terms of care, then, the intimate terrorist violates his obligation to give proper care to his partner. This is an important point, because the kind of care that we rightfully expect and usually receive from our partners is different from the kind of actions that a general respect for all persons requires of us. Victims of IT are deprived of the respect that they deserve as human beings and also the care that they deserve as intimate partners. This compounds the denial of dignity that is shown through the actions of the intimate terrorist—his partner is not worthy of the respect given even to strangers, nor is she worthy of the care given to one's partner. Again, the violation of the obligation to care serves to subvert the autonomy and agency of the intimate terrorist's partner: she does not deserve care, she does not deserve to have her own goals and projects, and she does not deserve support or help in forming or achieving those projects. The intimate terrorist uses his relationship and his connection with his partner, a relationship that is supposed to be caring and supportive, specifically to undermine her autonomy and agency.

Helping victims of IT, then, will involve restoring situations where the victims receive care. Sally Sholz argues that advocates for victims of domestic violence will need to care for those victims.[21] This involves working to help victims in a way that allows the victim to recover her sense of autonomy and so to make her own decisions.[22] We can generalize this point beyond the role of the advocate, however. Using Kantian theory and its requirement that the state act to support the autonomous action of its citizens, I will argue that the state is required to have public policies in place for victims of IT which serve the same purpose. These policies should support victims of IT in a way that allows them to regain their autonomy and agency.

IV. Understanding our Obligation to Help Victims of IT

Recognizing the threat to the autonomy and agency of victims of IT from the violations of respect and care enables us as individuals and as a society to better understand and thus meet our obligation to respond to some of the issues associated with IT. The means by which the abuser chooses to exercise control, such as intimidation, threats, and coercion are aimed at subverting the autonomy of the victim and reducing her agency. Recognizing this helps us think about what measures we as a society should take in order to help victims of IT. Johnson and Leone explain:

> because women subjected to intimate terrorism are more likely to suffer psychologically, sustain injuries, and miss work, they are at an increased risk of being unable to achieve and maintain self-sufficiency. . . . Thus, social policies that temporarily or permanently restrict a woman's income (such as time limits on receipt of temporary aid to needy families) may be especially detrimental to women entrapped in intimate terrorism because they are already at risk for being unable to secure self-sufficiency. These are the very women who are most likely trying to escape from their partner, and social policy needs to contribute to their self-sufficiency, not undermine it.[23]

Under Kantian theory, we have an obligation as individuals to help those who are victims of intimate terrorism. A central part of Kantian moral theory is the Categorical Imperative (CI), Kant's supreme principle of morality. The CI in the Formulation of Humanity as an End (FHE) requires us to "Act in such a way that you treat humanity, whether in your own person or in the person of another, always at the same time as an end and never simply as a means."[24] Onora O'Neill argues that in the FHE "the requirement of treating others as ends in themselves demands that Kantians standardly act to support the possibility of autonomous action where it is most vulnerable."[25] O'Neill's understanding of autonomous action is similar to what I have been calling autonomy and agency. Autonomous action is action based on principles and ends that we have chosen for ourselves. Our autonomy and agency are often compromised in some sense, according to O'Neill, because human beings are "*finite* rational beings," and our dependence on others often limits our ability for autonomous action or agency.[26] Appropriate care can help support our ability to be autonomous and to have agency by supporting us and helping us reach beyond our personal limits. In order to support the possibility of autonomous action, according to O'Neill, we should act in ways that provide others with "sufficient physical energy, psychological space, and social security for action."[27] The FHE, then, requires us to act in ways that promote the autonomy and agency of others. So, from a Kantian perspective, we have an obligation as individuals to work to restore and promote the autonomy and agency of others when that autonomy is vulnerable. In cases of IT, the autonomy and agency of the victim is especially vulnerable because of the violations of respect and care. As individuals, we have an obligation to work to restore and promote the autonomy and agency of victims of IT. We should work to support groups or organizations that provide victims of IT with the resources they need to set and pursue their own ends.

For the Kantian, though, this obligation goes beyond helping simply at the individual level. We see this by looking at Kant's Doctrine of Right, particularly at his description of the purpose and responsibilities of the state.

According to Kant, one of the duties we have is the duty to enter into society (the state) when we cannot avoid associating with others. We should do this in order to avoid harming others. In his discussion of the general division of duties of right, Kant lists three duties. The first duty is to assert our own worth in relation to others. Kant says this duty can be expressed in the following way: "Do not make yourself a mere means for others but be at the same time an end for them."[28] The second duty is a duty not to wrong others, even if this would require that we stop associating with others and "shun all society."[29] The third duty is related to the second: Kant says, "(If you cannot help associating with others), *enter* into a society with them in which each can keep what is his."[30] In his explanation of this, Kant says that we should think of it as saying that we are to "*Enter* a condition in which what belongs to each can be secured to him against everyone else."[31] Though this may seem at first to indicate that the purpose of the state is only to protect property, given the phrase "what belongs to each," we can also understand it as saying that we have a duty to join with others to create a civil society in order to secure just treatment for everyone.[32] The laws of our society should be based on the idea that each individual has worth and should not be treated as a mere means. Rather, each individual should be treated as an end in herself. After all, we are all to act in such a way that we "do not make [ourselves] a mere means for others but [are] at the same time and end for them." Each individual is an end, and the laws should recognize and reflect this fact. Practically speaking, then, when we join together into a society, laws should be framed in such a way that no one is made a mere means by any of the laws. Part of joining together into a state, then, will include making laws that secure just treatment for everyone.

The idea that the laws of the state should secure just treatment for everyone is echoed in Kant's discussion of the right of a state: "The sum of the laws which need to be promulgated generally in order to bring about a rightful condition is *public right.*—Public right is therefore a system of laws for a people . . . which, because they affect one another, need a rightful condition under a will uniting them, a *constitution* . . . , so that they may enjoy what is laid down as right."[33] The purpose of the state, then, is to provide laws which will establish and maintain what Kant calls "a rightful condition" to govern how people treat each other. Earlier in the Doctrine of Right, Kant defines 'right' as "the sum of the conditions under which the choice of one can be united with the choice of another in accordance with a universal law of freedom."[34] This universal law of freedom, or the universal principle of right, states that "Any action is *right* if it can coexist with everyone's freedom in accordance with a universal law, or if on its maxim the freedom of choice of each can coexist with everyone's freedom in accordance with a universal law."[35] At the very least, then, I am free to act in whatever ways I see fit unless my actions interfere with the freedom of another. Indeed, Kant says that the universal law of right tells us to "so act externally that the free use of your choice can coexist with the freedom of everyone in accordance with a universal law."[36]

With the goal of promoting freedom in mind, Kant says that coercion can be used to limit the freedom of individuals under certain conditions: "If a certain use of freedom is itself a hindrance to freedom in accordance with universal laws . . . coercion that is opposed to this (as a *hindering of a hindrance of freedom*) is consistent with freedom in accordance with universal laws, that is, it is right."[37] The state, then, can make laws that limit our freedom as long as the purpose of those laws is to promote freedom generally. That is, the state can prohibit us from acting in ways that negatively affect the freedom of others.

At a minimum, the state is justified in making laws against the kinds of actions in which intimate terrorists engage, and the state has a responsibility to get involved when one's citizen's actions—those of the intimate terrorist—are hindering the freedom of another citizen. Because the intimate terrorist's actions limit the autonomy and agency of his partner, they limit her freedom. The state, then, should be involved in separating the intimate terrorist from his partner and in protecting the victim from her abuser.

But the state's purpose is not simply to keep us from harming each other or from interfering with each other's freedom. As part of securing just treatment for everyone, Kant says that the state has the right to impose taxes on its citizens to help with the preservation of fellow citizens: "To the supreme commander [of the state] there belongs *indirectly*, that is, insofar as he has taken over the duty of the people, the right to impose taxes on the people for its own preservation."[38] He explains this further by saying, "The general will of the people has united itself into a society which is to maintain itself perpetually; and for this end it has submitted itself to the internal authority of the state in order to maintain those members of the state who are unable to maintain themselves."[39] In a sense, then, the state is responsible for making sure that those who need support in order meet the basic challenges of living receive support from the state because the resources needed for basic maintenance are necessary for autonomy and agency.

According to Sarah Holtman, one of the ways we can understand the state's duty is as a duty to provide citizens with the resources they need in order to be independent—that is, to provide citizens with they need in order to be self-governing individuals who can exercise their autonomy in the state.[40] In other words, part of the responsibility of the state is to provide citizens with the resources needed to support the autonomy and agency of its citizens. If its citizens are going to enter into partnered relationships that have a potential danger of negatively affecting the autonomy and agency of its citizens, then the state should make provisions for restoring autonomy and agency to its citizens when they enter into these caring relationships and those relationships end up subverting autonomy and agency.

As citizens of the state who are potentially unable to maintain themselves when they first leave their abusers, victims of IT have a right to be supported by the state. They have a right to services and policies that will help restore their autonomy and promote their agency. These services and policies are, in essence, a form of care, and will include financial assistance, housing assistance, possibly educational assistance, and physical and legal protection from their former partners. The state has a responsibility to its citizens to have in place policies that work to restore the independence, or autonomy, of those who are victims of IT. As citizens, we have a responsibility to work for and support laws and policies, including welfare policies, which take into account the situational complexities of victims, as well as agencies and policies that work to restore what O'Neill calls "the possibility of autonomous action" for, or agency of, victims.[41]

Furthermore, as citizens, we have a responsibility to secure just treatment for everyone. In the context of IT, this requires us to work to change the attitudes and social practices that lead to IT. Because the state is supposed to secure just treatment for all its citizens, all parts of the state, including the individual citizens, have a vested interest in countering such attitudes and in working for policies that promote and secure the autonomous action of all its citizens, regardless of gender.

V. Conclusion

Intimate terrorism involves violations of respect and care that undermine the autonomy and agency of the victim. I have argued that an understanding of the purpose of the Kantian state helps us understand the obligations the state has to help victims of IT; namely, that it must have policies, laws, and agencies that will help restore and promote the autonomy and agency of victims of IT. In addition to this, as citizens of the state, we have a responsibility to work for social conditions that secure just treatment for all. This includes countering social attitudes and practices that support or lead to IT.[42]

Marilea Bramer, Minnesota State University Moorhead

Notes

1.   The National Institute of Justice, part of the Office of Justice Programs in the U.S. Depart- ment of Justice, published a report in 2004, "When Violence Hits Home: How Economics and Neighborhood Play a Role" that discusses the link between economic strain and domestic violence. The resport is available at http://www.ncjrs.gov/pdffiles1/nij/205004.pdf. See Mary R. Laub and Sue Else, "Recession can be Deadly for Domestic Abuse Victims," *The Boston Globe* online edition, Dec. 25, 2008, http://www.boston.com/bostonglobe/editorial_opin- ion/oped/articles/2008/12/25/recession_can_be_deadly_for_domestic_abuse_victims/. Accessed Oct. 27, 2010. Also see Peg Hacskaylo, "No Recession for Domestic Violence," *The Washington Post* online edition, May 8, 2009, http://voices.washingtonpost.com/local- opinions/2009/05/no_recession_for_domestic_viol.html. Accessed Oct. 27, 2010.

2.   See Michael P. Johnson and Kathleen J. Ferraro, "Domestic Violence in the 1990s: Making Distinctions," *Journal of Marriage and the Family* 62.4 (Nov. 2000): 948–63. The other three types of domestic violence are situational couple violence, violent resistance, and mutual violent control. Situational couple violence occurs when both partners in a couple are violent towards each other, but the violence is not used to control the behavior of the other partner. Violent resistance occurs when a victim of intimate terrorism begins to use violence as a response to the intimate terrorist's attempts to control her. Mutual violent control occurs when both partners are engaging in intimate terrorism and is very rare.

3.   Ibid., 949.

4.   Michael P. Johnson and Janel M. Leone, "The Differential Effects of Intimate Terrorism and Situational Couple Violence: Findings from the National Violence Against Women Survey," *Journal of Family Issues* 26.3 (April 2005): 322–49, at 324. Johnson and Leone base this list on Pence and Paymar's "Power and Control Wheel" in E. Pence and M. Paymar, *Education Groups for Men who Batter: The Duluth Model* (New York: Springer, 1993), 185.

5.   The following statistics about IPV in the United States outline some of the effects of IPV and intimate terrorism on both the victim and on society as a whole: Each year, women experience about 4.8 million intimate partner related physical assaults and rapes. Men are the

victims of about 2.9 million intimate partner related physical assaults. See "Understanding Intimate Partner Violence Fact Sheet 2006," Atlanta, Georgia: Centers for Disease Control and Prevention, www.cdc.gov/ncipc/dvp/ipv_factsheet.pdf. Accessed May 5, 2008). IPV also affects the society in which the victims live. According to the National Center for Injury Prevention and Control, the estimated financial costs of IPV each year exceeds $5.8 billion, $4.1 billion of which is direct medical and mental health care services. See *Costs of Intimate Partner Violence Against Women in the United States,* Atlanta, Georgia: Centers for Disease Control and Prevention, 2003), www.cdc.gov/ncipc/pub-res/ipv_cost/ipvbook-final-feb18 .pdf, 8. Accessed January 12, 2009. The costs also include $0.9 billion in lost productivity from paid work and $0.9 billion in lifetime earnings lost by victims of IPV homicides.

6.   Because most instances of IT are directed towards women, I will refer to the abuser as 'he' and the victim as 'she.'

7.   Immanuel Kant, *Grounding for the Metaphysics of Morals,* trans. James W. Ellington, 3rd ed. (Indianapolis: Hackett, 1993). Translation based on Karl Vorlander's German text as it appears in Vol. III of the *Philosophische Bibliothek* edition of Kant's works, and Paul Menzer's text as it appears in Vol. IV of the Prussian Academy of the Sciences edition of Kant's works. Citations refer to volume and page number of the Prussian Academy edition. Hereafter *Grounding,* 4:440.

8.   For further discussions of Kantian autonomy, see Thomas E. Hill, Jr. "The Kantian Conception of Autonomy," in *Dignity and Practical Reason in Kant's Moral Theory* (Ithaca: Cornell University Press, 1992), 76–96; Thomas E. Hill, Jr,. *Autonomy and Self-Respect* (Cambridge: Cambridge University Press, 1991), especially chap. 3 "Autonomy and Benevolent Lies," and chap. 4 "The Importance of Autonomy"; Stephen Darwall, "The Value of Autonomy and Autonomy of the Will" *Ethics* 116 (January 2006): 263–84; and chaps. 4–6 of Andrews Reath, *Agency and Autonomy in Kant's Moral Theory* (Oxford: Clarendon, 2006).

9.   Immanuel Kant, *The Metaphysics of Morals,* trans. Mary Gregor (New York: Cambridge University Press, 1996). Translation based on text of *The Metaphysics of Morals* edited by Paul Natorp, vol. 6 (1907) of the Prussian Academy of the Sciences edition of Kant's work. Citations refer to volume and page number of the Prussian Academy edition. Hereafter *MM,* 6:462 (emphasis in original).

10.   Others may describe an agent's autonomy and agency as self-determination, where self-determination is one's ability to choose the goals for one's life and to take action to meet those goals. I use the terms 'autonomy' and 'agency' here because Kant discusses autonomy in his work. Any actions which negatively affect one's autonomy and agency, then, also negatively affect one's self-determination.

11.   We might have legitimate reasons to act in ways which limit someone's autonomy and agency—for example, incarcerated prisoners have limits placed on their autonomy and their agency. If the incarceration and the limits are just, though, this would be a much different kind of case than the limitations on autonomy and agency involved in IT.

12.   There is a question of how responsible we can hold the abuser for this violation of respect and the denial of dignity. The assumption is that the abuser has full autonomy of the will. But research shows that some individuals who abuse others were either abused themselves as children or were witnesses to domestic violence between adults in their homes. If this is the case, can we say that the abuser is fully culpable for his actions? Certainly, he bears some

responsibility for the violation of respect, but how much? The cycle of violence complicates the picture of moral responsibility in cases of domestic violence. This is an important part of understanding the moral culpability of the abuser and should be examined, but it is beyond the scope of the current project.

13. Kant, *Grounding*, 4:429.

14. Ibid., 4:428.

15. Anna Quindlen, *Black and Blue* (New York: Dell, 1998).

16. Ibid., 209–10.

17. *Violence and the Family: Report of the American Psychological Association Presidential Task Force on Violence and the Family* (Washington, DC: American Psychological Association, 1996), 36.

18. Care ethicists differ in whether they refer to our obligation to care or whether they characterize it as a responsibility to care. Rita Manning, Sarah Clark Miller, and Daniel Engster all refer to our obligation or duty to care, while Joan Tronto and Virginia Held refer to our responsibility to care. Whether they refer to it as a responsibility to care or an obligation to care, care ethicists agree that, in personal relationships, the source of the obligation or responsibility is the relationship itself. See Rita Manning, *Speaking from the Heart: A Feminist Perspective on Ethics* (Lanham, Maryland: Rowman & Littlefield Publishers, 1992); Sarah Clark Miller, "A Kantian Ethic of Care?"in *Feminist Interventions in Ethics and Politics*, ed. Barbara Andrew, Jean Keller, and Lisa Schwartzman (Lanham, MD: Rowman & Littlefield Publishers, 2005), 110–27; Daniel Engster "Rethinking Care Theory: The Practice of Caring and the Obligation to Care," *Hypatia* 20.3 (Fall 2005): 50–70; Joan Tronto, *Moral Boundaries: A Political Argument for an Ethic of Care* (New York: Routledge, 1993), 131–3; Virginia Held, *The Ethics of Care: Personal, Political, and Global* (New York: Oxford University Press, 2006).

19. See Nel Noddings, *Caring: A Feminine Approach to Ethics and Moral Education*, 2nd ed. (Berkeley: University of California, 2003), 19; Held, *The Ethics of Care*, 10; and Hilde Lindemann, *An Invitation to Feminist Ethics* (Boston: McGraw Hill: 2006), 92–3 for further descriptions of moral caring.

20. Manning, *Speaking from the Heart*, 103–4.

21. Sally Scholz, "Peacemaking in Domestic Violence: From an Ethics of Care to an Ethics of Advocacy," *Journal of Social Philosophy* 29.2 (Fall 1998): 46–58.

22. Ibid., 53.

23. Johnson and Leone, "The Differential Effects" 346.

24. *Grounding* 4:429.

25. Onora O'Neill, "Ending World Hunger," in *World Hunger and Morality*, 2nd ed., ed. William Aiken and Hugh LaFollette (Upper Saddle River, New Jersey: Prentice Hall, 1996), 85–111, at 98. Though O'Neill makes this point in relation to a Kantian's duty to work to reduce hunger and poverty, the point applies here also because her overall claim is that we have a duty to help those who are vulnerable or whose autonomy is threatened. Victims of IT certainly fit into that group.

26. Ibid., 98–9.

27. Ibid., 105.

28. *MM*, 6:236.

29. Ibid.

30. *MM*, 6:236.

31. Ibid.

32. Sarah Holtman interprets this passage in the same way. See her "Kantian Justice and Poverty Relief," *Kant-Studien* 95 (2004): 86–106.

33. *MM*, 6:311.

34. *MM*, 6:230.

35. Ibid.

36. *MM*, 6:231.

37. *MM*, 6:232.

38. *MM*, 6:325–6.

39. Ibid.

40. Holtman, "Kantian Justice," 98.

41. Sally Scholz specifically provides guidelines for advocates of those victimized by domestic violence that include a guideline to be an advocate for all who are victimized by domestic violence, not just one particular individual who is requesting advocacy. Scholz makes this argument from a care ethics perspective, but her guidelines to care in solidarity and to promote the autonomy of the woman who has been victimized fit very well with Kantian theory. See Scholz "Peacemaking in Domestic Violence: From an Ethics of Care to an Ethics of Advocacy" *Journal of Social Philosophy* 29.2 (Fall 1998): 46–58.

42. Thanks are due to anonymous referees for this journal.

Sexual Abuse, Modern Freedom, and Heidegger's Philosophy

NATALIE NENADIC

Abstract: The sexual abuse of women and girls, such as sexual harassment, battery, varieties of rape, prostitution, and pornography, is statistically pervasive in late modern society. Yet this fact does not register adequate ethical concern. I explore this gap in moral perception. I argue that sexual abuse is conceptually supported by an ontology of women that considers a lack of bodily integrity as natural and by a sex-specific idea of freedom that considers sexual violations as liberating. This conceptual framework is pernicious because it supports abuse and interferes with our moral perception of harm, encouraging us to see harms as normal and as positive. I argue that Heidegger's idea of philosophy and the resources of his epistemological and ontological project in *Being and Time* can help show the pernicious function of this conceptual framework and thus help us better understand this abuse.

I. Introduction

The sexual objectification and abuse of women and girls that pervades late modern society is a major ethical challenge of our time. It ranges from the dehumanizing images and attitudes that saturate everyday life to the statistically common practices of sexual harassment, battery, varieties of rape, prostitution and pornography.[1] These abuses are becoming increasingly "normalized" through a culture that is becoming more pornographic, meaning it portrays sexual abuse as something that women and girls enjoy and as entertainment. Through technology such as the Internet and an expanding array of digital gadgets, these images have a reach into our lives today that is historically unprecedented, which incites the growing practice of these abuses.

These facts however do not register adequate ethical concern. They do not appear to most people as evidence of harm but as evidence of sexual expression that is both natural to women and is sexually liberating. I explore this gap in moral perception. I argue that sexual abuse of women and girls is conceptually supported by both an ontology of women and a sex-specific idea of freedom that is distinctive of the modern era. This conceptual framework is pernicious not only because it supports abuse, but also because it interferes with our moral perception, encouraging us to see abuse and its psychological consequences not as harms but as normal and as positive. A lack of bodily integrity is construed as natural and sexual violations as liberating. I argue that Heidegger's idea of philosophy and the resources of his epistemological and ontological project in *Being and Time* give us a way to respond to this problem, which can help show the pernicious function of this conceptual framework and thus help us better understand this abuse.

II. Sexual Abuse and Ontology

One way to think about today's pervasive sexual objectification and abuse is that it undermines the bodily and psychological integrity of women and girls while casting this condition as natural to them. They are treated and portrayed as sexually malleable and violable in myriad ways, especially when they express these characteristics assertively. Indeed, not to have bodily boundaries is how they are said to have bodily self-possession, in contrast with such a condition in men, in whom it is more often recognized as a lack of self-possession. Whatever its degree, this circumstance severely limits, thwarts, and usurps women's choices in life, especially in the realm of intimate relationships.

Over the last several decades, feminism has attained a better understanding of this situation by grappling with the phenomena of women's resistance to it and has accordingly been dismantling this ontology. Its pernicious function in obscuring harm is especially perspicuous in the most extreme expressions of this lack of bodily boundaries, which feminism has revealed not as ontological, but as typical signs of sexual abuse, usually beginning in childhood. We see such expressions, for example, in the young teen who is in repeated sexual encounters with boys or men, who are re-doing upon her the violating kind of sexuality that was done to her earlier in life and who often seek out girls exhibiting this type of vulnerability. We see this dynamic in the adult who, regardless of her social status, "picks up" man after man in bars or elsewhere, in a similar replay of earlier sexual abuse, with little or no clarity on why she is doing this.[2] Often, she convinces herself that she is now "in control," that she thereby evinces her "sexual agency" and "power" by "choosing" what is, in effect, her abuser, though she cannot change the dehumanizing character of the sexual dynamic, only her attitude towards it.[3]

We now recognize such compulsive reenactment of earlier sexual abuse as a post-traumatic response aimed at gaining some control, this time around, over a situation that originally left her completely powerless and over a life that feels out of control, a response however that is self-destructive and ultimately ineffective. It is a way of coping with lingering and overwhelming post-traumatic symptoms like flashbacks, depression, hyper-vigilance, constant anxiety, and suicidal thoughts and attempts. A typical self-protective response during sexual abuse is to withdraw into the mind to dissociate or mentally separate from what is actually happening, resulting in a condition of numbness that persists well after the actual abuse is over. When the abuse occurs in childhood, it is especially damaging to one's later identity, often resulting in various identity disorders (e.g., multiple personality), which is a kind of semi-permanent scrambling of a person's interiority. Accordingly, survivors oscillate between not feeling anything and being unable to stop the post-traumatic effects that they don't have the psychological resources to cope with.

Therefore, subsequent self-harming sexual encounters are often ways of feeling something instead of, unbearably, feeling nothing or "dead," in a practice that is related to other self-harms associated with earlier sexual abuse like repeated cutting of the skin.[4] Other times, these encounters are ways to numb or blot out the overwhelming post-traumatic symptoms, in a practice tied to the self-numbing drug use common among survivors, from prescription pain killers and tranquilizers, to alcohol and street drugs. Part of the "narcotic" effect is the immediate external affirmation she receives in such encounters, in a culture in which such degradation is the principal way that women are valued. And affirmation is especially desperately needed by someone who already has deep feelings of worthlessness, often believes she doesn't deserve any better, and usually is not far from suicidal thoughts, that is, from something worse.

This dynamic is of course more complex than I can do justice to here. But my point is simply to indicate the oppression behind such lack of bodily boundaries, oppression often marked by deep, complex, and distinctive psychological dimensions, which is said to be ontological to females. We now recognize its most extreme forms as signs of having had one's bodily and internal self so broken-in that one now "limps along" as this apparently seamless embodiment of that lack of boundaries. They are signs of harm and distress and accordingly are an ethical summons.

The approach of superficially reading off harms as ontological characteristics of a group, and therefore as benign, is not new. Aristotle reasoned thus about slavery (and about women), thereby imposing upon them a conceptual framework that interfered with people's moral perception of harm. The slave's obedience, obsequiousness, his apparent harmony, contentment and lack of resistance to his condition were proof of its naturalness. They were part of slaves' ontological difference from masters and moreover were virtues to be further cultivated. By contrast, in the natural master such characteristics were recognized to reflect his dehumanization.[5]

A neo-Aristotelian approach to slavery and slave-like oppression that treated signs of harms as ontological and positive features of a group extended well into the modern period when it was the common sense among professional philosophers and political and legal theorists. Rousseau and a handful of other philosophers of this era sought to dismantle this traditional ontology by pointing to the phenomena of force and abuse that it concealed.[6] He seems also to have had some sense of the internal oppression that slavery can produce, which can incapacitate resistance and cause a slave to identify with masters, though he does not develop this point. He indicates that it was not uncommon for his opponents to cite examples of enslaved peoples, perhaps even recently freed slaves, in which they approve of slavery or have little sense of how to function as free persons, which was then taken as evidence of its naturalness. Such response exploited the fact that this internal dimension of slavery's oppression hadn't yet been philosophically mapped, a dimension that left Rousseau baffled and groping for how to understand it and better counter these pro-slavery positions.

Accordingly, he sometimes writes of the "degradation of enslaved peoples" and of "enslaved peoples [who] do nothing but boast of the peace and tranquility they enjoy in their chains."[7] Elsewhere he says that a person who consents to slavery simply "does not have his wits about him," as consent to something that is such an extreme objective harm makes no sense.[8] It seems that the only way that Rousseau could get his head around this dimension of oppression was to consider it a sign of madness. And "[m]adness," he says, "does not bring about right."[9] Reaching a point of apparent frustration, he concludes, "I sense that it is inappropriate for slaves to reason about liberty."[10]

Rousseau could not explain, in a more comprehensive manner, why enslaved people sometimes appeared in harmony with their condition. Yet he stayed close enough to the phenomena of abuse, which in turn pointed to a more universal standard for harm, to conclude that "from every point of view, the right of slavery is null."[11] He thereby played a central role in dismantling the ontology that concealed harms as benign and as positive attributes of slaves, an ontology at the heart of a multitude of rationalizations for slavery circulating in his time.

III. Sexual Abuse and Modern Freedom

As I have noted, today's common sense also considers the consequences of sexual objectification and abuse as evidence of this condition's naturalness for females and therefore as benign and positive. Accordingly, it has taken enormous efforts to break through this conceptual framework to make these harms visible as such. This difficulty is compounded by the fact that this condition is further conceptually obscured through being cast as the way that women experience their freedom or sexual liberation, which is said to be naturally different from the way men experience it. Thus, sexual harassment, varieties of rape, prostitution, and pornography are not harms systematically deployed against females but are merely the ways that they are "liberated," especially when they actively embrace this state, while men are "liberated" when they treat women in these ways. If each sex thus manifests the freedom that is natural to it, then women are not harmed here.

Many of these abuses have of course existed in some form throughout history, as expressions of the male dominance of that history. However, what significantly distinguishes them in the late modern era is that now they seem to require rationalization in terms that pertain to freedom, equality, or some other manner of parity with men. This development has added another layer of conceptual interference in our moral perception of harm, which has helped these destructive practices and the social inequality they reflect to persist relatively unrecognized and arguably to expand.

Speaking historically and admittedly with broad strokes, before the modern political era there wasn't this kind of need for rationalization. Political inequalities, both among men and between men and women, such as slavery, serfdom, and sex inequality were considered natural. They were facts of life, existing from time immemorial that would never change. Accordingly "pre-modern" polities didn't have to address or explain such inequalities the way modern ones are more obligated to do. Enlightenment political philosophy and the French Revolution dismantled this "pre-modern" worldview and the traditional ontology on which inequalities among men were based by recognizing the Rights of Man. These developments recognized, in theory, political equality among men (*Liberté, Egalité, Fraternité*) while denying it to women, though they finessed the latter by dressing it in obfuscating modern garb.

In her 1792 work *A Vindication of the Rights of Woman*, the English philosopher Mary Wollstonecraft referred to this garb as a bewildering and malicious "alchemy."[12] It was deployed in the popular culture and by most philosophers of the day like Rousseau to deny women political equality by treating conditions and characteristics that reflect objective harms into positive, empowering, and natural ones for women. Thus, qualities such as obsequiousness, submissiveness, lack of critical thought, cunning, and inherently lesser reasoning capacities were women's natural "strengths." They evinced women and girls' special feminine "power," their natural sexual difference, to be celebrated and cultivated. They were said to give women a kind of parity with men such that they didn't need political liberty.[13] This position is part of the emerging popular and philosophical view, a view reflected, for example, in Rousseau philosophy and in Hegel's that women had their own special kind of freedom that was naturally different from men's. A woman's freedom was experienced in modern man's domestic, private sphere while a man's freedom was exercised principally in the public sphere and was guaranteed by law,[14] which included a right to do virtually anything to women in his private sphere.

Wollstonecraft criticized having two standards for virtues and liberty, instead of a single one, as "un-philosophical" and claimed that they perniciously concealed harms to women and girls.[15] Perhaps we may consider the late modern state of sexual objectification and abuse as a next stage of this modern phenomenon. We may say that it has evolved in neo-Hegelian fashion from an earlier modern ontology of women that was wrapped up in a sex-specific notion of freedom to a late modern version of this package. Through a more recent "alchemy," conditions that would more likely be considered oppressive if most men experienced them now evince not only women's natural lack of bodily boundaries but also their distinct form of freedom or sexual liberation. It is their feminine "sexual difference," a strength and positive attribute, to be celebrated and cultivated.

Feminism's more systematic treatment of the phenomena of sexual abuse has taken its guidance from survivors' lived experiences that are covered up by this conceptual framework. As part of piercing through and dismantling this ontology, this work has renamed these experiences with terms like "sexual harassment," "domestic battery," "child molestation," "date rape," "acquaintance rape," and "marital rape" while terms like "sexual slavery" now describe dimensions of prostitution and pornography.

Yet the old conceptual framework remains formidable and in tension with this emerging one. We may say that we are at the beginnings of a "crisis in concepts" induced by our attention to phenomena of abuse that resist this old framework, which is now starting slightly to "totter" as a more adequate one is entering its place.[16] The latter reflects the beginnings of a fundamental shift in humanity's consciousness of freedom and oppression, something that, as Hegel reminds us, is a historical process that takes a long time to occur though, contra Hegel, is not inevitable. A testament to this fact is that even when we name the experiences in a manner that is more adequate to them, their reality is downplayed through the ensuing perception that the abuses are rare and anomalous rather than common as the empirical evidence shows. Accordingly, we need continuously to re-ground ourselves in these phenomena, against the overpowering late modern framework that casts them as evidence of female ontology and of women's sex-specific liberation. So here I refer very briefly to a few concrete instances that convey this tension between that framework and this emerging, more objective understanding.

Take, for example, the legal term "sexual harassment." It was coined in the late 1970s to name the pervasive workplace experience where typically male bosses (and co-workers) target female subordinates for sexually intrusive advances that exploit various power differentials as a condition of employment.[17] Although in the ensuing years the recognition of this abuse has emerged with greater clarity in the courts, still in the 1990s we can have the *Reed v. Shepherd* case, which is not atypical. The plaintiff Reed, a female jailer for the county, was "handcuffed to the toilet, the drunk tank, and inside the elevator; made the subject of lewd jokes and remarks; has her head forcefully shoved in her co-workers' laps, and an electric cattle prod forced between her legs—facts that were not disputed by the defense."[18] Yet the defense and the court still interpreted such treatment as something that a sexually uninhibited woman might welcome and enjoy.[19] Instead of recognizing the objective nature of the harms that would be deemed violating of any human being subject to them—and an approach more readily adopted in racial harassment cases[20]—here they were proof of her female nature and therefore as not necessarily harmful.[21] This approach contrasts with, for example, some factually similar abuses that took place in the very different context of the Abu Ghraib prison but which are recognized to violate men rather than deemed natural and perhaps liberating to them. This treatment is not considered something that people of a certain ethnicity might welcome and enjoy as their "ethnic difference."

In the late 1970s and early 1980s the prevalence of child sexual abuse, especially of girls, began to be uncovered. Yet it butted heads with psychoanalytically-shaped popular and professional views that the abuses weren't real but healthy and natural fantasies of girls wishing to "have sex" with their fathers or with father figures. As Nabokov and both his high and low brow popularizers have opined, girls are by their nature precocious "Lolitas"[22] who express their sexual freedom in a manner natural to their sex, which is to welcome a kind of sexuality that violates their boundaries and that is enhanced by the extreme power differential between a middle-aged man and a child. In this doublethink scenario, the female child seduces the helpless older man, rather than such men being recognized as the calculating sexual predators that they are. The American feminist writer Andrea Dworkin summarizes this situation. The existence of child molestation was denied as the sexual objectification of children, especially girls, was advanced "under the rubric of free sexuality for children" and efforts to protect them were thwarted as "a tyranny of the repressed."[23]

Although the crime of rape has recently begun to be recognized in a way that reflects the experiences of its victims,[24] it still remains obscured by the framework of women's natural lack of bodily boundaries and their sex-specific sexual liberation as a 1996 New York case exemplifies.[25] Here a woman and her date were at a restaurant and drinking heavily. She went to the bathroom where she passed out while her date, who waited for her to join him outside, fell asleep in his pickup truck. Four men then followed her to the bathroom, carried her out into a booth and took turns raping her, after which they returned to their beer and sandwiches. A defense attorney at trial claimed, and the court concurred, that it was reasonable to assume that she could have consented. She became drunk to a point verging on unconsciousness in order to liberate herself of her sexual inhibitions and engage in what might reasonably be construed as consensual activity, as each sex liberating itself in its own sex-specific way.[26] It wasn't concluded that such treatment might objectively violate any human being subjected to it.[27]

Finally, there have been significant efforts over the last few decades to make the misogynistic reality of pornography visible against the prevailing conceptual framework that it depicts harmless, healthy, free sexuality.[28] Today's top-selling pornography shows women enjoying sexual violence, for instance, being beaten, cut, bruised, bleeding, hung, tortured, gang-raped, and multiply-penetrated in horrific ways, which is presented as liberating for them, as their "sexual difference."[29] Researchers studying pornography's effects aren't able to find readily-available, commercial, heterosexual pornography that doesn't in some way show women submissive and degraded.[30] Much pornography records actual sexual abuses as they are taking place and is tied to trafficking in sexual slavery.[31] Moreover that degradation has gotten progressively worse in recent years,[32] with pornography now mainstreamed and exploding in reach with every new technological advancement and gadget.[33] It trains men and boys to perpetrate what they see in the pornography, with today's average age of boys' initiation into and regular consumption of pornography being eleven.[34] Meanwhile, women and girls experience trauma, internal breakdown, loss of a sense of self, and a progressive erosion of their bodily and internal integrity with little way to make sense of what is happening to them. They are left with less and less space in their lives where the men and boys they encounter aren't in some way shaped by, and so see them through, pornography. All of this becomes invisible when the traumatic outcomes of this violent processing system are then adduced as proof of this condition's naturalness for females.

To summarize, from the 1970s onward, most notably in North America, there were successive initiatives to make the harms of sexual abuse visible, from sexual harassment to battery, rape, prostitution, and pornography. At every step of the way, there was and continues to be organized opposition under the rubric of freedom, a development that even more deeply entrenches the supposed ontology that females lack bodily boundaries. Its alchemical machinery transforms these abuses into complementary, sex-specific, freed sexuality while proponents of this position cast themselves as freedom fighters and liberators against the forces of oppression and repression.[35] If however we hold more closely to the phenomena, which point to a more universal standard for harm, then we may cut through these conceptual barriers and recognize what is ethically at stake, namely that this traditional ontology and this aspect of modernity's freedom in fact advocate destructiveness, most directly against women and girls.[36]

IV. Heidegger's Philosophy

Heidegger's philosophy has a distinctive relevance to showing the pernicious function of this conceptual framework that supports sexual abuse and to helping us better understand that abuse. This relevance is tied to Heidegger's idea of philosophy's task, an idea which we may elicit from his practice of it in *Being and Time* and may summarize as follows. The philosopher delineates a contemporary philosophical problem through making visible some hidden dimension of what we think we so surely know. The new understanding that this dimension indicates must be wrested from a dominant traditional understanding, including through confronting its historical sources. The philosopher thereby situates a contemporary problem within philosophy's past, that is, within an established tradition, as he or she takes us beyond it. I claim that modern sexual abuse demands philosophical response of this order and that Heidegger's project in *Being and Time* provides a significant road map for such response.

Heidegger delineates and creatively responds to the contemporary crisis that he calls philosophy's forgetting of the question of Being. He means that in the late modern period and in its philosophy, we notably avoid facing the fact of our finite existence, and we thus evade assuming the freedom more fundamentally to shape our life to our own making. He claims that dislocations in our ordinary, everyday dealings in and understanding of the world are those triggers that compel us more directly to address the question of Being. Dislocations occur when I suddenly notice some aspect of an entity that is usually hidden, something Heidegger calls a "phenomenon."[37] It is something beyond what I thought I knew, which then forces me to step back and re-think how I understand and go about in the world. This moment can compel me to reflect upon my existence by bringing more sharply into view ways by which I may choose to be otherwise than how I usually am and by which I may have a more meaningful life.

Heidegger implicates traditional ontology's understanding of self and world, from Descartes onward, for this current state of amnesia in relation to the question of Being, an understanding whose problematic assumptions, he says, reach into the present-day to limit contemporary philosophy's work. For traditional ontology posits determinations of self and world that are reductive, definitive, timeless truths, and it designates as unreal or of significantly demoted reality whatever falls outside such determinations. Nothing hidden shadows what we know with such certainty, so there is nothing to dislocate us from our ordinary dealings in and understanding of the world and thus compel us to face the question of Being. Heidegger must accordingly confront traditional ontology, which, he says, stands in for and covers up[38] a more fundamental ontology of self and world that has room for "phenomena" or the hidden. He must wrest the latter from the former.

Dasein is Heidegger's term for this more fundamental understanding of self. This self is embodied and always existing within and constituted by relations with things and others in the world, in contrast to the Cartesian and neo-Cartesian subject who is disembodied and detached from the world and expresses his freedom by simplifying reality into the kinds of determinations in which nothing escapes his complete grasp. The Heideggerian subject assumes there is something real about self and world beyond what we so surely know instead of dismissing those dimensions from the outset. His way of knowing the world isn't inscribed with a tendency to cover up other dimensions of a domain of inquiry. Rather, he expects his understanding to continue to maintain some opening to the world, and therefore to be a little more tentative. *Dasein* is thereby perceptually and epistemologically cultivated to be more likely to notice what is usually hidden. His comportment towards and way of knowing the world has fewer barriers to the "phenomena's" affecting or doing their work on him so that, even in spite of himself, they may deliver him to tend to the question of Being or to his existence.

Tending to the question of Being may also take the form of pursuing more systematically the new understanding that a "phenomenon" indicates about a particular matter such that the result is philosophy or original thinking. For Heidegger, "phenomenology" refers to the work of drawing out and explicitly exhibiting, describing, and explicating a "phenomenon," that is, thematizing it.[39] It is, Heidegger says, philosophy's method.[40] Philosophy's source, like the source of facing the question of Being, lies in something unsettling in our immediate, everyday dealings in the world; in something that we thought we knew but that is thus revealed as not so well understood after all.[41] It now beckons and burdens the philosopher to articulate it as philosophy. As Heidegger says, "What is given to thinking [is something that] lies nearest . . . [and is] therefore constantly and already passed over."[42] It is a blind spot in relation to philosophy's established understandings, a spot that a "phenomenon" signals as a territory to chart phenomenologically.[43]

Accordingly, Heidegger describes "philosophy [as] universal phenomenological ontology."[44] He means that philosophy emanates from noticing a "phenomenon" within the wider or more fundamental ontology of a nearby entity and, through phenomenology, drawing out and making the understanding indicated there more universally intelligible.[45] That understanding makes evident a shortcoming in an existing conceptual framework and may precipitate a "crisis in concepts," in which a taken for granted framework, or part thereof, must now make room for a better one.[46]

This confrontation with a governing conceptual framework includes confronting its historical sources through which the philosopher situates a contemporary problem in relation to the tradition.[47] Heidegger refers to this turn to the past as a dismantling or "destruction" (*Destruktion*) of the tradition, which, he quickly clarifies, does *not* mean getting rid of the tradition or "bury[ing it] in nullity" but rather staking out one's own place in relation to it.[48] Elsewhere he describes this relation to the past as a "conversation,"[49] as "talk[ing] through with [the philosophical greats of the past] that about which they speak,"[50] and "as an adoption and transformation of what has been handed down to us."[51] He recognizes that contemporary philosophy has a complicated and ambivalent relation to its past. Contemporary philosophy is part of an existing narrative and needs the resources of its past, but that past can also significantly limit how we interpret the world by propagating assumptions that demand fundamental questioning yet are considered self-evident.[52]

Heidegger suggests that we may navigate our venture into the past, without losing our own ground in relation to it, if we journey there with a contemporary problem as our clue or source of orientation. Indeed, he says that his own project's "destruction" of the history of traditional ontology is about "today"[53] and that he goes to the past with "*the question of Being as our clue.*"[54] For a contemporary problem serves as our guide and gives timely purpose to our turn to a formidable past, which then helps us keep that past "within its *limits.*"[55] That is, this guide helps us maintain our boundaries in relation to the tradition's agenda, so that we do not allow it to pull us, like a rip current, into its stream and under. We may thereby take up the past in a "positive manner [by which we] make it productively [our] own."[56] In this case, this means that we may make it about today, about considering how our contemporary problem fits into the tradition but uses its resources to take us beyond it.

This compass of a contemporary problem points us towards and illuminates shortcomings in parts of the tradition that were not evident before, giving us new perspective on it and on where precisely a step beyond it might lie. In such places, Heidegger says, a "hardened tradition" start to loosen and "the concealments which it has brought about" start to dissolve.[57] A space opens to cast anchor and situate our present-day problem within a historical home, by which we attain a "bigger picture" view on our problem and a better sense of how to chart our new philosophical territory. In Heidegger's case, this territory is about a way by which to put us more squarely within the domain of the question of Being. "Remain[ing] in conversation with that to which the tradition delivers us," he says, is essential to discovering philosophy's present-day work.[58] And because philosophy as such is about charting new territory in a way that is also anchored in the tradition, it is a large and unwieldy undertaking, one that will initially be a bit rough-edged, as he suggests, somewhat "awkward" and "inelegant."[59]

The Heidegger scholar William Lovitt summarizes this idea of philosophy in relation to its history. He says that it is "thinking within the sphere of tradition"[60] but that, here, elicits the "unthought" from the thought.[61] "As such [thinking] is freed by tradition from being a mere thinking back, to becoming a thinking forward."[62] Philosophy so understood reshapes the past "in the *next* responsive on-writing of thought"[63] and thus "point[s] to some way or reality needed beyond what is now known."[64]

Modern sexual abuse requires philosophical response in this Heideggerian sense, which will help us better understand this problem. His subject is epistemologically better positioned than philosophy's traditional Cartesian and neo-Cartesian subject to notice a "phenomenon" or anomaly that shadows the prevailing understanding of sexual abuse as a manifestation of women's natural lack of bodily boundaries and as their freedom, an understanding that interferes with our moral perception of harm. Heidegger's subject, as a Being-in-the-world, is more proximate to what reveals itself beyond that understanding, for instance, through survivor testimonies or in the vacant eyes of a violated person than is the detached and disembodied Cartesian subject. Because Heidegger's subject assumes that there is something real beyond what we so surely know, she is more likely to recognize such examples that are so nearby that they are usually overlooked, and she is more likely to seek them out. Unlike the Cartesian subject, she is not epistemologically held back from making this move. Moreover, she recognizes that philosophy is about phenomenologically drawing out new understanding that is thus indicated, as the source of philosophical insight lies in such places. In sum, she has in this Heideggerian manner of inquiry a way to delineate this contemporary problem against a prevailing ontology and idea of freedom that conceal it.

This understanding is first indicated in more immediate, extra-philosophical areas of feminist inquiry such as consciousness raising, testimonial literature, sociology, psychology, trauma studies, and in developments in politics and in law. Together, they have been eroding this conceptual framework that supports and interferes with our moral perception of sexual abuse. Although philosophy that responds to this ethical challenge relies on these developments, its task is distinctive in that it translates them into philosophy, which, in this case, means using them phenomenologically to bring into sharper view this contemporary problem and the ontology and idea of freedom that obstruct this recognition. It means pushing the latter closer to the brink of a "crisis in concepts" and to a more effective dismantling of that ontology, which then makes room for a better understanding of the matter.

But Heidegger's idea of philosophy is bigger still, as furthermore it situates a contemporary problem within philosophy's past through a "destruction" of the latter. In this case, our venture into the past, guided by our present-day problem, significantly parallels Heidegger's own "destruction" of the history of traditional ontology. As I have shown, the ontology about women's lack of bodily boundaries and sex-specific freedom has sources in the early modern political era, in popular and philosophical views from Rousseau to Hegel and beyond. They consider characteristics that reflect objective harms to be part of women's nature, and therefore not harmful, and consider women's freedom to be expressed in modern man's private sphere in contrast to men's public political liberty. We may say that this framework has evolved over the modern era into today's version of these views.

A return to philosophy's past with the problem of modern sexual abuse as our clue illuminates shortcomings in the tradition and opens a space in which historically to anchor our problem. We may thereby stake out the tradition's positive possibilities in a way that is our own. We attain a bigger and better understanding of this present-day ethical challenge that we wrest from a traditional understanding, as we bring the tradition to bear on this problem in a way that might move philosophy today towards a next chapter.

Natalie Nenadic, University of Kentucky

Notes

I thank Karsten Harries, Michael Della Rocca, Sun-Joo Shin, and two anonymous reviewers for *Social Philosophy Today* for helpful comments.

1.   Approximately one in four women in America reports having been raped. Fourteen percent report having been raped in marriage. Forty-four percent of women in America report completed or attempted rape at least once in their lives. With regard to the last figure, numbers are higher among some ethnic groups, for instance, among Native American women (55 percent) and Jewish women (50 percent). Thirty-eight percent of girls report having been sexually abused before reaching age eighteen, most by men close to them or in positions of authority over them; age ten is the average age of the first abuse. Between forty and sixty-eight percent of female employees report experiencing sexual harassment in their workplaces. In secondary schools, eighty-five percent of girls were found to have experienced sexual harassment; sixty-five percent were touched, grabbed or pinched in a sexual way; sixty-six percent were subjected to at least one type of sexual harassment "often" or "occasionally." Battering of women by husbands, ex-husbands, or boyfriends is the largest single cause of injury to women in this country. These statistics and information are from many studies listed in Catharine A. MacKinnon, *Sex Equality*, 2d ed. (New York: Foundation Press, 2007), 753–4 (rape), 851 (sexual harassment), 675–6 (battery).

2.   The dynamic I describe in this section is more or less a common sense within the literature on sexual abuse trauma. E. Sue Blume, *Survivors: Uncovering Incest and Its Aftereffects in Women* (New York: Ballantine Books, 1991); Diana E. H. Russell, *The Secret Trauma: Incest in the Lives of Girls and Women* (New York: Basic Books, 1986); Judith Herman M.D., *Trauma and Recovery: The Aftermath of Violence—From Domestic Abuse to Political Terror* (New York: Basic Books, 1992), 33–86, 166–72; Sue Michael Silverman, *Because I Remember Terror Father I Remember You* (Athens, GA: The University of Georgia Press, 1999).

3.   Rebecca Whisnant offers a similar analysis of the general views of "third wave feminists." Unable to change such sexual dynamics, they instead change their attitude towards them. They say that they "choose" these conditions, which somehow makes the objective oppressiveness of these dynamics go away and the woman's position not only liberating but "feminist." Rebecca Whisnant, "Not Your Father's Playboy, Not Your Mother's Feminist Movement: Contemporary Feminism in a Porn Culture," delivered at the conference "Pornography and Pop Culture: Re-Framing Theory, Re-thinking Activism," Boston, March 24, 2007 available at http://www.saidit.org/archives/jun06/article5.html.

4.   Herman, *Trauma and Recovery*, 166.

5.   Aristotle, *The Politics*, in *Social and Political Philosophy: Classical Western Texts in Feminist and Multicultural Perspective*, ed. James P. Sterba (Belmont, CA: Wadsworth/ Thompson Learning, 2003), especially 60, 66–7.

6.   See, for example, Jean-Jacques Rousseau, *Discourse on the Origin of Inequality* in *The Basic Political Writings*, trans. Donald A. Cress (Indianapolis/Cambridge: Hackett Publishing Co., 1987), 72–3; Jean-Jacques Rousseau, *On the Social Contract* in *The Basic Political Writings*, 142–4.

7.   Rousseau, *Discourse on the Origin of Inequality*, 72.

8.   Rousseau's criticism here is more properly a criticism of a Hobbes's pro-slavery position though Rousseau considers the respective positions of Aristotle and Hobbes to be more or less the same. Hobbes criticizes Aristotle's claim that slavery is natural for some people, arguing instead that slavery is entered into by the consent of naturally free people. Aristotle

and Hobbes arrive at the same destination of slavery but use different avenues to get there. Thomas Hobbes, *Leviathan*, ed. Richard Tuck (Cambridge: Cambridge University Press, 1996), revised student edition, 107.

9. Rousseau, *On the Social Contract*, 144.

10. Rousseau, *Discourse on the Origin of Inequality*, 73.

11. Rousseau, *On the Social Contract*, 146.

12. Mary Wollstonecraft, *A Vindication of the Rights of Woman*, ed. Miriam Brody (New York: Penguin, 2004), 54, 57.

13. See, for example, ibid., 31–3, 38–9, 45–7, 99–112.

14. See generally G. W. F. Hegel, *Phenomenology of Spirit*, trans. A. V. Miller (Oxford: Oxford University Press, 1977), 266–89; G. W. F. Hegel, *Elements of the Philosophy of Right*, ed. Allen W. Wood (Cambridge: Cambridge University Press, 1991), 199–219. Hegel would continue with these basic Rousseauian ontological assumptions. In this regard, we may say about Hegel what Heidegger says of the traditional ontologies that came after Descartes, in that trajectory that Heidegger treats and criticizes. Hegel would elaborate Rousseau's ontological assumptions in his own way, that is, put his distinctive stamp on them and expand their reach in the world but would not fundamentally question them. They would be "merely material for reworking, as [they were] for Hegel." Martin Heidegger, *Being and Time*, trans. John Macquarrie and Edward Robinson (New York: HarperCollins, 1962, 2008), 43.

15. Wollstonecraft, *A Vindication of the Rights of Woman*, 28–9, 36–7, 46–8, 55–6.

16. Heidegger, *Being and Time*, 29.

17. Constance Backhouse and Leah Cohen, *The Secret Oppression: Sexual Harassment of Working Women* (Toronto: MacMillan, 1978); Catharine A. MacKinnon, *Sexual Harassment of Working Women: A Case of Sex Discrimination* (New Haven: Yale University Press, 1979).

18. Louise F. Fitzgerald, Suzanne Swan, Karla Fischer, "Why Didn't She Just Report Him? The Psychological and Legal Implications of Women's Responses to Sexual Harassment," *Journal of Social Issues* 51.1 (1995): 131.

19. Ibid., 131–2.

20. Ibid., 130.

21. Ibid.

22. Vladimir Nabokov, *Lolita* (New York: Random House, Second Vintage International Edition, 1997).

23. Andrea Dworkin, "Suffering and Speech," introduction to *In Harm's Way: The Pornography Civil Rights Hearings*, ed. Catharine A. MacKinnon and Andrea Dworkin (Cambridge, MA: Harvard University Press, 1997), 27; Judith Herman M.D., *Father-Daughter Incest: A Speak-out on Incest* (Cambridge, MA: Harvard University Press, 1981).

24. Stephen J. Schulhofer, *Unwanted Sex: The Culture of Intimidation and the Failure of Law* (Cambridge, MA: Harvard University Press, 1998), 3. Traditionally rape was considered a crime against men. "[A] husband was injured in his conjugal rights if his wife—loyal and not adulterous—was violated; a father's rights over his unmarried virgin daughter became worthless when she was ruined and despoiled. The crime was not against the rape victim but against her male owner. If the male owner raped her, it was not rape. Only when women

said what happened to them when they were forced was raped properly defined, understood, and prosecuted" Dworkin, "Suffering and Speech," 33.

25. Schulhofer, *Unwanted Sex*, 10–2.

26. For a related gang-rape case using this line of defense, see also the 1991 St. John's case in ibid., 14.

27. Ibid., 7–8.

28. MacKinnon and Dworkin, *In Harm's Way*, especially at 3.

29. See, for example, the recent documentary film "The Price of Pleasure: Pornography, Sexuality and Relationships," by Chyng Sun and Miguel Picker, 2008; see also almost all of the testimonies in MacKinnon and Dworkin, *In Harm's Way*.

30. See the testimony of Edward Donnerstein in MacKinnon and Dworkin, *In Harm's Way* 51, 292.

31. Donna Hughes, "The Use of New Communication Technologies for Sexual Exploitation of Women and Children," in *Not for Sale: Feminists Resisting Prostitution and Pornography*, ed. Christine Stark and Rebecca Whisnant (North Melbourne, Australia: Spinifex Press, 2004), 38–55.

32. See generally Gail Dines, *Pornland: How Porn has Hijacked Our Sexuality* (Boston, MA: Beacon Press, 2010).

33. Ibid.; Pamela Paul, *Pornified: How Pornography is Damaging Our Lives, Our Relationships, and Our Families* (New York: Henry Holt and Company, 2005).

34. Paul, *Pornified*, 174.

35. Dworkin, "Suffering and Speech," 27–8, 33.

36. Of course, it has long been recognized that many universal categories actually mask male experiences, prompting some feminists to advocate a "difference" approach. However, I am arguing for a more robust universalism along the lines of Catharine MacKinnon's, which centers on recognizing dominance or power hierarchies and considers both a biased universalism and a "difference" approach to reflect male bias and an inadequate situatedness in social reality. She claims that a "difference" approach tends to neutralize harms and powerlessness by reifying them as difference, an approach she claims will not register the worst harms to women because male dominance will have succeeded in making them appear natural. Catharine MacKinnon, "Dominance and Difference: On Sex Discrimination (1984)," in *Feminism Unmodified: Discourses on Life and Law* (Cambridge, MA: Harvard University Press, 1987), 32–45, especially 39, 242–3.

37. Heidegger, *Being and Time*, 59–60.

38. Ibid., 60.

39. Ibid., 59–61.

40. Ibid., 49–50.

41. Ibid., 36.

42. Martin Heidegger, "The Word of Nietzsche," in Martin Heidegger, *The Question Concerning Technology and Other Essays*, trans. William Lovitt (New York: Harper Torchbook, 1977), 111.

43. Heidegger, *Being and Time*, 30–1.

44. Ibid., 62.

45. Martin Heidegger, *What Is Philosophy?*, trans. Jean T. Wilde and William Kluback (Lanham, MD: Rowman & Littlefield Publishers, Inc., 2003), 75.

46. Heidegger, *Being and Time*, 29. Although Heidegger's specific point refers to major conceptual shifts in mathematics and in science, it is also relevant to philosophy and to smaller conceptual shifts.

47. Ibid., 41–9; Martin Heidegger, *The Basic Problems of Phenomenology*, trans. Albert Hofstadter (Bloomington, IN: Indiana University Press, revised edition, 1988).

48. Heidegger, *Being and Time*, 44.

49. Heidegger, *What is Philosophy?*, 71.

50. Ibid., 67.

51. Ibid., 71.

52. Heidegger, *Being and Time*, 41, 43–4.

53. Ibid., 44; see also Heidegger, *What is Philosophy?*, 71.

54. Heidegger, *Being and Time*, 44, italics in the original.

55. Ibid., italics in the original.

56. Ibid., 43.

57. Ibid., 44.

58. Heidegger, *What is Philosophy?*, 71.

59. Ibid., 63.

60. William Lovitt, "Introduction," in Heidegger, *The Question Concerning Technology and Other Essays*, xxxvii.

61. Ibid., xxxviii.

62. Ibid., xxxvii.

63. Ibid., xxxviii, italics added.

64. Ibid.

Critical Thinking, Autonomy, and Social Justice

Matthew R. Silliman and David Kenneth Johnson

Abstract: In a fictional conversation designed to appeal to both working teachers and social philosophers, three educators take up the question of whether critical thinking itself can, or should, be taught independently of an explicit consideration of issues related to social justice. One, a thoughtful but somewhat traditional Enlightenment rationalist, sees critical thinking as a neutral set of skills and dispositions, essentially unrelated to the conclusions of morality, problems of social organization, or the content of any particular academic discipline. A second interlocutor, steeped in "critical" pedagogy of Paulo Freire, insists that the problem is the pose of neutrality itself. On this view, all honest and effective approaches to teaching must confront the hegemony of unjust relationships, institutions, and conceptual schemes. The third character attempts to resolve the tension between these two opposed camps.

Alison: We've been speaking quite a lot about the fostering of autonomy—progressively thinking in a grounded way for oneself—as a central goal of teaching. I wonder what relation this has to the Freirean idea of liberation, understood as the sole legitimate aim of pedagogy?[1]

Jules: Be careful not to get me started on Paulo Freire and his followers, Alison! I'm a huge fan of his groundbreaking work on the profoundly political nature of all teaching and learning. Not only would he have liked our emphasis on developing student autonomy, he probably would have encouraged us to push it even further.

Russell: Forgive me, but I get suspicious of anything that comes with a radical *caché*, especially when it promises to push a sensible idea "even further." In my experience, this usually presages an exaggeration to absurdity, especially whenever politics pokes its nose where it doesn't belong.

Alison: Let's try our best to keep it civil, okay? I know you are both good-hearted, but your passion compels me to remind us all that we're here to try to answer these questions, not to score points or align ourselves one way or the other with intellectual trends.

Jules: I don't think either Russell or I were on the verge of incivility, Alison. But point taken; let's see what the Freirean, overtly political approach does or does not have to offer us as teachers.

Russell: I'm thinking not much, frankly, but I'm willing to give it its day in court. If you'll try to curb your enthusiasm, Jules, I will endeavor to suppress my scoffism.

Alison: That's the spirit, or as close as we get in a typical classroom at least!

Russell: I don't want to seem merely reactive, so let me begin with the positive claim that core learning is politically neutral. And what we call critical thinking, or thinking objectively and rationally about the products and processes of own thinking, bespeaks no particular content or political-ideological point of view whatsoever. To be a critical thinker is simply to pursue a life devoted to reason. To ignore this fact courts demagoguery in teaching.

Alison: I take it you are being deliberately provocative.

Russell: I'm just expressing an honest belief. I'm aware some people think otherwise, but by being definite and clear I hope to provoke no more than edifying conversation.

Jules: Actually, Russell, your very words are a tidy example of the ubiquity of political influence in all discourse. Your status as a professor of philosophy, your mastery of analytical thought, and so forth, speak volumes before you open your mouth. You amplify this whenever you express yourself with such rhetorical certainty and authority . . .

Russell: Oh, don't be silly, Jules. You're choosing to characterize my words that way just because you disagree with me!

Alison: Perhaps a less personalized example would be better.

Jules: Okay, okay. Consider a typical classroom, at any level you like, from kindergarten through graduate school: we can witness variations in the authority a teacher exercises, but the *fact* of authority seems constant.

Russell: I agree with you, Jules, whether it only seems to be or is in fact constant. I suspect the latter, since some kind of authority always informs teacher-student relationships.

Jules: What kind exactly?

Russell: Well, it's neither self-servingly manipulative nor arbitrary, but flows from the teacher's greater knowledge of the subject, wider understanding of the analytical tools of the discipline, and sustained experience reasoning well and clearly about the topic at hand.

Jules: You may be right in principle, but in actual practice the teacher's authority always has many other features, arising from social status, cultural history, personality, and especially institutional role.

Russell: I take such things to be genuine, if regrettable, intrusions on ideal pedagogical relations, but the best teaching goes a long way toward overcoming them.

Jules: The Freirean insight is that these influences, which you call regrettable intrusions, are endemic to any real-world teaching situation. These power relations and other sources of authority are part of who we are and cannot be erased even in principle, so we must acknowledge and work with them.

Alison: How would we do that?

Jules: By becoming progressively conscious of the dynamic of authority in the teaching-learning relationship, and use it consciously, deliberately, in an effort to liberate and empower our students.

Russell: Subtract off the revolutionary-sounding phrases, and maybe we're after the same thing . . .

Jules: I would hope so, Russell, but to maintain the fiction that we are approximating your ideal pedagogical relations only serves to conceal such "regrettable intrusions," and this invisibility makes them all the more powerful.

Alison: When you say that such authoritarian intrusions are endemic and cannot be erased, I take it you do *not* mean that we are helpless in the face of their deterministic force?

Jules: No, of course not. As we become aware of their influence on our thinking, we can make progressively more liberating choices in relation to our students. Why do you ask?

Alison: Because I wonder how it is any different from the Enlightenment emphasis on the power of reason. In fact, your suggestion that we think clearly about what influences our beliefs sounds to me a lot like Russell's description of critical thinking.

Russell: I had the same thought. You seem to want it both ways, Jules. On the one hand, you claim the illegitimate bases of a teacher's authority are ineradicable, so we have no choice but to try to use them for (what we take to be) good. On the other hand, you seem to presume that the methods of critical thinking can help students eventually liberate themselves from that authority.

Jules: Freirean liberation involves actually bringing about change in human relations and institutional and economic structures, so that students and others are no longer oppressed.

Russell: Well, good luck with that. But do you suppose for a minute that people will ever be free from oppression who cannot think for themselves?

Jules: I suppose not. Critical thinking as you describe it does seem necessary for liberation, but I agree with Freire that it is not by itself sufficient.

Russell: I won't dispute that, and I'm willing to admit that the critical task of overcoming prejudice is one we never wholly complete.

Alison: So it looks like we are in essential agreement after all?

Jules: There is still one thing I'm sure Freire would reject, and that's Russell's suggestion that anything, least of all Enlightenment-style critical thinking, "bespeaks no particular content or point of view whatsoever."

Alison: Why do you say that?

Jules: Because everything we say or do bears the mark of our unique, individual perspectives and histories. Maybe we can change or widen our points of view, and with careful attention choose more appropriate or liberating ones, but each of us thinks, speaks, and acts from a perspective that is in some way limited to who we are and where we've been.

Russell: This is old news, Jules. All living organisms, in contrast to gods or disembodied spirits, experience the world from some place or other. But since, as you say, we can with a little effort widen and improve our views, nothing about our original position prevents us from accessing perfectly general truths about the world.

Jules: No matter how much it improves, your view will always be your view, Russell.

Russell: I'm entirely willing to take responsibility for my views, especially the improved ones! Look, constructivist tautologies aside,[2] the fact that we must experience the world from some perspective or other tells us nothing about what we can or cannot know or experience.

Jules: I have already given you and Alison due credit for moving me beyond the pedagogical theory of radical constructivism.[3]

Russell: Well, then can we safely infer that you no longer subscribe to the radical relativism or "ontological agnosticism" with which it flirts?

Jules: You may.

Russell: Good. I take it that you are thus no longer shy about saying that we can know something about ourselves and the world?

Jules: Some connotations of the word 'know' still make me uneasy, but I think we can certainly come to understand some things about the world and ourselves, yes.

Alison: That's a refreshing distinction, Jules. In my teaching, I am usually less concerned with what my students know, purely in terms of data or factual information, than with how they understand it, which includes making sense of it, grasping its importance in context, and keeping an open mind. The gerund 'understanding' has a suitable ring of ongoing process and intellectual activity—and by suggesting a particularity of context, it includes the political issues that concern Jules.

Russell: 'Understanding' is a perfectly serviceable term for what contemporary epistemologists are after, and I think it's especially appropriate in an educational context. But there's nothing "post-modern" or especially new about it. In fact, early modern philosophers of knowledge favored the term.[4] Think of Locke's *Essay Concerning Human Understanding*.

Jules: Or Hume's *Enquiries Concerning Human Understanding and the Principles of Morals*. I'm glad we're in agreement, Russell, and with that small terminological caveat, I think we are safe from the threat of any sort of radical relativism.

Alison: What point were you making, then?

Jules: I'm merely defending what we might call a moderately relativist or perspectivalist view: given our unique perspectives on the world, we are always subject to presuppositions, ideas, and influences that we have not yet deconstructed—or if you prefer, thought critically about—so we're never entitled to think we're above politics, especially in relationships as complex as teaching.

Russell: As a healthy statement of fallibilism, I won't quibble with those claims, Jules. I worry, though, that they might conceal a dangerously slippery slope. Good-hearted, humanist teachers like yourself will surely interpret even "moderate" relativism as *carte blanche* to impart to your students what you take, perhaps rightly, to be good politics and a sense of social justice.

Jules: Thank you. I struggle to do exactly that.

Russell: But suppose a particular teacher's politics were something you or I would find abhorrent—advocating genocide or torture, for example—would he or she be justified by your principle to teach from that warped perspective?

Alison: I take it your point is that the principle "all teaching is irreducibly political," and the alleged license it gives us to make teaching an overtly political act, seems to embody no necessary boundaries on what sort of politics would be beyond the pale?

Russell: Just so.

Jules: But the principle, as articulated by Freire and others, does contain such boundaries, and they are more than enough to constrain any unjust politicization of the classroom or slide into an "anything goes" radical relativism. The boundaries are built into the very purpose and point of education itself, which is the liberation of students from all arbitrary authority—whether that of the teacher, the culture, or their own insecurities.

Alison: That's a tidy move. If we assume that the principal reason we educate is to free students from any authority but their own informed and autonomous deliberations—another way of framing the development of autonomy we have discussed—perhaps we *could* identify meaningful constraints on what counts as good pedagogical politics, and thus admit overt politics to the classroom in a controlled manner.

Russell: Many, perhaps most teachers and students, do not operate on this assumption, so it will need a rigorous defense before we're done. But even if it were a broadly shared understanding of the end of education, I fear this would not effectively banish our *genocidaire*. Consider a typical middle-class German child in the 1930s, empowered by the friendship and support of Hitler Youth activities, receiving a rigorous and expansive education in music, art, history, languages, mathematics, and so forth, and in some of the best public schools in the world.

Jules: Those schools imposed rigid social formalities and curricula, and were strictly elitist and authoritarian to a degree that would shock many of us today.

Russell: True enough, or so I've heard. My point is that nonetheless such schools did empower many students in Germany, in effect liberating them from the constraints, for example, of having to refrain from torture and genocide.

Jules: That's clearly not what Freire means by liberation or empowerment!

Alison: Of course it isn't, but Russell has a point. We might even say that the events of September 11, 2001"liberated" many U.S. politicians and their supporters from previous, long-standing prohibitions on torture and preemptive war. Obviously, we need to do more than offer nice-sounding words like 'liberation' and 'student autonomy.' These ideas need specification and defense. And, as Russell would probably agree, their adequate defense can come only from critical thought that seeks objective reasons to prefer one interpretation of liberation or autonomy over another.

Russell: Exactly, Alison. Teaching toward students' autonomy sounds nice, but at the very least we must ensure that the empowerment we foster in them is coherent with the like empowerment of everyone else.

Jules: Freire was influenced by Marx, and by the Liberation Theology movement, so of course he agrees that liberty is socially grounded and justified, rather than a reductively individual acquisition. He and his followers are fiercely opposed to the popular model of education as job training for individual advancement or economic development, for example.[5]

Alison: To hear our political leaders talk, economic advancement is the only reason they can imagine for supporting schools, and sadly many educators drink this same Kool-Aid.[6]

Russell: I hope all teachers agree that learning is its own reward, but we shouldn't go overboard. Liberation from material want, which in our world means being qualified to work and able to find some, is no trivial matter. My father was a machinist and my mother a janitor, and they got their educations where they could find them.

Alison: But Russell, surely you could not have become an intellectual if they had not valued education beyond earning a weekly paycheck?

Russell: They were not unsupportive, and Iowa City was a wonderful place to learn in those days, but I don't think they ever really understood why I didn't do something they would have seen as more practical.

Jules: I think Freire would say this attitude is a measure of their oppression. There's nothing wrong with knowing how to earn a living, of course; but learning and life don't stop with bare survival.

Russell: I didn't mean to suggest they were narrow people—my mother loved music and books as much as I do. We should avoid any artificial division between some notion of pure education and learning how to make one's way in the world.

Alison: I can agree with that wholeheartedly, and I wouldn't expect someone influenced by Marx to doubt it.

Jules: Fair enough, so long as we also agree that employment and economic growth are not the main point of learning. But let's not lose sight of our target here: Russell's allegation that critical thinking is ideologically neutral, along with the Freirean insight that such an attitude covertly reinforces prevailing structures.

Russell: Jules, you and I are hardly ideological soulmates, but the very possibility of our carrying on this conversation obviously presupposes our shared commitment to reason.[7] We often disagree, but it's not just dueling ideologies; we listen to each other, and are persuaded (or not) by the quality of the reasons we give and how clearly we present them. We are precisely, and to this extent, educated persons—liberated, autonomous, reasonable, call it what you like.

Jules: Do you really think the devotion to "reason" is not an ideological stance? Don't even get me started on the history and sociology of science . . .

Russell: I concede that some people have treated a thing they called reason as a rigid ideology, but there's something off about that—reason makes a strange object of fanaticism.

Alison: I would say the social cultivation of reasonableness is a very good thing to be passionate about.

Russell: Sure, passion is important, but I don't think it's reasonable to be blindly fanatical about *anything*, especially reason itself. Critical thinking, properly understood, really does transcend ideology.

Jules: I'm from Missouri. Show me.

Alison: No you're not! You told me you grew up in Greenwich Village.

Jules: Washington Square born and bred. "I'm from Missouri" is only an expression.

Alison: I'm just teasing you. You were starting to sound a little combative again.

Russell: No Problem. It's a fair request, Jules, so here's a solid example. One objective feature of reason is its built-in, structural requirement of self-correction. No ideological standpoint has this feature, except to the extent that it subjects itself, extra-ideologically, to critical examination.

Jules: This is just the sort of thinking the Freireans resist: setting up Reason-with-a-capital-R as a kind of über-ideology that everyone must worship! Talk about meta-narratives!

Russell: Your overheated rhetoric misses the point. Reason is neither an ideology nor a meta-narrative, whatever that is.[8] It's just a fairly pedestrian set of tools—hammer, saw, measuring tape, chalk line—without which no one could build much of anything substantial.

Jules: If that really were all reason amounted to, how is it that the European colonialists managed to carve up the planet in its name? Reason is no mere hammer; it's a demand for obedience![9]

Russell: I have already conceded that it is possible to misuse a hammer as though it were a weapon, but to do so is anything but reasonable. Someone who views the world as nothing but a field of ideological power-plays can't help but interpret the demands of reason in that way, but such a reductive view of the world is a mistake.

Jules: How so?

Russell: In the first place, the principles of sound reasoning do not originate as a system of ideas in the usual sense: we do not invent them, we discover them.

Jules: I don't recall ever seeing a piece of reason lying about in nature awaiting discovery! The principles of reason are *our* principles; we actively generate them in the course of thinking about and experiencing the world.

Russell: I smell a red herring, Jules! Of course the principles of sound reasoning are ours. But they are discoverable features of the world of organized, human thought, just as the number *Pi* expresses our discovery of the fixed relationship between the circumference and the diameter of circular things.

Alison: And in the second place?

Russell: This point will seem like a direct affront to Freire's so-called critical pedagogy, I'm afraid. In the same way that correcting an error presupposes the existence of a truth, the neutrality of critical thinking is in fact a condition of the possibility of liberatory pedagogy.

Jules: Well, you're right about it being an affront!

Russell: Bear with me. If the social world really were, as some followers of Freire suggest, an arena of nothing but competing power blocs and ideologies, its full Hobbesian implications would follow: a war of all against all, life brutal and short, etc. We would then need a sovereign power of some sort capable of bullying us into détente.

Alison: A shockingly autocratic and paternalistic result . . .

Russell: Certainly not a world view that could effectively foster liberation, in its pedagogy or anywhere else.

Jules: I'm not sure Freire actually holds such a simplistic view, but I see that anyone who did would have a problem, according to your reasoning.

Alison: To be fair to the spirit of our conversation, Jules, that last qualifier is out of line. If you understand the reasoning and agree that its conclusion follows, then it's not just Russell's reasoning, but yours as well. I take it that this is part of what he means by the independence of reason.

Jules: Now who's sounding combative?

Alison: I'm not taking sides here, Jules. This isn't even about sides! But I want to get back to Russell's claim about teaching critical thinking.

Jules: I would expect it to be perfectly clear. If as Russell says reason is ideologically neutral, it would follow that we can and should teach it that way. He clearly insists that anything else is demagoguery.

Alison: I don't think any such thing follows.

Russell: You don't?

Alison: Not at all. For one thing, the nature of a topic always underdetermines the teaching methods we need to convey it effectively. History is long, but it would be silly to schedule a longer class period for it on that account. Biology—your field, Jules—has all sorts of creepy, slimy, and infectious features that we don't necessarily replicate in the lesson plan.

Russell: I take your point.

Alison: Good. Secondly, as you both well know from experience, understanding something and being able to teach it are radically independent, in part because it can be difficult to recall empathetically what it was like *not* to understand it. This is why teaching is an art, and being an expert in your field is not equivalent to being a good teacher of it.

Jules: You can say that again! I've heard this referred to as the "Curse of Knowledge."[10]

Alison: That phrase makes it sound universal or inevitable. I don't think it's so much a curse as a bad habit, arising from an underdeveloped sense of empathy and imagination—the ability to step outside of yourself, listen to others, and craft a narrative trail from their understandings to yours.

Russell: Those skills do seem to be in short supply in our culture. Most people can't seem to give a stranger adequate directions in their own communities. But this related insight aside, what conclusion were you about to draw from your two premises?

Alison: Spoken like a true logician. And someone who sometimes has trouble finding his way around.

Russell: I am those, and other things, too.

Alison: Sorry, just teasing, again. In fact, I recognize and admire your skill in articulating the nature of critical thinking while employing it in this very conversation.

Russell: Thank you. But what *was* your conclusion?

Alison: My own intuition as a teacher is that trying to teach critical thinking skills without embedding them in some fairly robust content that is familiar and engaging to the students would likely be a disaster. Moreover, I suspect that much of this content needs to be drawn from the richly political and personal stuff of real life, as this is just the area where students will most need to learn how to think clearly and systematically.

Russell: Well, I'm not sure about your last point. Such real-life commitments, along with fraught matters of justice and equity, are precisely where thinking critically is most difficult to do, because we have such deep emotional investments in them. You need to learn to garden before you buy the farm . . .

Alison: Nice metaphor, Russell. But don't you agree that these are the central personal and social issues about which we most need to learn to reason well?

Russell: Yes, of course. We can't omit such content, but I think it is important first to learn the skills on easier issues, and then apply them to such emotionally intense matters when the students are more mature.

Alison: And I suspect just when and how to do so is a tactical question about which good teachers can disagree.

Jules: Excuse me, but are you both saying what it sounds to me like you're saying, that you agree with Freire about the profoundly political nature of teaching and learning?

Russell: Not the way I took him to mean it, but maybe in the more limited sense that Alison describes.

Alison: I think I mean to say precisely that, Jules.

Jules: So it turns out that the alleged neutrality of critical thinking is completely consistent with a pedagogy devoted to liberation and social justice?

Russell: The neutrality of critical thinking is a fact, not an allegation, but if Alison's teacherly instincts are correct, it looks like we can balance these ideas in practice. I must insist, however, that the barest hint of ideological indoctrination is an abuse of our authority.

Alison: . . . and an assault on students' autonomy. We can neither tell students what to think nor bully them into agreeing with us. But this hardly prevents us from expressing and exemplifying our social consciences in the classroom, or explaining the reasoning that we believe leads us to the sense of justice that motivates us.

Jules: In my experience, a heavy-handed approach to such matters backfires anyway. Many students fiercely resist when they think I'm preaching to them, and reject whatever I say for that reason alone.

Russell: Good for them! Their anti-authoritarian impulse may only be a precursor to thinking critically, but it's a healthy first step.

Alison: I have an intuition about how it happened that you two seemed initially to disagree about critical thinking. You, Russell, use the term 'critical' in something like Kant's sense, don't you?[11]

Russell: Yes. A critique is a systematic investigation and assessment of the strengths, weaknesses, presuppositions, and implications of our concepts.

Alison: More simply put, that sounds like thinking carefully about something.

Russell: Basically, yes.

Alison: Whereas, like Freire, you mean something a little different by critique, don't you Jules?

Jules: I think of critique as a rigorous political-ideological investigation of our knowledge, pedagogy, and many other things, in the context of a systematic criticism of the *status quo.*

Alison: And by 'criticism' you thus mean thinking carefully about the *status quo*—with the main goal of figuring out what's *wrong* with it?

Jules: There is not, nor is there soon likely to be, a shortage of things wrong with the prevailing power structure that need figuring out and changing.

Alison: I take it that this negative insight, and accompanying notion of criticism, is just what motivates theorists like Freire. Notice how similar it is in practical content, however, to Russell's more neutral notion of critique, and how as a consequence you might only appear to be at cross-purposes when your actual views and practices are not that far apart.

Russell: I'm still a very long way from Jules's and Freire's radical *chic.*

Alison: I can tell, Russell. But doesn't your commitment to critical thinking as a process of systematic questioning reveal to you any injustice in our world, or any need to do something about it?

Russell: I'll take that as a rhetorical question.

Alison: And I'll take *that* as a concession to Jules's insistence that the classroom is not, in this important sense, a neutral zone. Of course, how we manage the competing intuitions about justice in any actual classroom is a different and sensitive matter, but I submit that you two are on the same team, whether you like it or not.

Matthew R. Silliman, Massachusetts College of Liberal Arts

David Kenneth Johnson, Massachusetts College of Liberal Arts

Notes

Special thanks to the three anonymous reviewers, whose thorough and perceptive comments helped us to clarify our reasoning. A version of this dialogue will appear as a chapter in our forthcoming book *Bridges to Autonomy; Paradoxes in Teaching and Learning*.

1. Paulo Freire (1921–1997), a Brazilian educator and theorist who ranks among the most influential educational thinkers of the twentieth century. His *Pedagogy of the Oppressed* (1970) and many other works emphasize the social dynamics of learning, and place respectful dialogue among equals as the paramount educational method.

2. Constructivists of a "radical" stripe often pretend to derive antirealist or relativistic conclusions about knowledge ("I cannot know the way the world really is") from simple tautological premises ("I can only know what I know").

3. See Johnson and Silliman, *Bridges to the World* (Sense Publishers, 2009), especially chapter 15, "Ontological Agnosticism and Solipsism."

4. Harvey Siegel, "Gimme That Old-Time Enlightenment Meta-Narrative: Radical Pedagogies (And Politics) Require Old-Fashioned Epistemology (And Moral Theory)," *Inquiry: Critical Thinking Across the Disciplines* 11.4 (1993).

5. Jeremy Rifkin explicitly links the worker-training model of education with a reductively individualist notion of autonomy in *The Empathic Civilization* (New York: Jeremy P. Tarcher/Penguin, 2009).

6. See Martha Nussbaum, *Not For Profit:Why Democracy Needs the Humanities* (Princeton: Princeton University Press, 2010).

7. Hervey Siegel, *Educating Reason* (New York: Routledge, 1998).

8. Not all meta-narratives are avoidable or inherently oppressive. See Harvey Siegel, *Rationality Redeemed? Further Dialogues on an Educational Ideal* (New York and London: Routledge, 1997).

9. For a famous example of this view, see Umberto Maturana, "Reality: The Search for Objectivity or the Quest for a Compelling Argument," *Irish Journal of Psychology* 9.1: 25–82, who reduces all truth claims to demands for obedience (which, of course, has the paradoxical implication of so characterizing his very account of truth).

10. Chip Heath and Dan Heath in *Made to Stick: Why Some Ideas Die and Others Survive* (New York: Random House, 2007).

11. See Immanuel Kant, *Critique of Pure Reason* (Cambridge: Cambridge University Press, 1999).

Part IV:

AUTHOR MEETS CRITICS:
JAN NARVESON AND JAMES P. STERBA,
ARE LIBERTY AND EQUALITY COMPATIBLE?

Précis of *Are Liberty and Equality Compatible?*

JAN NARVESON AND JAMES P. STERBA

The issue between us in this book[1] would easily appear, from the title, to be very large. We hope, however, that we are in enough agreement about the general shape of the question as we see it, that our area of agreement can be narrowed down quite considerably. Sterba opens the discussion with his lengthy essay, "Equality Is Compatible with and Required by Liberty"; Narveson continues with "The Right to Liberty is Incompatible with the Right to Equality." Both really accept that the formulation in terms of rights is more perspicuous, for Narveson points out that *conceptually* there is no necessary incompatibility between the two ideas as such. The issue for both of us is whether the claim that the fundamental principle of justice is a general right of all to maximum liberty is compatible with the claim that we have a right to equality, especially when it is equality of the sorts of things that people are able to produce by their efforts—food, clothing, housing, medical care, and the like. We both intend by 'rights' moral statuses such that to have a right is in principle to be eligible for coercively provided provision, if that should be necessary. Thus politically provided welfare programs, supported by taxes, would be just if Sterba is right, and at least *prima facie* unjust if Narveson is. As Narveson notes at the end of his essay, if we go by what is currently done, there is no contest, since welfare states are now the norm throughout the developed world. So Narveson is a critic of the established ways, in one direction. Sterba, on the other hand, wants the equalizing efforts of governments to be much greater than they actually are, and so he is a critic of those ways in the other direction. We are both, it seems, relatively radical on practical issues. But this is a book about theory, and only about practice insofar as it issues from theory.

Narveson thinks that the fundamental principles of justice should do no harm and be the object of a "social contract" in the currently accepted, more or less Rawlsian, sense. Sterba thinks such principles should not violate the "ought implies can" principle and should not be question-begging. Sterba argues that property rights do not extend so far as to justify denials by the "wealthy" of provisions needed by the "poor." His claim is that when the chips are down, and there is no alternative to fulfilling their needs by involuntary transfers from people who have more than enough, the people who have that more-than-enough are obliged to stand aside and allow the poor the necessary access. He argues, specifically, that the moral claim that the poor have no right to fulfill their needs in that way runs up against the "ought implies can" principle: a moral duty to refrain from taking what you need for the basics of life from those who have more than they need is one that cannot be expected to be adhered to by those in desperate straits. Here would be an "ought" that cannot be fulfilled; therefore, it cannot be a rationally acceptable "ought."

How does this relate to the liberty principle on which we claim to agree? That principle has it that everyone is entitled to the maximum liberty compatible with a like liberty for all (in a suitably classic formulation): that is, that we have a right to do whatever we wish provided only that in doing so we impose no harm, no undermining of liberty, on the part of others. This means, as both agree, that our rights are fundamentally "negative": that is, they require people essentially to *refrain* from *preventing* others from acting in various ways, including under that concept their bodily condition as something not to be damaged or otherwise interfered with by others. Very well: but, says Sterba, in the case he has crucially in mind, we have a *conflict of liberties*: the liberty of the poor not to be interfered with in taking from the surplus of the rich, vs. the liberty of the rich not to be interfered with in doing what they please with their possessions including the "surplus" parts of those possessions. So it is a question, he says, of which of these liberties is the more morally valuable. And he believes that if we put it that way, then the case is hands down in favor of the poor.

So now the issue becomes: is there indeed a conflict of the relevant kind, and is the right way to adjudicate such conflicts to award it to the one whose liberty is "most valuable"?

On the first question: it is inconsistent, of course, to say both that Jones may not to be interfered with in taking something from Smith and that Smith may not to be interfered with in keeping it if he wants. Now, both authors agree that there is just the one basic principle, of maximum liberty. So one way to view the issue is whether we have "maximum liberty" when we let the "poor" win. But Narveson denies this. He argues that since liberty is absence of interference, then those agents who are doing various things which, looked at in themselves, do no harm to others, may not be interfered with by others in the doing of those things. The others in question would therefore be interfering with these agents, and thus not permitted by the liberty principle to engage in those activities.

To this Sterba would counter that the wealthy who won't allow the poor to help themselves from their surplus goods are in fact interfering with the liberty of the poor, who after all cannot live (by hypothesis) without the goods in question. But Narveson responds to this by pointing out that whether A is "interfering" with

B in doing x is not a question of which interests A is attempting to satisfy by his actions, but only of whether A is indeed interfering with activities of B that are intrinsically harmless to others. Sterba accepts this.

Of course, a definition of "harm" is needed here, and Narveson supplies what he takes to be a perfectly normal one: harming is *worsening*. A "harms" someone, B, only if A does something that makes B *worse off* relative to the status quo ex ante. Sterba accepts this, too.

If that status quo were to include various entitlements against A, of course, then A would harm B by nonfulfillment of those entitlements. But to posit that people have an antecedent entitlement to whatever they need in order to sustain their lives would, of course, be to beg the question altogether. In the cases Sterba is concerned about, Narveson points out, the rich by refusing to allow the poor to supply themselves with necessities that are in A's legitimate possession do *not* make the poor *worse off*; instead, they merely leave the poor where they, by hypothesis are—viz., in very bad shape.

Sterba contests this. He claims that the rich by stopping the poor from acquiring just those resources the poor require to meet their basic needs and have a decent life do make them worse off. Without the interference of the rich, the poor would be able to meet their basic needs and to have a decent life. Sterba concedes that if the rich simply do not help the poor, they would not be harming the poor or making them worse. For him, it is the rich's actively stopping the poor from acquiring just those resources the poor require to meet their basic needs and to have a decent life that harms the poor and makes them worse off.

Sterba sees a further problem here. If the reason why Narveson thinks that the rich by stopping the poor from acquiring just those resources the poor require to meet their basic needs and have [A] decent life do not make them worse off is that the rich do not just possess, but have already been determined to legitimately possess, that is, have a right to, those resources against the poor, then who is harmed or made worse off is parasitic on a pre-determined set of rights, not the other way around, as Sterba had been understanding Narveson to be arguing. In that case, Sterba would clearly question the grounds for that prior determination of rights. Mere initial possession, absent some story about harming or making worse off, does not, all by itself, establish continuing rightful possession and rightful ownership.

Now it may be that all Narveson means by "legitimate possession" here is that the rich did not acquire these possessions in question by any illegitimate means. Sterba could accept this for the sake of argument. What Sterba would definitely challenge is that this "legitimate possession" thereby entitles the rich to "legitimately retain" those possessions against the poor, independently of some argument about the rich, and only the rich, being harmed and made worse off in the context.

Narveson responds to this, however, by denying that the rich get rich by taking things from the poor, including resources. What the poor take from the rich are things the rich have literally made—they are things which would not exist if it were not for the voluntary activities of many people. Or insofar as they use natural resources found in the areas where the poor might live, they have, after all, bought from them (or their governments—alas) the right to utilize those resources, which the poor of themselves would be entirely unable to do. Thus the activities of the rich do not worsen the lot of the poor (instead, they normally better it, if anything), whereas the poor's taking from the rich is a net interference, in his view, with what he claims are the harmless activities of those rich persons.

To this, Sterba responds that it was never denied that the rich produced the surplus in question. That was assumed. Rather, what is at issue is whether the rich harm the poor or make them worse off when they deny the poor access to that surplus when having access to it is the only way for the poor to meet their basic needs and have a decent life. Clearly, it does because if the poor were not denied access they would be able to meet their basic needs and have a decent life. Sterba allows that what the rich might be doing in other areas of their lives and with respect to other people might be of some relevance here, as Narveson suggests. Nevertheless, we still have to face the hard fact that given our agreed upon assumption that we do not already have established property rights here, the rich would be harming the poor and making them worse off when the they deny the poor who are in need access to their surplus. Now Sterba agrees with Narveson that the rich too are harmed and made worse off when the poor are successful in taking from the rich's surplus. His main point is just that the harming and making worse off goes both ways so that we must take this into account when we are determining what rights people have in these contexts.

The libertarian, as both authors agree, can be all in favor of charity—let the rich help the poor out of the goodness of their hearts. But Narveson ponders whether the libertarian can really allow that the luxury goods of the wealthy are, as it were, of such inferior moral status as compared with the enablement of continued life to the poor that the latter are actually *entitled* to take them, and their putative owners not even *permitted* to defend themselves against those actions—even though the actions of the poor in this case are clearly intended to leave the rich *worse off*—though, again by hypothesis, still very well off.

As Sterba sees it, if we give priority to the liberty of the rich in these conflict situations, the poor are harmed and made worse off, and if we give priority to the liberty of the poor, the rich are harmed and made worse off. For these conflicts of liberty, Sterba further claims that the "ought implies can" principle and the principle of nonquestion-beggingness favor the liberty of the poor over the liberty of the rich.

Favoring the liberty of the poor over the liberty of the rich, Sterba claims, will give rise to a positive right to welfare. Agreeing with libertarians that basic rights are universal rights, Sterba extends this right to welfare to distant peoples and future generations. He further argues that, barring a technological fix, respecting this right requires that we use no more resources than we need for a decent life so that distant peoples and future generations will also, as much as possible, have the resources they need for a decent life. And this, he claims, will lead to an equality in the use of resources over space and time. In short, Sterba argues that the libertarian's own negative right to liberty leads to the requirements of a substantive ideal of equality.

Narveson does not take up the issue of distant people or future generations here, but he denies that what the rich do is "harming." Insofar as there is an issue of fact about using resources and so forth, that issue remains undiscussed in the exchanges in these pages, Narveson is simply assuming that people are able to "get rich" without thereby harming anyone, and denying that whether one person interferes with the liberty of another has any logical relation to how much the persons in question either need or want the various things they are attempting to get. Sterba agrees that whether one person interferes with another has no logical relation to what people need or want, but he contends once it has been determined that interference will occur one way or the other, we may use a standard of meeting the basic needs of the deserving poor to determine which interference we should sanction.

To justify his view Narveson appeals to the general thesis of the social contract, which he develops, at some length, along Hobbesian lines. We cannot, he argues, impute to people in the base line situation, the so-called "state of nature," any antecedent morality nor more than the minimal amount of fellow-feeling. Our project in this exercise, he holds, is to come up with the set of moral requirements that literally *everyone* would support, or at least, everyone who would support any such set at all. The background is that everyone (virtually) is capable of (a) inflicting various evils on others, up to and including death, but also (b) of being useful, up to and including being extremely useful, as when we save someone's life—or, in another direction, help build his Rolls Royce. What each individual wants, says the Hobbesian, is to maximize the input of net benefit from others. We want them to do as little harm and as much good as possible. Now, often we can at least apparently promote our own good *at the expense* of others, but that, of course, generates conflict and "war"—at the limit, Hobbes's famous "war of all against all." In order to avoid such suboptimal outcomes, we need to give up our liberty to damage, destroy, and despoil, thus confining ourselves to mutually agreed exchanges. Given our comparable vulnerability, if we ask what set of restrictions does best, the answer is, then: prohibitions on *harms*, that is, *inflicted worsenings* on others.

Sterba allows that Narveson's social contract approach might have been able to provide us with a mutually beneficial resolution if the harmings and worsenings between the rich and the poor did not cut both ways forcing us to decide which harmings and worsenings are acceptable. Thus, as Sterba sees it, in these conflict situations, if we give priority to the liberty of the rich, the poor would be harmed and made worse off and if we give priority to the liberty of the poor, the rich would be harmed and made worse off. Regarding the social contract approach as ill-suited to deciding who should be harmed and made worse off in contexts where the harming and making worse off can go both ways, Sterba uses instead the "ought implies can" principle and the principle of non-question-beggingness which can be shown to favor the liberty of the poor over the liberty of the rich, and thus the harming and worsening of the rich over the harming or worsening of the poor in these conflict situations.

So when all is said and done, there are really just two fundamental issues over which Narveson and Sterba disagree. They are:

1) Where and when are harming and making worse off occurring and
2) What normative standard(s) should be used to determine what should be done about the harmings and worsenings that do occur.

Does this mean that a resolution might be in the offing? Surely that would be a welcomed event. Meanwhile, the reader will have to judge—and, no doubt, await further developments!

Jan Narveson, University of Waterloo

James P. Sterba, University of Notre Dame

Note

1. Jan Narveson and James P. Sterba, *Are Liberty and Equality Compatible?* (New York: Cambridge University Press, 2010).

The Compatibility of Liberty and Equality: Sterba vs. Narveson

ALISTAIR M. MACLEOD

The project Jim Sterba and Jan Narveson undertake in their book, *Are Liberty and Equality Compatible?*,[1] is an important one, in that they are trying to determine whether (and how far), despite their deep differences—Sterba is an "egalitarian" and Narveson a "libertarian"—philosophical assumptions to which they are both committed can be interpreted and developed in ways that diminish the sharpness of their initial disagreements about the precise content of, and relations between, the ideals of liberty and equality. The general strategy they adopt is in principle an admirable one, provided shared philosophical assumptions can be found that are relevant to the articulation and defense of libertarian and egalitarian doctrines. The risk, however, is that the assumptions, while nominally the same, will be understood by them in different ways—indeed in ways that already anticipate to some extent their own distinctive political philosophies. One of these ostensibly shared philosophical assumptions is the assumption that the doctrine of "negative liberty" provides the best initial account of the freedoms we have reason to value.[2] The risk they run in taking this doctrine to provide the agreed starting point for their discussion is that they will want to interpret it in different ways—and (more discouragingly) in ways that reflect the gulf between the positions in normative political theory that their strategy is designed to bridge.

In view of the hazards of a strategy that seeks to identify common philosophical ground, it would arguably be more promising to try to identify the common pre-philosophical convictions (and practices) that provide an important part of the underpinning for the positions philosophers adopt even when their positions turn out to be incompatible. Since the aim being pursued in the book is to clarify the content and mutual relations of two socio-political ideals—the liberty ideal and the equality ideal—common pre-philosophical ground might be looked for in our ordinary understanding of concrete everyday uses of the terms "free" and "equal" and in the (relatively uncontroversial) everyday judgments in which these terms are embedded. It ought to be possible to identify a range of these

Social Philosophy Today, Volume 27   147

ordinary uses—and a range of the judgments in which these terms are put to use—about which there is, as between libertarians and egalitarians, no disagreement.[3] After all, philosophical accounts of the concepts of freedom (or liberty) and equality—and the normative doctrines of freedom and equality philosophers articulate in what they have to say about the liberty and equality ideals—must arguably be consistent with (and thus "checked" for adequacy against) what we already know to be the case about the uses of the terms "free" and "equal" as well as what we know about the everyday judgments in which these terms are put to use. When the search for common ground between Libertarians and Egalitarians is approached in this (rather more cautious) way, it becomes apparent (arguably) that the philosophical doctrine of negative liberty offers a potentially contentious reconstruction of the pre-philosophical uses we make of such terms as "freedom" and "liberty" in our everyday judgments. This should not be viewed as surprising: everyday judgments are typically made without any knowledge of (let alone any vested interest in) any of the special axes philosophers may be grinding when they get round to propounding their theories. The difficulty of finding common ground in what philosophers have to say about "negative liberty" is compounded, of course, by the fact that there is no single canonical version of the doctrine of negative liberty.

In the first section of this paper, I raise some questions about the starting point—the ostensibly agreed starting point—of the Sterba-Narveson debate on the compatibility of liberty and equality. In Section 2, I discuss Narveson's remarks about the nature and source of the value that attaches to liberty when it is taken to require nothing more than non-interference by others in the lives we seek to lead in the light of our own conceptions of the good life. These remarks have implications that are congenial to Sterba's view that the state is justified in sponsoring (at least certain sorts of) welfare programs—though not necessarily to the line of argument for this view he develops in *Are Liberty and Equality Compatible?* By the same token, these implications run counter to the kind of Libertarianism Narveson thinks is entailed by commitment to the doctrine of negative liberty. In Section 3, I offer some brief reflections on the relationship between the ideals of Liberty and Equality. Unlike both Sterba and Narveson, I argue that it is a mistake to think of them either as mutually incompatible or as systematically interrelated. Rather, since they provide possible answers to different but complementary normative questions, there is no barrier to the endorsement of both ideals. However, each can be sponsored in many competing versions and there is no good reason to think, antecedently, either that there is any single way of articulating theses about the compatibility or incompatibility of liberty and equality, or that there is any single line of argument that will enable us to identify the preferred versions of both ideals.

I. The Doctrine of Negative Liberty—An Agreed Starting Point?

Both Sterba and Narveson claim to begin with "negative liberties"—liberties that individuals enjoy when they are not subject to acts of interference by others. There are, however, several respects in which—even if this starting point is not challenged[4]—it remains unclear what precisely it amounts to. Given these unclarities, the possibility looms that Sterba and Narveson may not be adopting identical interpretations of the putative starting point. This would jeopardize (it seems) the project on which—ostensibly—they are jointly engaged, which is to determine whether, in light of the arguments they develop from an agreed starting point, it is Narveson's libertarianism or Sterba's egalitarianism that should be endorsed. If, despite appearances to the contrary, their arguments do not take off from the same starting point, it may not be surprising that we are conducted by these arguments to different destinations.

A. What Counts As a "Negative Liberty"?

One unclarity has to do with the scope of the "negative liberties" that constitute, ostensibly, the agreed starting point. Are absolutely all the actions that individuals (given their abilities and wants) might be in a position to perform when others don't interfere to be counted as determining the scope of the negative liberties that provide the putative starting point? If the answer is "yes," then a would-be murderer can be said to be at liberty (in the negative sense) to commit an act of murder provided he is free from interference by others in committing such an act.

Narveson seems not to want to give recognition to this possible construal of the starting point: he seems to want to restrict the interferences from which individuals are protected when they enjoy negative liberty (properly so-called) to interferences that are not themselves interferences with interferences. On this reading, the would-be murderer's "freedom to commit an act of murder" doesn't count as one of the negative liberties he might be thought to have. His negative liberty (in the sense crucial to specification of the putative starting point) is not being interfered with (in the sense deemed relevant by Narveson) when the state either forbids or prevents acts of murder. While the existence of a law prohibiting such acts and diligent efforts by the police to enforce it constitute obstacles to the commission of acts of murder, these obstacles to freedom to commit acts of murder don't count as "interferences" with "negative liberty"—given Narveson's understanding both of "negative liberties" and of what count as "interferences" with these liberties.

Sterba, on the other hand, seems to want to launch his argument—the argument from "negative liberty" to "substantial equality"—by allowing both "the liberty of the poor from interference by the rich when they seek to take from the surplus of the rich in order to satisfy their basic needs" and "the liberty of the rich from interference by the poor when they seek to use the surplus they have to secure luxury goods for themselves" to count as "negative liberties." The question whether the negative liberty of the poor or the negative liberty of the rich should be accorded precedence when they conflict is consequently the question Sterba takes up.

Narveson's response, essentially, is to deny that there is ever any such conflict of negative liberties, because (in his view) the poor are not at liberty (free, that is, from interference by the rich) to seek to take the surplus possessions of the rich in order to satisfy their basic needs. That is, the poor have no such "negative liberty" as Sterba is positing here. It's the rich who have a negative liberty in these circumstances: they must be seen as enjoying the freedom not to be interfered with by the poor when they use their surplus to secure luxury goods for themselves.

In short, when Narveson and Sterba "face off"—at the beginning of the first round in their debate—they seem not to be operating with the same understanding of the negative liberties that are supposed to provide the agreed starting point for the debate. For Sterba, an individual can be said to enjoy the negative liberty to X for all values of X (where X is an action she is capable of performing and wants to perform)—provided, of course, she is not "interfered with" when she seeks to X. For Narveson, an individual has the negative liberty to X for only a certain sub-class of the values of X: excluded, as possible values of X, are all those actions that take the form of interfering with the actions of others.

But what if it should be claimed[5] that while Sterba and Narveson have the same understanding of what a "negative liberty" is, they simply sponsor different views as to which "negative liberties" qualify for recognition under the doctrine of negative liberty? On this account, Sterba's preferred list of the "negative liberties" protected by the doctrine simply doesn't coincide with Narveson's preferred list.

This would still be a puzzling response, in at least two respects. First, what, precisely, is the agreed understanding of what is meant by talk of "negative liberties" if they are disagreed about the liberties that count as "negative liberties"? It does indeed seem to be the case that Sterba and Narveson disagree about which particular liberties are to count as liberties protected by the doctrine of negative liberty—presumably because the doctrine of negative liberty can be taken to be a normative doctrine and they don't agree about the content of that normative doctrine. But if they don't agree about what is to count as a "negative liberty"—in the sense crucial to the articulation of the doctrine of "negative liberty"—where precisely is the "common ground" on which they stand about the meaning of talk about "negative liberties"?

Second, if the doctrine of "negative liberty" is understood by both of them as a normative doctrine—which is presumably the case if they sponsor different lists of the liberties protected by the doctrine (the differences between the lists being traceable, presumably, to the fact that they disagree about the value of some of the liberties that might be listed)—what becomes of the claim that the doctrine of negative liberty constitutes part of the agreed starting point for their exploration of the points at which libertarians and egalitarians part company?

When attempting to support his rejection of the objection that there is perhaps no common ground between himself and Narveson in the doctrine of negative liberty, Sterba cites a passage from Narveson's part of the book. Narveson writes:

> The libertarian case is that the fundamental right is a right to liberty, but in being so it is automatically a prohibition of the liberty to do certain things: namely, acts that infringe liberty. . . . [From t]he fact that it is the liberty of the poor [not to be interfered with when taking] from the rich that is being restricted, then, it does not follow that what we have is a clash of liberties in the relevant sense: namely, a clash of liberties that the theory protects. It is, instead, a clash between a familiar kind of liberty that it is the very essence of the theory to forbid and another kind of liberty that it is the very essence of the theory to protect.[6]

Is Sterba claiming, when he appeals to this passage, that he and Narveson are working with the same notion of negative liberty (and thus that it is false to say, as I have suggested, that they are perhaps working with different notions of negative liberty) and that this (agreed) sense is the normatively neutral sense of the term "liberty"? In this sense of the term, an individual A can be said to be "free" (or "at liberty") to X provided there is (in fact) no interference with A's Xing, it being a further (and independent) question whether it's either the case (a) that it's a good thing (in principle) for A to be free to X, or (b) that A has a right to X.[7] It's true that Narveson refers, in the passage Sterba quotes, to this sort of liberty as a "familiar kind of liberty." However, in the preceding sentence in the same passage, Narveson indicates that "liberty" of this "familiar kind" is not liberty "in the relevant sense." This makes it clear that, unlike Sterba, Narveson is not prepared to take as his starting point the existence of negative liberties in the normatively neutral sense of "liberty."[8] The passage from Narveson that Sterba quotes should consequently be read, not as supporting Sterba's claim that he and Narveson are working with the very same understanding of the notion of "negative liberty" but rather as showing that they are not.

It is important to be clear, however, that their not having the very same understanding of the notion of "negative liberty" is perfectly consistent with its being the case—as Sterba can rightly claim by citing the passage he quotes from Narveson—that Narveson doesn't deny that the term "liberty" can be used (correctly) in a normatively neutral way. After all, Narveson doesn't say, of Sterba's reference to the "liberty of the poor to be free of interference when they take from the rich," that it embodies a meaningless use of the term "liberty." On the contrary, he acknowledges that Sterba is referring to "a familiar kind of liberty." Nevertheless, Narveson's recognition that the word "liberty" can be used in this way does not show that he's prepared to allow this use of the term in the articulation of the "common ground" between himself and Sterba. If he were prepared to take this line, he'd go along with Sterba's claim that there's a clash of "liberties"[9]—liberties of this "familiar kind"—when we have to choose which of Sterba's clashing" liberties we should seek to protect. But, as is clear from the passage itself, Narveson rejects the claim that there's a clash of liberties in the relevant sense—the relevant sense being, that is, the sense of "negative liberty" that he (Narveson), proposes to work with. The "liberty of the poor to be free from interference when they take from the rich" simply is not, for Narveson, a "negative liberty" in the relevant sense. There is consequently, for Narveson, no such thing as a clash of "negative liberties" in the relevant sense. Rather there's a clash between a genuine "negative liberty"—viz. the liberty of the rich to be free of interference by the poor when they seek to enjoy the luxury goods they own—and a liberty of "the familiar kind" (the kind that doesn't qualify, according to Narveson, as a "negative liberty" at all).

B. What Counts As "Interference" with Liberty?

There's a second (related) unclarity in the doctrine of negative liberty they both say they are prepared to take for granted at the outset because there is an ambiguity in what is thought to count as "interference" with negative liberty. On a narrow (and arguably correct) understanding of what it means to interfere with (or restrict) the freedom or liberty to X of some individual A, the interference must take the form of doing something that makes it impossible (or at any rate difficult) for A to X. Typically, acts of interference (so understood) would include rules or laws prohibiting X, threats of harm to A (or to others) if A Xs, physically preventing A from Xing, and the like. However, both Narveson and Sterba say they understand interference in a broader way.[10] They claim that in this broader sense (if sense it be) A's negative liberty to X can be "interfered with" not only when A is prevented from Xing (by rules, threats, physical interventions, etc.) but also when A is harmed by the actions of others or when A is rendered worse off by their actions.

The trouble with this broader understanding, however, is that A can be harmed (for example, injured, whether physically or psychologically, or in respect of his reputation) without any diminution in his liberty to X. Thus, where the liberty to X is (say) the liberty to join in a rally protesting the government's decision to go to war, A can be harmed (or made worse off) in all sorts of ways without losing the liberty to X. For example, participants in a (competing) pro-war rally may launch a physical attack on A—bloody his nose, or kick his shins—without thereby "interfering with" his liberty to X (in the strict—i.e., the narrow—sense of "interfere"). Again, they may publicly accuse A of being unpatriotic—or even of being a traitor to his country—without thereby interfering with his liberty to take part in the anti-war demonstration. Indeed, even if they shoot and kill him, it's (at least) misleading to represent the act of killing as an act of "interference" with his liberty to take part in the anti-war demonstration. While it's true that the dead can't take part in anti-war demonstrations, it's surely stretching things to try to represent the murder of an anti-war demonstrator as one of the ways in which this particular liberty can be restricted or limited.

It might be thought that a defense of the broader understanding of what counts as "interference with liberty to X"—and thus a response to the objection that it's a mistake not to distinguish between interfering with a person's freedom or liberty and "harming" that person (or making that person "worse off")—can be provided by questioning one part of my argument when I deploy the "anti-war demonstration" example. Part of the argument, it will be recalled, is that a demonstrator can have his or her nose bloodied while participating in an anti-war protest without that demonstrator's freedom to take part in the protest being interfered with: the demonstrator is "harmed" (or made "worse off") by the bloodying blow, but he or she can be "harmed" (or made "worse off") in this way without his or her freedom to take part in the anti-war demonstration being interfered with. The response to this argument might be that, in being "harmed" (or made "worse off") in this way, the demonstrator *is*—in a sense—having his or her freedom to participate in an anti-war protest interfered with. This is because, while there's a sense (perhaps) in which it can be said that the demonstrator's freedom to take part in the protest is not being interfered with (in that he or she can continue, as before the blow, to take part, even though, now, it's with a bloodied nose), the freedom to take part in the protest "without having his or her nose bloodied" *is* being interfered with.

To see whether this response really blunts the point I'm making, it's worth noting that in my deployment of the anti-war demonstration example, I was trying to make the case for distinguishing between acts that interfere with someone's freedom to perform some particular action and acts that "harm" that person (or render that person "worse off"). I presented two versions of the example. The first version poses the question whether the bloodying of the nose of a demonstrator (or the kicking of the demonstrator's shins) can be regarded as (necessarily) an act of interference with that demonstrator's freedom to take part in the anti-war rally. The second version poses the crucial question in a slightly different way—by asking whether the demonstrator's freedom to take part in the anti-war rally is being interfered with if he or she is said (in shouted remarks from the ranks of pro-war demonstrators) to be acting "unpatriotically" in opposing the war. Now it seems to me that this second version of the example I was providing cannot be handled in the way Sterba thinks might suffice for dealing with the first version.[11] Even if the freedom to participate in an anti-war rally can be glossed (as it is by Sterba) as the freedom to participate "without having one's nose bloodied," it certainly cannot be glossed as the freedom to participate "without being called unpatriotic."

Why the difference, then? Perhaps the explanation is that bloodying someone's nose—since it's an act of assault—is a violation of the right not to be assaulted (which at least lends color to the suggestion that a demonstrator should be free to take part in an anti-war demonstration "without having his or her nose bloodied") whereas calling someone "unpatriotic," while hurtful no doubt, isn't one of the banned exercises of the right to freedom of speech.

However, even if the "bloodied nose" version of the "anti-war demonstration" example is potentially less effective as a counter-example to the claim that whenever someone's freedom is interfered with that person is being "harmed" or rendered "worse off"—and it is still somewhat problematic to hold that it provides no support at all for the drawing of a distinction between "restricting someone's freedom" and "harming" them—at least the second version of the example (the version in which the anti-war demonstrator is merely the target of hurtful remarks about being unpatriotic) isn't subject to this criticism. However, more needs to be said both to clarify and to vindicate the distinction between "restricting someone's freedom" and "harming" her (or making her "worse off").

The need for the distinction can be supported in two ways. First, it can be shown that there are acts of interference with the freedom of others that cannot be regarded (defensibly) as acts that "harm" them or that render them "worse off." Second, it can be shown that there are acts that "harm" people or render them "worse off" that cannot be regarded (defensibly) as acts that restrict their freedom.

1. Restricting Freedom without Harming

Consider, first, the point that an account of what liberty or freedom amounts to must make allowance for cases where individuals can be said to be free (or at liberty) to perform some action X even if X is an action they have no desire to perform (and no interest in performing) given their own conceptions of the good life. If A has no interest in Xing—no desire to X—because Xing plays absolutely no role in the living of the good life as A conceives the good life, then while a rule that forbids anyone to X will have to be characterized as a liberty- or freedom-restricting rule (and thus as a rule that restricts *A's* freedom or liberty to X), its adoption and enforcement won't "harm" *A* or render *A* "worse off." In determining what counts as "harming" A, or in rendering A "worse off," reference can plausibly be made to A's conception of the good life. However, no such reference is needed to determine whether a rule prohibiting X restricts A's freedom or liberty to X.

More importantly (and tellingly) there's a second (arguably rather large) class of important counter-examples to the view that all acts that restrict someone's liberty or freedom are acts that "harm" that person or render her "worse off." This is the class of paternalistic acts. These are acts that restrict liberty or freedom (for example, the freedom of young children to decide whether to go to the dentist or whether to attend school on a regular basis) but that are designed to promote the wellbeing or welfare of the person whose liberty or freedom is being restricted. The view that all acts that restrict someone's liberty or freedom are acts that harm that person or render that person "worse off" would rule out the very possibility of defensible paternalistic acts. At best, parents who restrict their children's freedom in order to promote their children's wellbeing or welfare would have to be represented either (i) as believing (albeit falsely) that their freedom-limiting actions promote the wellbeing of their children (when the truth is that such actions always in fact "harm" their children and render them "worse off"), or (ii) as holding, that while paternalistic acts of these benignly-motivated kinds do indeed "harm" children and render them "worse off," such acts can be justified on balance if there's good reason to think that the (long-term) good they do is sufficiently great to outweigh the (short-term) "harm" they inflict. Both (i) and (ii), however, embody implausible explanatory hypotheses. The first ([i]) is implausible because it seems plainly false that parents who act paternalistically in the way here supposed are always acting on the basis of false beliefs about how to promote the wellbeing of their children. The second ([ii]) is an implausible hypothesis because when paternalistic acts are in fact justified, it isn't because those who perform them have made judicious "balancing" judgments: the well-being of children, both in the short and in the long run, is typically being promoted by their parents when they are required to have dental check-ups or to go to school on a regular basis.

It should go without saying, of course, that allowance has to be made for foolish and indefensible paternalistic acts—acts that are believed to be (or are represented as) beneficial to those whose freedom is being restricted, when the truth is that the acts are actually harmful to those affected by them and render them "worse off." However, it is obvious that not all paternalistic acts can be characterized, dismissively, as foolish and indefensible.[12]

It should also be noted that the claim that (judicious) paternalistic acts are counter-examples to the view that all freedom-limiting acts "harm" those whose freedom is being limited cannot be dismissed on the ground that paternalistic regulation of the lives of young children doesn't yield any examples of freedom-restricting acts because young children are not fully autonomous agents; and for two reasons. First, it's false that it's a necessary condition of a person's freedom being restricted that that person can be correctly described as a fully autonomous agent: even though young children are not fully autonomous agents, their freedom *is* being restricted when they are required by their parents to have regular dental check-ups or to go to school (as is particularly clear in cases where children are taken to the dentist or to school against their will). Second, even on the view that paternalistic treatment of adults is always open to objection, the rationale for the objection, typically, is that it's an affront to the autonomy (and thus to the freedom or liberty) of adults for them to be required to do things it may well be in their interest to do. The argument is not that paternalistic treatment of adults is wrong because such treatment is not in their interest. Even staunch opponents of paternalism recognize that it's possible for freedom to be restricted without the infliction of "harm."

2. Harming without Restricting Freedom

What, then, of the claim that that there are acts that "harm" people or render them "worse off" that cannot be regarded (defensibly) as acts that restrict their freedom? It too seems to be a claim that can be readily supported.

When someone is assaulted (punched in the face, for example), the blow may be painful (and thus "harmful") without in any obvious way restricting that person's freedom or liberty. Again, even if the blow is injurious in some way (for example, if it leaves a nasty bruise), a distinction still needs to be drawn between (i) the victim being injured, and (ii) the freedom or liberty of the victim being impaired. An incapacitating blow is a special case. Precisely because it is "incapacitating" (in some way)—and not (merely) because it is a "blow"—it no doubt restricts the victim's liberty or freedom by making it impossible or difficult for actions of certain sorts to be performed, viz. actions rendered impossible or difficult by the incapacitation associated with the injury that has been inflicted. Even in these special cases—arguably—it may still be important to distinguish between the complaint that the victim has been "harmed" (suffered an injury; experienced pain, etc.), and the complaint that the victim's freedom has been restricted. (The distinction has a certain importance when, for example, victims of reputation-undermining statements are suing for damages.) In any case, not all cases are "special" cases.

C. The *Value* of Negative Liberty and the *Right* to Negative Liberty

There's a third unclarity in the presupposed doctrine of negative liberty, this time because of a distinction that is needed but (apparently) not drawn (at any rate in any explicit way). This is the distinction between the question whether negative liberty has value (and is therefore worth protecting) and the question whether there's a right to negative liberty. Both of these are of course expressly normative questions, but they shouldn't be treated as one and the same question: the possibility has to reckoned with that there are negative liberties to which some value attaches even if it isn't the case that individuals have a right to their protection. A given individual's "negative liberty" to pursue some project P1 might have value (because[13] P1 plays a role in A's effort to give effect, in living his life, to his own conception of the good life) and yet it may turn out that A cannot be said to have a right to pursue project P1 (because A's pursuit of project P1 is incompatible with the pursuit by other individuals B, C, D, etc. of various projects that have roughly comparable value because of the role they play in their efforts to implement their conceptions of the good life). When a choice has to be made between allowing or enabling A to pursue project P1 and allowing or enabling B, C, D, etc. to pursue their projects—and the choice should be made (arguably) by appeal to considerations of distributive fairness—they cannot all be said to have a right to pursue the particular projects in question, but there is no need to withdraw the claim that value attaches to pursuit of all these projects.

There's an objection, consequently, to the glossing of the distinction between the question whether negative liberty has value and the question whether there's a right to negative liberty, as is in danger of being done if a distinction is drawn—merely—between a descriptive doctrine of negative liberty (that is, a doctrine that sets out what it means to say that given individuals actually enjoy particular negative liberties) and an expressly normative or evaluative doctrine (that is, one that identifies that sub-class of the class of negative liberties for the endorsement of which good reasons can be given).

II. The Instrumental Value of Negative Liberty and the Welfare State

When negative liberty is taken (as it is by both Sterba and Narveson) to be something we have good reason to endorse—and this is the case whether negative liberty is seen as something we have reason to value or as something to which we have a right[14]—how do they set about supporting it? Since negative liberty (on one familiar account to which they both subscribe) consists in "absence of interference by others," what precisely is it that makes it important for "non-interference" in people's lives to be aimed at whenever possible?

There is an interesting feature of what Narveson says about this question—which he takes up expressly at the very beginning of Part II when he is framing the issue between himself and Sterba[15]—to which I want to direct attention. While the focus will consequently be on Narveson's view, I don't think it's a view from which Sterba would dissent. It's worth examining Narveson's treatment of the issue not only because the line of argument is one he might not be expected to take but also because it seems to have implications that imperil his defense of the sort of "libertarianism" that sets him apart from Sterba.

A. The Instrumental Value of Negative Liberty

What, then, is Narveson's view of the rationale for the importance we attach to the protection of negative liberty, understood as freedom from interference by others? And does his account of the value that attaches to "non-interference by others" provide support for the narrow (merely negative) doctrine of liberty he favors?

Narveson writes:

> Liberty is not properly viewed as *a value* on a par with real values such as good music, a hard day's work well done, and no end of other things. Indeed it is fair to say that liberty, taken by itself, has no value at all. That is because liberty is the absence of hindrance or impediment to the actions that are what we really do value, or whose results we value.[16]

This is a truly remarkable passage, both for the explicitness of its denial that liberty has any intrinsic value ("Liberty, taken by itself, has no value at all") and for the reason Narveson offers in support ("That is because liberty is the absence of hindrance or impediment to the actions that are what we really do value, or whose results we value").

When Narveson says that we "really do value" the actions that individuals are in a position to perform when they enjoy liberty (conceived as non-interference by others) and that we "really do value" the results of those actions, both the actions in question and their results are thought to have value because of the contribution they make to the realization of individual conceptions of the good life.[17] Thus while liberty conceived merely negatively (as consisting in non-interference by others) has no value in itself, it has instrumental value because it facilitates the living of the good life as that life is conceived by the individuals seeking to live it.

B. Non-interference by Others As the Only Social Condition of Liberty?

Since it's clear that interference by others does constitute an obstacle to the living of the good life (again, of course, the good life as conceived by those whose life it is), removal of this obstacle clearly has instrumental value in just the way Narveson claims. But if the rationale for negative liberty is that it facilitates the living of the good life by removing an obstacle to the living of that life, shouldn't Narveson be prepared to recognize that value of just this sort attaches to the removal of other obstacles to the living of the good life?

Before these other obstacles can be identified, however, it has to be noted that there are two respects in which they must resemble the obstacle to which Narveson gives recognition when he identifies interference by others as an obstacle to the enjoyment of liberty and thus to the living of the good life. If they are to be given recognition alongside interference by others—and if Narveson's representation of interference by others as the only obstacle to the enjoyment of liberty to which recognition need be given is to be contested—the potential (additional) obstacles must be both (a) comparable and (b) comparably important.

To be comparable in the present context they must be obstacles that share a couple of features with "interference by others." First, they must be obstacles that individuals are unable to overcome through the adoption of measures it is wholly within their power as individuals to adopt. Second, they must be obstacles that can (or at any rate can most effectively) be overcome through the adoption by the state of appropriate policies or through the establishment of appropriate institutional arrangements or through the enactment of appropriate laws and so on.

For putative additional obstacles to be comparably important it would have to be as crucial to the enjoyment of liberty by individuals (and thus to their being in a position to implement effectively the conceptions of the good life they favor) for these obstacles to be overcome as it is for the obstacle presented by interference by others to be overcome.

1. Non-interference by Others and Additional Obstacles to Liberty as Comparable

Take, first, the question whether additional obstacles that might be posited—additional obstacles to the enjoyment of the liberty to implement effectively a favored conception of the good life—are comparable to the obstacle presented by interference by others in the two ways indicated. It would certainly be rather surprising if it turned out that that there are no such (additional) obstacles and that the only obstacle of this sort to the living of the good life is interference by others. However, the truth here is not surprising in this way, because the answer surely is that there *are* additional obstacles that are fully comparable to interference by others in the two respects noted. Consider two examples.

First, there's the obstacle to the living of the good life presented by lack of opportunity to acquire the economic resources needed for the effective implementation of conceptions of the good life. Notice that the obstacle here is lack of opportunity to secure the requisite economic resources, not lack of economic resources as such. The point is that while it's obvious that lack of economic resources *is* an obstacle—a familiar obstacle—to the living of the good life, it's not an obstacle that resembles interference by others in the first of the two respects noted above. This is because it is sometimes (though of course by no means always) reasonable to assume that individuals who lack the resources they need are themselves responsible for the lack: they have simply not availed themselves of the opportunities they had for the securing of these resources. With lack of opportunity to secure needed economic resources, however, it's quite different. While individuals can perhaps be held responsible for exploiting (or for failing to exploit) the opportunities for the acquisition of economic resources they have, they cannot (coherently) be held responsible for not being given (or afforded) such opportunities. Like interference by others, lack of opportunity to acquire needed economic resources is an obstacle to the living of the good life that cannot be overcome by individuals who are left to their own devices, no matter how strenuously or impressively they might try. Also—and this is the second respect in which the two obstacles are comparable—the collective efforts of other people, typically (and perhaps most effectively and reliably) through measures adopted by the state in their name and on their behalf, can contribute significantly to the contraction (even if not to the elimination) of these obstacles.

A second obstacle to the living of the good life that resembles interference by others in the two respects noted is lack of opportunity to develop the skills and competences needed for the effective realization of conceptions of the good life. Here too a distinction has to be drawn between simply not having the requisite skills and competences and not having the opportunity to develop these. Individuals can be held responsible for failing (or refusing) to take advantage of available opportunities for the development of the skills and competences they need to implement the conceptions they favor of the good life, but it's incoherent to suppose that, as individuals, they are responsible for not having the opportunity to develop the skills and competences in question. Like interference by others, consequently, lack of opportunity to develop needed skills and competences is an obstacle to the living of the good life that individuals on their own are powerless to overcome. And again, like interference by others, lack of this sort of opportunity is an obstacle that can be overcome, at least to some reassuring extent, by the actions others can take when they adopt appropriate collective strategies, generally through state action in their name and on their behalf.

2. Non-interference by Others and Additional Obstacles to Liberty As Comparably Important

I turn now to the question whether these additional obstacles to the living of the good life—lack of opportunity to acquire needed economic resources and lack of opportunity to develop required skills and competences—have an importance comparable to that of the obstacle presented by interference by others. It will be recalled that to say that these obstacles are comparably important to the living of the good life (and thus to the enjoyment of liberty, when liberty is seen to get its value from the role it plays in facilitating the living of the good life) is to say that it is as crucial (or essential) to the effective implementation of conceptions of the good life for individuals to be provided with opportunities of these two sorts as it is for them to be protected from interference in their lives by other people. The basic issue is an empirical one: is it in fact the case that interference by others and lack of opportunity of the kinds in question make it difficult or impossible on a reliable basis over time for individuals to give effect, in the living of their lives, to the conceptions of the good they favor, and consequently is it in fact the case that the removal of these obstacles is essential to their being free to implement their conceptions of the good?[18] But while empirical evidence of the relevant sorts would ideally have to be assembled to provide a definitive answer to this question, a simple thought experiment can point to what the answer would be bound to be—viz. that the comparable importance criterion *is* satisfied (and to about the same degree) by measures aimed at overcoming all three obstacles. Imagine someone who lacks opportunities of the two kinds in question—and who is consequently not well-positioned to realize, even to a modest extent, his own conception of the good life—being told that he should be grateful for the knowledge that at least other people are going to be prevented, on a reliable basis, from interfering in the life he might endeavor to lead. Even if he would be worse off if he were not protected from interference by others, it would be not unreasonable for him to feel that mere non-interference in his life by the other members of his society is hardly something he should be expected to celebrate, or be grateful for, when the life he is in a position to lead is bound to be a greatly impoverished version of the good life as he conceives it because he lacks the opportunity to acquire both the economic resources and the skills and competences that are indispensable to the effective implementation of his own conception of the good life. There would be no good reason for him to be satisfied with life in a society that denies him these crucial opportunities while assuring him, merely, that he will be left to his own devices in the living of his life, secure in the knowledge that at least others won't be allowed to interfere.

C. Non-interference by Others, Liberty, and the Living of the Good Life

Now to the claim that removal of all three obstacles is crucial to the realization of the ideal of individual liberty it might be objected that it is one thing to show that lack of opportunity to acquire needed economic resources and lack of opportunity to acquire needed skills and competences are obstacles to the living of the good life that are both comparable to, and as important as, the obstacle presented by interference by others and another to show that removal of these obstacles enhances the liberty (or freedom) of individuals. Thus it might be maintained that it is only the removal of one of these obstacles—viz. the obstacle presented by interference by others—that contributes to the living of the good life by enhancing the liberty or freedom of individuals. That is, even when it is conceded that the removal of the other putative obstacles would also facilitate the living of the good life, it may still be insisted that only the provision of effective guarantees of non-interference by others does so by protecting individual liberty. This is what seems to be implied by Narveson's view that liberty consists in "absence of interference by others."

Against this, however—and thus against Narveson's attempt to establish a definitional link between an individual's "liberty" and "non-interference in that individual's life"—it is worth pointing out how odd it is to hold that the liberty (or freedom) of individuals to implement their own conceptions of the good life can be enhanced by effectively enforced non-interference rules aimed at enabling them to live the good life as they conceive it but not by either the provision of opportunities for the securing of the economic resources needed for the implementation of conceptions of the good life or the provision of opportunities for the development of the skills and competences that are indispensable to the effective realization of conceptions of the good life—when these opportunities are as crucial or essential to the living of the good life as measures offering protection from interference by others. If the rationale for institutional arrangements for the effective prohibition of interference in people's lives is the contribution such arrangements make to the living of the good life by the individual members of society, and if this is also the rationale for institutional arrangements that provide opportunities of types (a) and (b), it's difficult to see on what basis it can be maintained that non-interference by others *is* but provision of opportunities for the living of the good life is not what liberty (or freedom) to live the good life requires.

Ready reinforcement of this point can be provided when it is noted that we cannot provide a merely negative formulation of the liberty (or freedom) that is here presumed to be a desideratum. Why? Because when liberty is said to consist in freedom from interference by others, the actions that are not to be interfered with have to be specified,[19] and the specification must be consistent with Narveson's claim that liberty, while not in itself valuable, is valuable instrumentally through the contribution it makes to the performance of actions that are valued by individuals for their role in the implementation of their conceptions of the good life. The actions that are to be protected from interference by others must consequently be understood to be the actions that help individuals to realize their conceptions of the good. It's because being free from interference by others is crucial to being free to live the good life in the light of our own conceptions of the good life that liberty, even when conceived negatively (as it is by Narveson) as absence of interference by others, is thought to have value.

Narveson's claim that negative liberty, while not valuable in itself, gets its value from the contribution it makes to the freedom of individuals to implement the conceptions of the good they favor leads naturally to the question whether non-interference by others in the freedom of individuals to implement their own conceptions of the good is a sufficient, or merely a necessary, condition of enjoyment of this freedom. Once it becomes clear that it is only a necessary (and not a sufficient condition), and once questions are raised as to what the other necessary conditions are, it's difficult to see how Narveson can deny that these other necessary conditions have just the sort of instrumental value non-interference by others is said to have. And if these other conditions have to be represented as having instrumental value in exactly the same way, and for exactly the same reason, as non-interference by others, then the fulfillment of these other conditions must of course be represented as crucial to the enjoyment by individuals of the freedom to give effect to their own conceptions of the good. That is, it cannot be insisted that while fulfillment of these other conditions is essential to the implementation by individuals of their conceptions of the good, it's only non-interference by others that can be represented both as essential to the implementation by individuals of their conceptions of the good and as instrumental to the enjoyment by individuals of the freedom to implement the conceptions of the good they favor.

And there's another point. Once it's noted that non-interference by others is only one of several necessary (but not also sufficient) conditions of the enjoyment by individuals of the freedom to implement their own conceptions of the good, the question is bound to be pressed what *set* of these necessary conditions would count as jointly sufficient to enable individuals to enjoy the freedom to implement their own conceptions of the good. And once even a preliminary answer to this question is provided, it's difficult to see what conceivable justification there could be for the view that greater importance attaches to the fulfillment of one of these necessary (and jointly sufficient) conditions than to the fulfillment of the others. If the value that attaches to any one of these necessary (and jointly sufficient) conditions is merely instrumental—if, that is, it gets its value from the contribution it makes to protection of the freedom of individuals to implement their own conceptions of the good—it isn't clear how any value can be held to attach to efforts to fulfill only one of these conditions, given that it would be clear in advance that these efforts could not result in individuals actually enjoying the freedom to implement their own conceptions of the good in the absence of fulfillment of the other necessary conditions.

It's worth noting, though, that even if there were some good reason[20] to link liberty (or freedom) exclusively with removal of only one obstacle to the living of the good life—viz. interference by others—the fact that the rationale for the liberty ideal (on this narrow version of the ideal) is identical with the rationale for the provision of opportunities of the two kinds mentioned above is a powerful argument for the programs (in employment and education) that provide these opportunities to all on an assured basis. These welfare state programs would then have to be defended by reference to some ideal or principle other than liberty (or freedom)—other than liberty (or freedom), that is, on the narrow interpretation under consideration here—but advocates of this narrowly specified liberty ideal would not be well-positioned to object to the programs themselves.

The upshot is that Narveson's account of the rationale for the negative liberty ideal seems to undermine the claim he would like to be able to make about Libertarianism in the version he favors being a corollary of endorsement of the ideal. While this gives Sterba an additional—perhaps unexpected—argument in support of (certain key) welfare state programs, endorsement of a right to welfare on this basis must still be distinguished from the sort of endorsement of this right Sterba's argument from negative liberty[21] is designed to establish. Moreover, the argument for a right to welfare suggested by Narveson's account of the rationale for the value that attaches to "negative liberty" cannot be regarded as lending support even indirectly to Sterba's argument: (an important part of) Sterba's conclusion is supported, but not his argument.

D. Implementing the Ideal of Liberty: The Question of Costs

While Sterba may not object to the case I have tried to present for seeing Narveson's argument for the value of negative liberty as committing him to the view that a society that is serious about protecting negative liberty would have to endorse instead of rejecting (at least a significant version of) the welfare state, he may think that the different argument *he* develops offers a more compelling critique of (Narvesonian) libertarianism. He may want to claim that libertarians will not be persuaded by my argument because, even if the adoption of welfare state measures (in education and employment) is conceded to be an additional condition of adequate protection of individual liberty, these measures cost too much. By contrast, measures to secure fulfillment of the non-interference condition, while not costless, are so much less costly than the welfare state measures needed for the adequate fulfillment of the other conditions for the realization of the liberty ideal that it would be perfectly understandable if the members of a society were willing to endorse interference-preventing measures while repudiating welfare-state measures.

This response would be puzzling, for at least three reasons. The first is that if the question under discussion is whether serious commitment to the ideal of negative liberty (as Narveson conceives of this ideal) requires support for welfare state measures as well as for measures to prevent interference in people's lives, it looks as though the question of what it would cost a society to implement the needed measures is simply a different question—and thus (strictly) irrelevant. Second, if—when the (quite different) question of cost is taken up—it should be found to be too costly to implement the needed welfare state measures, a social decision not to provide such measures might indeed have to be made. But it would then be necessary to concede that the commitment to implementation of the negative liberty ideal must itself be abandoned. (It would be thoroughly implausible to try to maintain that the commitment can still be met—through fulfillment of only the non-interference condition—on the footing that only affordable conditions for the implementation of the negative liberty ideal really qualify as conditions for the realization of the ideal!) Third, it seems clear that any objection to the costs associated with adoption of the welfare state measures mandated by the conclusion of the argument I have constructed using Narvesonian premises would be generated equally by endorsement of the argument Sterba has tried to construct. After all, the conclusion of that argument is the same as the conclusion of the argument I have suggested Narveson is committed to accepting—and it's the welfare state measures called for by this (shared) conclusion that are alleged to be too costly.

III. The Compatibility of Liberty and Equality

The larger aim of the Sterba-Narveson book—as its title indicates—is to determine whether or not the ideals of Liberty and equality are compatible ideals. The question of the mutual compatibility of these ideals can obviously take many determinate forms. Indeed, it can take as many determinate forms as there are determinate accounts of the content of these ideals—and it's clear, even from the discussion in this book, that Sterba and Narveson don't see eye to eye about their content. For example, despite the lip-service they both give to a merely "negative" construal of the content of the liberty ideal, they disagree about which the "negative liberties" are that the ideal should be taken to protect. And although Narveson, when he inveighs against the ideal of Equality seems for the most part to identify it as an ideal that calls for complete economic equality (for example, equality of income and wealth), this seems not to be the version of the ideal to which Sterba would be prepared to subscribe. One very general concern, consequently, about the discussion undertaken in this book of the question of the mutual compatibility of liberty and equality is that it rests on different—indeed, mutually incompatible—formulations of the question.

However, there are a number of more specific concerns as well. Let me here mention two that have to do with Narveson's handling of the question, and one that relates to the general argument Sterba mounts for the compatibility of liberty and equality.

One concern about Narveson's handling of this general question is that at times he seems content to take it to be the question whether the negative liberty ideal as he construes it can be reconciled with the version of the equality ideal for which complete economic equality (equality of income and wealth) is the crucial desideratum. He is of course quite justified in concluding that, when liberty and equality are construed in these ways, they are incompatible: a society in which the role of the state is limited to the meticulous enforcement of "non-interference" rules will not be a society in which there is strict equality of income and wealth, and a society in which the state attempts to enforce strict equality of income and wealth will not be a society in which there is full compliance with "non-interference" rules. But this is a Pyrrhic victory, surely, if (a) what is at stake in the Narveson-Sterba debate is the defensibility of the Narveson version of the negative liberty ideal, and if (b) Sterba would reject (as I assume he would) the idea that the equality ideal calls for strict equality of income and wealth.

A second concern is Narveson's surprisingly emphatic rejection of the view there is at least one version of the view that liberty and equality are compatible ideals that libertarians who share his view of the content of the (negative) liberty ideal can endorse—viz. the version that calls for equality in the distribution across society of the (negative) liberties protected by the (negative) liberty ideal. After all, this (modest) version of the equality ideal would require only two things: (a) that all the members of a society be beneficiaries of the non-interference rules generated by the (negative) liberty ideal, and (b) that all the members benefit equally from the enforcement of non-interference rules. That (a) and (b) are not trivial requirements—and that they are not infrequently violated, even in societies that pride themselves on giving a certain primacy to the enforcement of non-interference rules—can be seen by noting, for example, that such rules as those that prohibit physical assault are often unevenly policed by security forces and unevenly applied in the courts.

The difficulty I have with Sterba's treatment of the question of the mutual compatibility of liberty and equality is that he seems bent on constructing a single, multi-stage argument that is designed to lead anyone who is willing, initially, to accept a merely negative conception of the liberty ideal to endorse, at the end, an ideal of global equality. Quite apart from whether, in a piece-meal review of the many steps in this complex argument, doubts can be generated about some of its crucial "transitions," it is antecedently problematic whether Sterba's general strategy is defensible. The idea that the linkages between liberty and equality are so "tight" that a single argument, if patiently and ingeniously developed, can be expected to conduct us from rather modest premises about the importance of certain widely-accepted "negative liberties" to the conclusion that a very ambitious version of global egalitarianism must be embraced seems, among other things, to give insufficient recognition to a very simple feature of the liberty and equality ideals—viz. that they provide possible "answers" to different normative questions. To give content to the liberty ideal (taking it to be, as is commonly done, an ideal of individual liberty) is to be committed to asking about which the liberties or freedoms are that individuals ought to have if they are to live satisfactory lives—and this question clearly cannot be answered without exploration of what it is about these particular freedoms or liberties that makes them crucial to the living by individuals of a satisfactory and fulfilling life. To give content to the equality ideal, by contrast, is to be committed to asking how a society's institutions—social, economic, legal, political, etc.—ought to be structured if all the members of a society are to be afforded an equal opportunity to live their lives in a satisfactory and fulfilling way.

There are consequently at least two reasons for questioning the defensibility of Sterba's general "argument-from-liberty-to-equality" strategy. The first is that, while the answer to questions about the importance we have reason to attach to specific "negative liberties" obviously helps to set the stage for dealing with the question how institutions ought to be structured if these liberties are to be made available to all on an equal basis, this latter question—conceived as a question about the role institutional arrangements play in securing this or that determinate distribution of the things we value—goes well beyond those we have to tackle in the course of giving determinate content to the liberty ideal itself. The second reason for doubting the defensibility of Sterba's general strategy is that the preferred version of the equality ideal must do more than identify the institutional conditions for a defensible distribution of the particular liberties that are to be protected by the liberty ideal: distributive issues must also be faced about the proper distribution of all the conditions that must be fulfilled if individuals are to be in a position to live a satisfactory or fulfilling life. While the securing of the various liberties embedded in the Liberty ideal is obviously a very important condition, it isn't the only condition.

Alistair M. Macleod, Queen's University

Notes

1. Jan Narveson and James P. Sterba, *Are Liberty and Equality Compatible?* (New York: Cambridge University Press, 2010).

2. Another is the "ought implies can" principle—about the role of which in the book's central debate I shall have nothing to say in this paper.

3.   The agreement needed for this purpose wouldn't have to be agreement about all the uses and all the everyday judgments. It would be good enough if there were agreement about a reasonably broad range of more or less representative examples of these uses and judgments. (And it would be important to the securing of this sort of agreement for philosophically-motivated "cherry-picking" of uses and judgments to be avoided.)

4.   It might be challenged, for example, because talk about "negative liberties" is already technical philosophical talk—talk that incorporates potentially controversial philosophical claims about liberty. As I have already suggested in my introductory remarks, it would argu-ably be methodologically preferable—as well as more promising—for common ground about liberty between Libertarians and Egalitarians to be sought in the many non-technical—and thus pre-philosophical—uses to which we all put the terms "liberty" and "freedom." As ordinarily used (that is, when no philosophical axe is being ground) these terms do not seem to imply that an individual's liberty or freedom can be jeopardized only by "acts of interference by others."

5.   This point was made by Jim Sterba in his contribution to the symposium on *Are Liberty and Equality Compatible?* at the North American Society for Social Philosophy (NASSP) conference in Toronto (July 15–17, 2010).

6.   The passage from Narveson was cited by Sterba in the written version of his contribution to the book symposium on *Are Liberty and Equality Compatible?* at the NASSP conference in Toronto (July 15–17, 2010). The passage can be found on pp. 92–3 of the book.

7.   This further (two-part) question is, of course, by contrast, an expressly normative question.

8.   The point here is, not that Narveson doesn't recognize that there's a familiar normatively neutral use of the terms "freedom" and "liberty"—it's clear that this isn't something Narve-son denies—but that he doesn't take the existence of various "liberties" in this normatively neutral sense as providing the agreed "starting point" for his exchange with Sterba.

9.   That is, the clash between the liberty of the poor not to be interfered with in taking from the rich what they need to satisfy their basic needs and the liberty of the rich not to be interfered with when they use their wealth to purchase luxury goods.

10.   While there's clear evidence that they both commit themselves to this broader interpre-tation of the notion of interference, it's more doubtful whether either of them consistently uses the notion in this way. Indeed, since this broader use is clearly stipulative, while the narrower use corresponds to ordinary usage, there's some risk of unnoticed oscillation between the two uses.

11.   It was in the written version of his contribution to the book symposium at the NASSP conference in Toronto (July 15–17, 2010) that Sterba suggested that interference with the freedom to take part in an anti-war demonstration should be glossed as "freedom to take part in an anti-war demonstration without having one's nose bloodied." (Sterba wrote: "I would claim that the anti-war protestors do lose a liberty in this context. There is something that they are not free to do. It is protesting the war without being bloodied up in the process.")

12.   I owe this point to conversation with Colin Macleod.

13.   As Narveson recognizes in an interesting passage (see Sterba and Narveson, *Are Liberty and Equality Incompatible?*, 127).

14. As noted in part C of Section 1, it's important for these questions to be distinguished.

15. See the section on "Liberty: Values and Rights" in Sterba and Narveson, *Are Liberty and Equality Incompatible?*, 127.

16. Sterba and Narveson, *Are Liberty and Equality Incompatible?*, 127.

17. As Narveson makes clear in his later discussion of what he takes to be "definitive of philosophical *liberalism*"—a position he says he and Sterba "also agree about"—each of us seeks "*to do the best we can with our life, **in our own understanding** of what makes that life go well*" (Sterba and Narveson, *Are Liberty and Equality Incompatible?*, 160; italics and emphasis mine).

18. The question what the social or institutional conditions in fact are for implementation of the ideal of liberty is an empirical question in that it can be asked and answered whether or not the ideal of liberty is thought to be defensible and whether or not its implementation through the establishment of the necessary institutions is thought to be a desideratum of public policy. It needs to be known, of course, what content is being assigned to the ideal of liberty for the purpose of asking about the social conditions of its implementation, but the assignment of that particular content to the ideal is not thereby assumed to be normatively acceptable.

19. It's false—as Narveson, e.g., correctly notes—that, in emphasizing the importance of preventing interference by others in people's lives, the doctrine of negative liberty imposes a ban on all acts of interference. On the contrary, acts of interference with acts that are themselves acts of interference are not subject to any ban under this doctrine.

20. The stipulation implicit in Narveson's elucidation of the concept of liberty—the stipulation that purports to establish a definitional connection between "liberty" and "absence of interference by others"—doesn't provide a "good reason" of the sort that is needed.

21. A central feature of Sterba's argument is his attempt to draw out the implications (especially for our attitude towards certain features of the welfare state) of the approach he thinks there is good reason to adopt towards resolution of the conflict between the "negative liberty of the poor not to be interfered with in taking from the surplus possessions of the rich what they require to meet their basic needs" and "the negative liberty of the rich not to be interfered with in using their surplus for luxury purposes" (Sterba and Narveson, *Are Liberty and Equality Incompatible?*, 254–5). If this conflict is resolved (as Sterba argues it should be) by assigning priority to the negative liberty of the poor, we are led, inexorably, to endorsement of certain key features of the welfare state—features that Narvesonian "libertarianism" cannot accommodate.

Putting Liberty and Equality
Back Together Again: Responses to
Alistair Macleod and Helga Varden

James P. Sterba

I. Introduction

Thanks very much to Alistair Macleod and Helga Varden for their very interesting comments that raise important questions about the character and the resolution of the debate in which Narveson and I are engaged. Surprisingly, Macleod and Varden demonstrate quite different approaches to critiquing Narveson's and my views. As things turned out, they both had a chance to revise their comments in light of Narveson's and my responses, and to remove any inaccuracies and improve upon their critiques in any way they wanted, before publishing them in *Social Philosophy Today*. Unfortunately, only Macleod chose to do this.[1] Varden decided to quickly publish her comments as an online book review[2] while not addressing at all, for example, my complaint that she mistakenly identifies me as a libertarian, something no other critic of my work on libertarianism over the years has ever done. That one mistake—identifying me as a libertarian—is so fundamental that it really renders incoherent the structure of my argument against libertarianism. For example, how can I explicitly reject left libertarianism, as I do, and yet be, as Varden maintains, a left libertarian myself!

So, Macleod and Varden have presented me with quite different challenges in trying to respond to their comments. My response to Macleod will be quite straightforward. He has improved upon his critique from the one he gave in Toronto, and I try to do the same in my revised response. With respect to Varden's comments, I will respond to them in the reconstructed form they would have to take if she had not mistakenly indentified me as a libertarian.

II. Macleod

Now Macleod raises four fundamental worries about how Narveson and I are construing our debate. First, he is concerned that I am using a broader notion of negative liberty than Narveson is—that Narveson means by negative liberty only morally approved noninterferences, whereas I count all noninterferences as negative liberties, although I only approve of some of them. But I think I have found evidence in Narveson's work that we share the usage I employ; we both distinguish between (negative) liberties and approved or legitimate (negative) liberties

In the book, I quote Narveson as saying:

> The libertarian case is that the fundamental right is a right to liberty, but in being so it is automatically a prohibition of the liberty to do certain things: namely, acts that infringe liberty. . . . [From t]he fact that it is the liberty of the poor [not to be interfered with when taking] from the rich that is being restricted, then, it does not follow that what we have is a clash of liberties in the relevant sense: namely, a clash of liberties that the theory protects. It is, instead, a clash between a familiar kind of liberty that it is the very essence of the theory to forbid and another kind of liberty that it is the very essence of the theory to protect.

In commenting on this passage, Macleod allows that the notion of (negative) liberty in the unapproved sense is regarded by Narveson as "a familiar kind of liberty," but then claims that Narveson holds that it is not liberty "in the relevant sense." But I hold this as well. Liberties in the relevant sense for both Narveson and me are approved liberties, and so we are back to the distinction between approved liberties and unapproved liberties, although Narveson and I don't agree about what liberties belong to each group.

What really seems to be bothering Macleod here, however, is that if Narveson and I just share the notions of approved and unapproved (negative) liberties, but don't agree about what liberties belong to each group, in what sense then are we proceeding from "common ground?" It is true that all that is common here is that we share two notions of negative liberty. Still, there is more than this that Narveson and I do hold in common. For example, we both agree that the standard for determining what count as approved liberties should not ultimately be morality. This is because we both recognize that different moral views would favor different liberties and that it is difficult to show that one moral view is preferable to all others. So we both want to ground the determination of approved liberties in something that is still more fundamental. Here, I ultimately appeal to a standard of nonquestion-beggingness, and Narveson appeals to self-interest. But Narveson contends, while I deny, that his appeal to self-interest is nonquestion-begging as well. So putting all this together, there is quite a bit that Narveson and I share in common, while still, in the end, disagreeing about what are the approved (negative) liberties.

Second, Macleod thinks that both Narveson and I may be, in another way, sharing too broad a notion of negative liberty, according to which whenever a person is harmed her liberty is restricted. Macleod allows that whenever a person's liberty is restricted, there is something that it is now impossible for the person to do, but he then contends that there are ways that people can be harmed without having their liberty restricted.

Now while Narveson may be committed to equating harming with restricting liberty, I myself am only committed to their generally going together. However, let us just suppose for the sake of argument that Narveson and I were both equating harming with restricting liberty, and consider why Macleod thinks that this is problematic. Macleod initially suggested that participants in an anti-war rally might not lose their liberty to so participate even when pro-war protestors bloodied them up a bit and thus harmed them while they were exercising that liberty. I responded at the meeting in Toronto that the anti-war protestors did still lose an additional a liberty in this context. I claimed that there is something else that they were not free to do. It is protesting the war without being bloodied up in the process. In his revised response, Macleod allows that this might be the case, but then he suggests that the protestors would still be harmed by shouted remarks that they are unpatriotic without being deprived of any additional liberty. But, as I see it, there is still a liberty related to this harm that the protestors are still being deprived of. It is the liberty to participate in their protest without being called unpatriotic. That is an action that in this context they cannot do. So I don't see anything particularly problematic about equating these particular instances of harming and restricting liberty.

Yet Macleod has other examples. He cites acts of justified paternalism as when parents force their children to undergo regular dental check-ups. Macleod claims that such acts restrict the freedom of children without harming them in any way, even in the short run. I am not so sure that we would get confirmation of this conclusion from many of the children who have undergone such check-ups and the cleanings and drillings that go with them. Still, Macleod is probably right that there are some restrictions of our liberty so unconnected with anything that would be for our good, either now or in the future, that they would not cause us any harm. I just think that such cases are very untypical. Restrictions of liberty and harming do tend to go together.

Third, Macleod raises an objection to Narveson's libertarian view that he thinks offers a better way of defeating Narveson's anti-welfare conclusions than the one that I offer. Macleod points out that Narveson allows that negative liberty is just a means to a good life. He then notes that there are other, comparably important, means to a good life, in particular, the opportunity to acquire the economic resources needed for the effective implementation of one's conception of the good life and the opportunity to develop the required skill and competences needed for the effective implementation of one's conception of the good life. So why not, Macleod argues, provide individuals with these comparably important means to a good life as well a right to liberty? Isn't Narveson, asks Macleod, committed to providing just these opportunities needed for implementing one's conception of a good life by the logic of his argument for a right to liberty?

Unfortunately, as I see it, Narveson is not committed to providing these additional means for implementing one's conception of a good life in the way Macleod indicates.[3] This is because although Narveson acknowledges that liberty is a means for living out one's conception of a good life, that it is a means for living out one's conception of a good life is not his justification or rationale for a right to liberty. His justification or rationale for a right to liberty is that not to support such a right is to fundamentally harm people. By contrast, failing to support the two opportunities for living out one's conception of the good life to which Macleod draws our attention does not harm people, it just fails to benefit them. It is on the basis of the distinction between harming and nonbenefiting that Narveson purports to support the negative liberties he favors without being committed to also supporting the opportunities that Macleod favors, although Narveson readily admits that these opportunities are also means needed for living out one's conception of a good life.

Yet while Narveson can escape Macleod's argument for securing the basic opportunities that people need for living out their conceptions of a good life, fortunately, he cannot escape my argument for much the same conclusion because my argument is all about securing negative liberties and what we need to do in order to avoid harming other people. What my argument manages to do is transform Macleod's concern for the basic opportunities that people need for living out their conceptions of a good life to a concern about negative liberties whose exercise can effectively secure those very same opportunities that Macleod favors. Thus Macleod's opportunity to acquire the economic resources needed for the effective implementation of one's conception of the good life is reconstituted as the liberty not to be interfered with when acquiring the economic resources needed to effectively implement of one's conception of the good life. The latter social good has the form of a negative liberty, so Narveson cannot simply dismiss it, given that he trades in negative liberties. So this negative liberty has to be assessed against other negative liberties with which it conflicts, such as the negative liberty of the rich not to be interfered with when using their surplus for luxury purposes. I claim that a nonquestion-begging evaluation of these competing liberties will favor the liberty of the poor over the liberty of the rich, and that this will justify a right to welfare, such that when distant peoples and future generations are taken into account will lead to substantial equality. Accordingly, there is a way to justify what is essentially the social agenda that Macleod wants to support against Narveson's libertarian view, it is just not the way that Macleod wants to do it.

At the very end of his comments, Macleod raises two overall problems for my view. The first is that my liberty to equality argument is a multi-stage argument, making it difficult to assess as a whole. The second is that the ideals of liberty and equality that I want to reconcile actually provide answers to different normative questions. According to Macleod, the liberty ideal is properly concerned with what basic freedom each of us should have, whereas the equality ideal is properly concerned with the basic opportunities that each of us should have. Thus, Macleod suggests, it would be bad form to run these two ideals with their different questions together, as I do. Yet run them together is just what Macleod himself does when he attempts to show that Narveson's argument for a right to liberty should also support a right to equal opportunity. So my argument from liberty to equality conforms more to the way Macleod actually argues against libertarians than with the way he here tells us we should be arguing against them.

As for my argument being a multi-stage argument that is difficult to access, I actually think that it is a comparatively simple argument, and that it is its basic simplicity that probably works against it. Surely, we think there must be something wrong with an argument that simply argues:

1) There are conflicts of negative liberty between the rich and the poor.

2) A nonquestion-begging weighing of these conflicting liberties will favor the liberty of the poor over the liberty of the rich, giving rise to a right to welfare.

3) Extending this right to welfare to distant peoples, and particularly to future generations, will require us, absent a technological fix, not to use any more resources than we need for a decent life so that as much as possible future generations will also have the resources they will need for a decent life.

III. Varden

Turning to Varden's comments, as I mentioned at the beginning of my responses, Varden mistakenly assumes that I am defending a form of left-wing libertarianism in my debate with Narveson, even when I made it very clear that I only start with libertarian premises so as to not beg the question against Narveson. Thus, what my argument is designed to show is that the libertarian ideal itself leads to requirements that are strikingly similar, although not identical, to those endorsed by welfare liberals or socialists. By thus showing that the practical requirements of both the libertarian ideal and the welfare liberal or socialist ideal are so similar, I hope to move libertarians, so to speak, " to throw in the towel" and join forces with welfare liberals and socialists about what should be done in practice.

It is also a mistake to label me a left libertarian, as Varden does, since left libertarians start with self-ownership, which is compatible with the negative liberty principle favored by Narveson , but then join it with common ownership of natural resources, which is not compatible with that principle. That is why right libertarians, like Narveson, do not take them that seriously, they simply have more content in their premises than right libertarians want to endorse.[4]

In any case, I only assumed the premises of right libertarians, like Narveson, for the sake of argument.[5] I never commit myself to the view that they are as fully adequate as the premises of welfare liberalism or socialism, although an important part of an adequate defense of the latter premises is the surprising conclusion of my argument that libertarian premises with the addition of a few fully compatible epicycles, like negative welfare rights and Robin Hoods, turn out to have much the same practical requirements as can be derived from those welfare liberal or socialist premises.

So a significant misunderstanding of my argument against libertarianism is to object to it on the grounds that it does not defend welfare rights in as straight-forward a way as do welfare liberal and socialist views. Instead, what should be noted is how, proceeding from libertarian premises, as it does, my argument ends up defending the same sort of requirements that welfare liberals and socialists defend. In this way, the argument effectively eliminates the libertarian's claim to be able to provide a real practical alternative to welfare liberalism and socialism.

So let me go on to consider Varden's objections, having now corrected the overall misinterpretation of my view within which she raises those objections.

First, Varden objects to my appeal to modern-day Robin Hoods to transfer resources from the rich to the poor so that the poor can meet their basic needs. Varden claims this would not be legitimate unless the modern-day Robin Hoods had the actual consent of the poor to act on their behalf. Before our session in Toronto, Varden e-mailed me about this issue, and I responded that I did not think actual consent was required before such Robin Hoods could act on behalf of the poor. In her comments, Varden affirms that actual consent is required, principally on the authority of John Simmons. But Simmons, in fact, commented on an earlier version of my argument, and he did not raise the objection that Varden is making on his behalf. The reason for this, I think, is that Simmons's view is that political obligations require consent, but we are not talking about political obligations here. What modern-day Robin Hoods would be doing would not be done out of political obligation, and if the poor don't like what they are doing, the poor are free to object, and faced with such objections, Robin Hoods would have to cease their activities on behalf of the poor, although I don't see why the poor would object to such help. Surely, the poor didn't object in and around Sherwood Forest.

Second, Varden objects to what she refers to as my non-relational conception of rights. However, I don't see why she would regard my view this way since I am assuming for the sake of argument that the only wrong here is a certain sort of interference—that sounds pretty relational to me. But what Varden really seems to be objecting to here is that I do not affirm straight off a positive obligation to help the poor. Here again we are getting the objection why don't I argue like a welfare liberal or a socialist. And my answer, as I have indicated, is that I trying to convince libertarians that they should endorse comparable conclusions to those that welfare liberals or socialists endorse. So I have a roundabout way of getting to such positive obligations. And in view of my project of arguing with libertarians, I cannot just start off by affirming such positive obligations. If I am to be arguing with libertarians, I must first get to what I call negative welfare rights and then ground positive welfare rights and correlated positive obligations in those negative welfare rights. If Varden wants me to start off with positive rights and obligations, she is asking me to give up arguing with libertarians in a way they cannot ignore because it appeals to the same ideal of negative liberty they themselves endorse.

Third, Varden maintains that she finds the idea of rights tracking non-existent persons inconsistent with a libertarian, negative conception of freedom. I don't see this. Suppose the present inhabitants of Toronto decide to bury tons of highly radioactive nuclear waste under the city deeply enough that it wouldn't percolate up and render the area uninhabitable until 150 years from now. Wouldn't the present inhabitants, assuming that they could maintain decent lives for themselves without doing anything comparable, have violated the rights of those presently non-existent future inhabitants of Toronto who will only happen on the scene just when the nuclear waste starts percolating up? I maintain that a conception of negative rights permits such claims.

Fourth, Varden wonders how I am able to get a right to welfare that covers a right to access basic goods such as food, shelter, medical care, protection, companionship, and self-development from a right to freedom, negatively understood. This parallels a worry that Varden expressed earlier—basically how I get from negative rights, even negative rights to welfare, to positive rights. I discuss this derivation in the book.

I start off by noting that it might be objected that the right to welfare that my argument establishes from libertarian premises is not the same as the right to welfare endorsed by welfare liberals and socialists. Now I grant this. We could mark this difference by referring to the right that this argument establishes as "a negative welfare right" and by referring to the right endorsed by welfare liberals as "a positive welfare right." The significance of this difference is that a person's negative welfare right can be violated only when other people through acts of commission interfere with its exercise, whereas a person's positive welfare right can be violated not only by such acts of commission but by acts of omission as well. Nonetheless, I claim, this difference will have little practical import because in recognizing the legitimacy of negative welfare rights, libertarians will come to see that virtually any use of their surplus possessions is likely to violate the negative welfare rights of the poor by preventing the poor, either now or in the future, from rightfully appropriating (some part of) their surplus goods and resources. So, in order to ensure that they will not be engaging in such wrongful actions, it will be incumbent on them to set up institutions guaranteeing adequate positive welfare rights for the poor. Only then will they be able to use legitimately any remaining surplus possessions to meet their own nonbasic needs. Furthermore, in the absence of adequate positive welfare rights, the poor, either acting by themselves or through their allies or agents, would have some discretion in determining when and how to exercise their negative welfare rights. In order not to be subject to that discretion, libertarians will tend to favor the only morally legitimate way of preventing the exercise of such rights: They will set up institutions guaranteeing adequate positive welfare rights that will then take precedence over the exercise of negative welfare rights. For these reasons, recognizing the negative welfare rights of the poor will ultimately lead libertarians to endorse the same sort of welfare institutions favored by welfare liberals and socialists.

Fifth, Varden criticizes me for presumptuously claiming to know that, given our present trajectory, at some distant point in human history, it will be impossible for future generations to meet their basic needs. However, I thought we all knew this. After all, doesn't modern science tell us that this has to be the fate of distant human inhabitants of the earth as the earth becomes more and more uninhabitable for life forms like us? So I don't think it would be presumptuous for me, or anyone else, to endorse this conclusion of modern science.

Yet in my discussion, I don't actually make this unobjectionable claim. Rather, what I claim is that, unless we have a technological fix, or are just using renewable resources, we have an obligation not to use any more resources than we need for a decent life, so that future generations will also, as far as possible, have the resources they will need for a decent life. The "as far as possible" clause allows for the idea that at some point resources will run out and the earth will become uninhabitable. So the moral requirement on us, after we have secured a decent life for ourselves, is just not to do anything to hasten that fate for future generations. And this follows, I claim, from the libertarian's own ideal of liberty.

Finally, it is important to note that Varden's critique of Narveson, like my own, appeals to an appropriate distribution of liberty, but unlike my own, hers requires buying into a Kantian universal law/categorical imperative perspective, that Narveson and other libertarians reject. By contrast, my critique, which supports an even more egalitarian conclusion, ultimately appeals to nothing more than a standard of nonquestion-beggingness to achieve that result, certainly not a standard that libertarians are likely reject.

James P. Sterba, University of Notre Dame

Notes

1. Varden gave as an excuse that she was up for tenure this year, and hence, could not even spend an afternoon revising her comments.

2. See http://ndpr.nd.edu/review.cfm?id=20927.

3.   Narveson, however, is committed to providing much the same additional means to those in need, I believe, by the force of the argument that I direct against his view.

4.   Narveson does not like the distinction between left and right libertarians, but it has some relevance in the limited way I am employing it.

5.   Notice I don't even assume the premises of left libertarians, making it doubly difficult for me to be, as Varden claims, a card-carrying member of the group.

Discussion of Helga Varden's Review and Alistair MacLeod's Comments

Jan Narveson

I. Helga Varden

I shall have to leave Helga's interesting criticisms of Jim's part of this discussion to Jim, not only because it's his bailiwick but more importantly because her arguments against my view are much too interesting to be left with a less than full-tilt response.

I will begin, no doubt forlornly, by entering my usual objection to being called "right wing." That is a political term in current use for which I hold absolutely no brief. My position is and always has been: a pox on both their houses—the "left-wingers" and the "right-wingers." It seems to be too much to hope that even otherwise acute philosophical discussants would not fail to see the distinction between the libertarian view and the absurdities inevitably associated with the "right" and the "left." But we will have to await another day to sort that out.

So, first: she proposes this:

> The only solution I see to the problems currently characteristic of Narveson's position, which solution is also consistent with a commitment to freedom, is to embrace Kant's requirement for the establishment of a public authority. Moreover, in order to establish the necessary public authority, what is enforced by it cannot merely be private right, but must also be public right. Private right concerns the rights and duties private individuals hold against one another, whereas public right concerns claims citizens have on their public institutions. And importantly for this discussion on economic justice (where issues of equality and liberty are often seen to conflict), public right includes certain redistributive measures to secure all citizens' systemic freedom, equality and independence. Importantly, however, if this argument concerning the necessity of public right for rightful relations is successful, the libertarian conception of justice fails. That is, if public right is necessary for liberty, then the compatibility of liberty and equality is not one that can be envisioned at the individual level—it requires us also to explore the institutional structure of the just state.

Now, first, I take Kant to be basically with me, since his fundamental principle of justice is, precisely, the libertarian principle.[1] So the question is, where do we go from

Social Philosophy Today, Volume 27   179

there? This idea that there is a "public authority" that is wholly distinct from private right is one which Kant, despite his very overt advocacy of that idea, can hardly allow, given his starting point. After all, Kant also seems to be (claims to be) a contractarian, like me. There is no "public level" if it's to be regarded as wholly underivative from the "private level." So in order to have a "public authority" which would uphold rights other than those evidently stemming from the libertarian idea, you have to show that private persons would accept such structures in their interests. But would they? And in particular, why would they have to accept structures that contravened the very liberty that Kant seems to agree with me that they have, basically? (I take Anthony de Jasay to have essentially shot this version of contractarianism out of the water.[2])

Having said this, let's admit that Kant comes on as virtually a fascist in his support of kingly authority. So the question is not whether he does that, but whether he has any business doing so. I claim not. It seems to me that if any sort of public "authority" is allowed, it is only to do what Bastiat says it is to do: act as the collective upholder of our individual rights, which are to live our lives as we see best, compatibly with the right of all others to do likewise—with, Bastiat puts it, the "collective right of self-defense."[3] And how are you defending people if you allow some to attack others?

So I deny that "if public right is necessary for liberty, then the compatibility of liberty and equality is not one that can be envisioned at the individual level—it requires us also to explore the institutional structure of the just state." What I deny is that the just state would be compelling people to promote "equality."

If, of course, you could establish that people did indeed have positive as well as negative basic rights, that would be a slam dunk. But we don't start there, and the question is whether you can get there from here. I don't, frankly, see how, other than by the usual methods of making agreements with particular people, in which case the relevant duties are to the people you make the agreement with, rather than the public at large.

Now, Helga says, "Without enforceable rights, the possibility of each individual's freedom is subject to other persons' consent, which is inconsistent with freedom to set and pursue ends of one's own choosing." Something is missing here. Each individual's freedom ends at the next person's right to his freedom, and that does indeed include his consent: you may visit my house if I consent, otherwise not. Surely she cannot be maintaining that if the individual's consent is ever definitive for how other people may act, then there is no freedom? Surely it's the other way around: If I have any freedom at all, it lies in the status that there are things others cannot do to the individual without that individual's consent.

On the other hand, the rules for the public are not, of course, a matter of individual consent: they are a matter of general consent. Perhaps that is what she (and Kant) had in mind. But in that case, what needs to be shown is that we would all consent to some "public authority" telling us all what to do. I should think it fairly obvious that we would not. We would, instead, consent to setting up authorities that would endeavor to prevent, or perhaps punish, incursions of one individual upon another.

Now we come to her general characterization of my view, which is in some respects perfectly correct—but not others, I think. "Remember that the original puzzle for libertarians is to explain enforceable, individual rights to material resources on a model of reciprocal freedom. Yet it seems that such a commitment to reciprocal freedom is inconsistent with some person being forced into a situation in which there is no freedom at all." Now, first, I don't think I recall that being "the original puzzle." Instead, it is to explain enforceable individual rights, period. We claim, like Kant and Hobbes and the others, that the fundamental right is a right to liberty, in general. It is not a right to some material goods; it is right to, among other things, attempt to use and shape various material things to one's own purposes. The claim is that nobody may compel you to refrain from availing yourself of opportunities afforded by nature: they may only compel you to refrain from availing yourself of what others have already created and/or are currently using (such as their own bodies.)

One of the standard fantasies recent philosophers employ in discussing the acquisition of natural resources involves envisaging a very tiny world, such as Helga's island, in which there is very, very little for anyone to attempt to acquire. Creating a highly abstracted artificial scenario on that little island with its specified but tiny set of resources is, of course, going to bring up tricky problems of "distribution." But the real world, of course, was never like that: it was, originally, almost entirely a very huge wilderness, as Locke characterizes America. And as Locke also noted, the effects of human work on what was originally wilderness have generally rendered it such that almost anyone of whatever rank would prefer remaining in the world where things are already owned by others to the world in which he can strike out for himself and make what he will and can of the wilderness. Why is this? Well, basically it's because people are (or at least can be) actually useful to each other. I deny that the Mafia, or Genghis Khan, have the right idea about other people and their things. The right idea is had by the entrepreneurs, especially: the potential voluntary activities of other people are sources of value, and the thing to do is to find out what they can do, and then make them an offer, so that both you and they benefit from this.

Of course there is the important and basic question whether "original property owners may choose to offer nothing." Since they may, then, she says, "Even from a Hobbesian point of view, this must be insufficient as it simply cannot be seen to be in their rational interest." Insufficient for what? For satisfying the suppliants, certainly. But what about satisfying the interests of those first-comers and first-developers? Why do the former automatically get to overrule the latter?

If she is right in that claim, then of course I am wrong. But is she? Hobbes has made it crystal clear that the problem in the state of nature is violence, and his cure for that, which seems the obvious one, is to outlaw the use of violence to get our ends. This outlawing should be across the board: everyone benefits from everyone else's peaceability. But the enterprising and the first-comers, on her and Sterba's idea of it, do not—their benefits are severely limited, by the "needs" of their fellows. Why would that have been part of the bargain? It's hardly obvious.

Helga says, "voluntary charity or provision of employment by some to others cannot in principle take the place of enforceable property rights." But of course! Voluntary employment and charity do not take the place of enforceable property rights: on the contrary, their very possibility is a consequence of such rights. Such rights say that people can own various things, which is to say that others are not allowed to seize those things for their own purposes. Consequently, everyone's choice is either to (a) make one's own way somehow, or (b) offer one's powers to others in an agreed-on exchange that is sufficient for one's purposes, or (c) become an object of others' charity. To go farther than that and add a fourth: (d) when you really need something, then take it from someone else, whether they let you or not—is, in my view, to head us back toward the state of nature.

I do have to point out that these choices are existential. Helga criticizes Jim for being elitist. On the contrary, it is the leftists who are elitist: unlike the "elites" such as Bill Gates, who act entirely within the terms of respect for others' liberty, the socialists get together and proclaim a right to compel everybody else to do their bidding in presumed support of the poor (or more precisely, the enormously larger class that they designate as qualifying for the benefit of other people's cash).

"According to Kant, the main problem with a unilateral account like Narveson's is the implication that the restrictions on interaction issue from unilateral choices rather than from universal law, which is inconsistent with a commitment to individuals' right to freedom." But where does that come from? Under no circumstances am I claiming that the principles of justice are "unilateral": unilateral principles of justice are nonsense. What we're talking about are social principles, and in the nature of the case such principles cannot possibly be "unilateral." Obviously, they are multilateral, coming, as I (and Kant) claim, from everyone. The Varden-Sterba view, on the other hand, cannot, as we have seen, be universal, for it involves authorizing some (the poor) to trample on others, without the latter's consent. But the individual's right to freedom is the right to the maximum freedom consistent with the extension of the same freedom to all—exactly as Kant's foundational principle has it. Now, the claim that the universal law is inconsistent with this right is the claim that Kant's position is incoherent from the word go. I suggest, on the contrary, that this conception of what Kant says is what is inconsistent.

Thus she says, "in contrast to Narveson, Kant argues that there must be an additional, third step if my unilateral acquisition is to be become rightful appropriation, that is, consistent with everyone's freedom." But this is not a "third step"—consistency with others is operative from the start. Nobody is allowed to take anybody else's property, to invade and despoil others to make his way in the world. Far from being "third," it is the very essence of the idea, which, remember, is the idea of general—that is, universal—liberty.

Now, the claim, which Kant does indeed make, that "Only such an authority can yield restrictions on everyone that are consistent with a basic commitment to each individual's right to freedom" is unclear in one crucial respect. According to Locke, in the state of nature, everyone has the right to enforce the law of nature. (Not, of course, to enforce whatever he should happen to think is the right of nature, but what is the right of nature, which Locke thinks—optimistically—everyone by common reason is aware of.) When Jones accosts innocent Smith, Robinson has the right to attempt to compel Jones to desist, and to punish him (if he can) if Jones does not. Locke thinks this leads to "inconvenience" and so he thinks we need to create public authorities. Yes—but those authorities have no authority that we did not already have. What's happened—so the idea goes—is that we have all given (some of) our already existing authority over to a central authority, who acts as our agent. But just as we are not to exceed it, in principle, so neither is he. He can't do anything it wouldn't have been right for us to do, if only we could have done it. This indeed is the touchstone, the guiding thread, of political liberalism: that government is limited; it does not have any godlike extra-human powers or authority. It is our servant—if it is anything at all.

And so consider this: "For Kant, therefore, once the state establishes a monopoly on coercion—as it must—it cannot simply enforce citizens' provisional private rights against each other. Instead, it must set itself up as a public authority that provides conditions of right for all by ensuring that the coercive system of law as a whole is consistent with each citizen's right to freedom." The words "for Kant" should be significant here. They should mean: "it follows from Kant's professed fundamental principles that . . . ." We should not infer from the fact that Kant often talks like a fascist that fascism is actually consistent with his principles. What the public authority should be doing is enforcing people's rights against each other, and these rights are rights to the maximum liberty that is consistent with the liberty of all others. The right in question is to do whatever doesn't involve aggressing in some way against anyone else. Dealing with such aggression—with crime—is the first concern of the state. Is it, as I claim, the only concern? Given this fundamental principle, shared between me and Kant (and so many others), it is at least hard to see how it could be anything else, at root.

Now consider her version of the welfare state: "Only the guarantee of unconditional poverty relief can ensure that no one citizen is dependent upon another citizen's consent to access means legally." Well, again to the contrary. The independence from others that she wants has the problem that it is gotten at the cost of imposing on free people. She may think that the implorings of people on the edge of starvation are not arbitrary, and in one sense, no doubt, they are not—but then, neither are the interests of the more successful. A regime such as Helga advocates here is certainly one that subordinates the productive to the unproductive. Creating a welfare state ensures that we will be treated according to the whims of the arbitrary authorities who happen to have been hired by the people that an arbitrary majority happens to have elected. The appeal to high principle here is out of place. Helga's faith that the state will see to the fulfillment of this supposed right is touching, but after all, the state in question will be the bureaucratic state, interested in lining the pockets and entrenching the powers of its bureaucrats, with scant interest in the actual rights or conditions of the people they supposedly serve. Insofar as it does what it is supposed to do, it protects people from incursions by others—be those others starving or not (and I for one don't trust it all that much to do that either, as witness the treatment of many hundreds of peaceable protesters at the hands of the police during the G20 meetings in Toronto.) Helga seems to have grabbed from the blue the equation of "universal law" with the arbitrary edicts of a *soi-disant* "public" institution. Universality by no means requires a welfare state. It assures us, rather, of mutual compatibility of our lines of actions—some of which will, of course, not be successful, and when not, we will have to appeal to our fellows to help us out. But that the appeal can properly be accompanied by the sword is not obviously part of the bargain. Indeed, I think it pretty obvious that it is not part of the bargain.

It is principle that matters here. And that principle, stemming from general reflection on our situations, is that people do not have the right to gang up on people and use force to promote their way in life—neither individually nor collectively. Whether that is really possible as a political condition in the world we live in is an interesting question. That doesn't keep it from being right, though.

II. Alistair MacLeod

Alistair has three general criticisms. (1) He thinks that Jim's and my differences aren't real, because we are somehow dealing in different notions of liberty; (2) he disputes the assimilation of harm to interference with liberty; and (3) he wants to ascribe to us as our fundamental interest that of identifying "which the liberties or freedoms are that individuals ought to have if they are to live satisfactory (fulfilling, etc.) lives"—as if that was what our disagreement is about. In all of these, I deny all charges.

(1) Let me begin, again, with a very slight cavil, about the term 'negative liberty': it is negative rights that we (or at least I) are concerned to push here. To say that people have a "negative" right is to say that they have a right to the nonactions of others in certain respects: namely, those which would interfere with the actions (or, therefore, the persons) of the rightholders in question. What makes it "negative" is that it's a right to others' refrainings rather than to their doings. They have this right only on condition that they themselves refrain from such interfering actions themselves, of course. When they don't refrain, they of course lose the benefits intended to be conferred by possession of a right.

It would, as I say at some length in *The Libertarian Idea*[4] be possible to turn liberty into a value to be promoted by government—at the expense of its constituents. This is not something that libertarians allow. Taxing Bill in order to extend Sam's liberty from someone or something (other than the malevolent actions of Bill himself, of course) is not acceptable under the liberty principle.

Alistair rightly asks that our uses of terms be consistenct with ordinary uses of terms, and he complains that our employment of the notions of freedom and equality, especially, do not do this. However, Alistair states his complaint in an ambiguous way: "the pre-philosophical uses we make of such terms as "freedom" and "liberty" in our everyday judgments." Now in this sentence fragment, he refers both to the judgments and to the use of such terms. But there is the possibility that the ordinary person does not make the right judgments about these things, even though we are using the terms in the same way. And of course that is just what I do claim.

He asks, concerning "the scope of the "negative liberties" that constitute, ostensibly, "the agreed starting point," this: "Are absolutely all the actions individuals might be in a position without interference to perform (given their abilities and wants) to be counted, at least initially, as determining the scope of the negative liberties that provide the putative starting point? If the answer is 'yes,' then a would-be murderer can be said to be at liberty (in the negative sense) to commit an act of murder provided he is free from interference by others in committing such acts." Now, I am unclear what he means by "initially" and "starting point."

(i) Of course it is possible for a person to be at liberty to commit murders. It happens, alas, all too often. If Alistair is asking whether such actions are logically within the scope of the concept of liberty, then of course the answer is "yes." So if he is referring to the "starting point" of the Hobbesian "state of nature," then of course the answer is "yes."

(ii) Or did he mean, what is our agreed moral "starting point," in the sense of the first principle of morals (which is the product of our hypothetical state-of-nature social contract deliberations)? Well, of course, the libertarian principle—like all theses about rights—is a thesis about which actions we are to be prohibited from performing. If the question is, which if any of those are we interested in prohibiting, then the answer is: actions that interfere with the peaceable actions (and persons) of others. A recursive judgment is required: if someone, A, proposes to perform one of these interfering actions, then is the intended object of his incursions, B, deserving of this, or not? The libertarian principle says that if B has himself not interfered with (or is in process of interfering with) other innocents (that is other non-interferers), then he is not deserving of it, and the proposed action is one that agent A does not have the right to perform. But if he is the performer of some previous or ongoing interference of the type, then some sort of correctional, hence interfering, action is justified. It is hard to put this in a noncumbersome way, but I think the idea is reasonably clear. What the libertarian principle says is that we are entitled, we have the right, to do whatever does not interfere with innocent others (their "innocence" being assessed in precisely the same way.)

But Alistair, as it seems to me, clouds this matter when he says, "Narveson seems not to want to give recognition to this possible construal of the starting point: he seems to want to restrict the interferences from which individuals are protected when they enjoy negative liberty (properly so-called) to interferences that are not themselves interferences with interferences. On this reading, the would-be murderer's "freedom to commit an act of murder" doesn't count as one of the negative liberties he might be thought to have, even initially."

But, as I say: obviously, if this is intended to be a question about the logical scope of the term 'liberty,' then of course murder is something that a person could be at liberty to do. But if by 'initially' he means, "is it among the things basically ruled out by the libertarian principle?," then the answer is, of course, "yes." There is no problem with either of these—unless we confuse the two issues and suppose that when somebody says that something is wrong, he also has to say that it isn't even logically possible for it to happen!

Thus Alistair: "While the existence of a law prohibiting such acts and diligent efforts by the police to enforce it constitute obstacles to the commission of acts of murder, these obstacles to freedom to commit acts of murder don't count as "interferences" with "negative liberty"—given Narveson's understanding both of "negative liberties" and of what count as "interferences" with these liberties." But of course they are attempts to interfere with any such liberties—hopefully, successful ones. They are interferences with a possible liberty that we don't want people to have—obviously.

The difference between libertarian and other views is that the list of considerations that would justify the use of force (which is what it amounts to) against others is larger in these other views than in ours. The difference is, again obviously, not that we don't allow anything to justify the use of force. Such a view would be moral nihilism; or more generally, just nonsensical. (Like Thomas Hobbes's so-called "right of nature,"which logically cannot be a genuine and universal right.) What justifies the use of force, i.e., interferences with liberties, is that liberties in question are liberties to interfere with the liberties of others who, in their turn, are not interfering with yet others. (As I say, the principle has to be applied recursively. We restrict liberty only in the interests of liberty. It is freedom of each in relation to all others that is being advocated.)

Alistair then goes on to express Sterba's view as follows: "(b) Sterba, on the other hand, seems to want to launch his argument—the argument from 'negative liberty' to 'substantial equality'—by allowing both "the liberty of the poor from interference by the rich when they seek to take from the surplus of the rich in order to satisfy their basic needs" and "the liberty of the rich from interference by the poor when they seek to use the surplus they have to secure luxury goods for themselves" to count as 'negative liberties.'" But, again, this is confused. Of both of course these things are negative liberties. The question is not whether they "count" as such, but whether they are both, on the libertarian view, allowable. To this, I take it, the answer is "no." If the rich are allowed to hold their "surpluses" then neither the poor nor anyone else are allowed to take them (without their permission). If the rich are allowed to own those surpluses, then they are allowed to forbid anyone else from taking them, if that's what they (the rich) want. As Sterba is well aware, I of course think that there is not only no objection, but normally positive merit, in the rich in question doing the desired allowing, at least now and then: but Sterba's claim is that it would actually be wrong, in the sense of an injustice, for the rich not to so allow them. That is what I do not accept, and where Jim and I disagree. Alistair's idea that there is no disagreement there is, so far as I can see, just a complete misconception. And so, he is surely also wrong to say that "In short, when Narveson and Sterba 'face off'—at the beginning of the first round in their debate—they seem not to be operating with the same understanding of the negative liberties that are supposed to provide the agreed starting point for the debate."

Alistair adds a note about Sterba's response: "while they [Sterba and I] have the same understanding of what a 'negative liberty' is, they simply sponsor different views as to which the 'negative liberties' are that qualify for recognition under the doctrine of negative liberty: Sterba's preferred list of the 'negative liberties' protected by the doctrine simply doesn't coincide with Narveson's preferred list." But this is just another way of recognizing that we actually disagree—it's not a verbal kefuffel, it's the real McCoy: Jim does not want to protect the liberty of the rich to do as they wish with their riches, whereas I do. That isn't because he doesn't call those things liberties and I do. Nor is it because I don't call the liberty of the poor to take people's stuff without asking a liberty. So he's entirely off base to say, "But if they don't agree about what is to count as a 'negative liberty'—in the sense crucial to the articulation of the doctrine of 'negative liberty'—where precisely is the 'common ground' on which they stand about the meaning of talk about "negative liberties'?" The answer to this is that Jim thinks that we have to choose among conflicting liberties on some basis other than that one set of them is inconsistent with protecting liberty.

So there simply is not such lack of common ground. The meaning of talk about negative rights as well as liberties is not different here. There is, instead, a substantial disagreement between us: a disagreement about what's right and wrong, and what isn't. I agree that it is puzzling that there is this disagreement. For *prima facie*, if the poor take something from the rich which the rich have acquired without any interference with others, then those poor are attacking those rich, and thus violating their liberties—that is, they are if, as Sterba appears to think, the objections of the rich, on those occasions when they object to this incursion, are to be overruled in the interest of what he claims to be justice.

Alistair goes on to say,

> However, in the preceding sentence in this same passage, Narveson indicates that "liberty" of this "familiar kind" is not liberty "in the relevant sense." This makes it clear that unlike Sterba, Narveson is not prepared to take as his starting point the existence of negative liberties in the normatively neutral sense of "liberty." [see note]. The passage from Narveson that Sterba quotes should consequently be read, not as supporting Sterba's claim that he and Narveson are working with the very same understanding of the notion of "negative liberty" but rather as showing that they are not. (123)

> [note] The point here is, not that Narveson doesn't recognize that there's a familiar normatively neutral use of the terms "freedom" and "liberty"—it's clear that this isn't something Narveson denies—but that he doesn't take the existence of various "liberties" in this normatively neutral sense as providing the agreed "starting point" for his exchange with Sterba. (139n8)

To this he adds, shortly:

> The "liberty of the poor to be free from interference when they take from the rich" simply is not, for Narveson, a "negative liberty" in the relevant sense. There is consequently, for Narveson, no such thing as a clash of "negative liberties" in the relevant sense. Rather there's a clash between a genuine "negative liberty"—viz. the liberty of the rich to be free of interference by the poor when they seek to enjoy the luxury goods they own—and a liberty of "the familiar kind" (the kind that doesn't qualify, according to Narveson, as a "negative liberty" at all). (124)

But again, this is just a misreading, if perhaps a more forgivable one.

Talk of 'senses' is almost unavoidable here, to be sure. But it's not that Jim and I are using these words in different senses; nor is either of us, I think, using them in ways markedly contrary to ordinary language. To the contrary, I think it is plain common sense that the poor can "take" from the rich in a sense implying that they can dispossess the rich of things; but I do not see how it can be claimed that it is consistent with libertarianism to say that they not only can, but may do so, when the dispossession in question takes from the rich things which they have themselves acquired peaceably (rather than by, say, fraud or armed robbery). For libertarianism says that interferences with liberties to do things that are not themselves interferences are wrong. That is the sole ground on which libertarianism asserts that interferences are allowable: when someone takes the liberty to do what violates the liberty of others. (Again, at the risk of being boring, we just have to keep pointing out that [a] 'liberty' as such is a purely descriptive term, and [b] that it is possible to identify some actions, in various contexts, as being done without incursions against others, while other actions are not; and it is the latter that are not permitted in the libertarian scheme. Trying to support these principles by redefining terms is not on.)

Alistair goes on to say, "Thus, it may be the case . . . that Narveson doesn't deny that the term 'liberty' can be used (correctly) in a normatively neutral way."

I am extremely puzzled by this. I have always maintained that the term 'liberty' as such is normatively neutral and can only see Alistair's complaints as founded on a misreading of my texts. Well, or on the currently fashionable habit among philosophers of fudging issues by talking about 'conceptions' versus 'concepts' and such like. But I'm old-fashioned: I'd like to define my spades and then dig, rather than trying to dig by recasting definitions.

Another standard tendency, to be sure—and one which Alistair frequently enough instantiates, is to claim that negative liberty isn't really liberty, or isn't "enough" if one is interested in protecting liberty. People with too few resources, it will be said, lack freedom—when what is meant is that they can't afford to do some of the things the philosopher talking this way thinks he ought to be enabled to do. But if you think we should all be liable to funding people doing various things, why not just say so? Why instead insist on translating the thesis into one about the protection of liberty?

(2) A much more serious matter is brought up by Alistair's contentions about harm and liberty. He says, "Typically, acts of interference (so understood) would include rules or laws prohibiting X, threats of harm to A (or to others) if A Xs, physically preventing A from Xing, and the like. However, both Narveson and Sterba say they understand interference in a broader way. They claim that in this broader sense (if sense it be) A's negative liberty to X can be 'interfered with' not only when A is prevented from Xing (by rules, threats, physical interventions, etc.) but also when A is harmed by the actions of others or when A is rendered worse off by their actions."

Now, this gets to the heart of a matter, indeed. In my writings, I classify those who insist that the individual may rightly be "protected" from self-inflicted "harm" as 'conservatives.' Liberalism, I have said, consists in the view that the values of individuals that are relevant in the theory of justice and thus of politics, are the values of individuals themselves. But Alistair says, "The trouble with this broader understanding, however, is that A can be harmed (for example, injured, whether physically or psychologically, or in respect of his reputation, etc.) without any diminution in his liberty to X."

Now, it is intended by me not to be a "broader understanding." Should we say that my liberty to use my arm has not the least bit been interfered with if you stick a needle into it, causing considerable pain? I say, yes. That is: my arm here is being used in a way contrary to my wishes when you do that. Whether I can continue to lift objects despite the pain you inflict is a separate issue. So when Alistair says, "For example, participants in a pro-war rally may launch a physical attack on A—bloody his nose, or kick his shins—without thereby 'interfering with' his liberty to do X (in the strict—i.e., the narrow—sense of 'interfere')," I think that in the strictest and narrowest sense of the term 'liberty' they have obviously interfered with his liberty—not just necessarily (very much) to do X, but his liberty to do Y, where Y is, use his nose, shins, and so on as he wants rather than as someone else wants.

On Alistair's view, evidently, so long as you don't positively make it impossible for A to do X at all, you haven't interfered with A's liberty. But it's A's general liberty, not just his liberty to do some one thing, that is to be protected (not surprisingly) by a libertarian principle.

In this regard, I may indeed be departing from "ordinary judgments." Perhaps some would say that these are different things. But then, the two certainly have something in common: in both the case where you tie me up and the case in which you inflict various pains on me, you do what I do not want done with some part of myself. All liberty is liberty of the person, the will, in this sense. (And then we must quickly add that this is not to get into the metaphysical question which John Stuart Mill rightly separates from the subject of his essay *On Liberty.*)

And I doubt very much that ordinary judgments are on his side when Alistair even goes so far as to say, "Indeed, even if they shoot and kill him, it's (at least) misleading to represent the act of killing as an act of 'interference' with A's liberty to X. While it's true that the dead can't take part in antiwar demonstrations, it's surely stretching things to try to represent the murder of A as one of the ways in which A's liberty to X can be restricted or limited." Hmm. If someone shoots me, do I remain at liberty to, for example, play tennis? I should have thought it. It seems to me totally obvious that murdering A is "one of the ways" in which his liberty to do X, or indeed just about anything else one can think of, is interfered with—indeed, nullified. No doubt the term 'interfere' is often used in a sort of middle-window way, so that annihilation is not regarded as being much farther along the same spectrum as throwing cold water on the actor. But I doubt that any ordinary person would have any difficulty at all seeing that certainly is farther along—much, much farther along!

Alistair seems to think that so long as the demonstrator's capability of demonstrating at all is intact, then is liberty hasn't been interfered with. But after all, demonstrating at antiwar rallies is not the only thing a demonstrator wants to do, and if a whole lot of those other things are interfered with by, say, police actions or any other, then we say that he has a complaint, although it isn't the same complaint as that he was prevented (altogether) from demonstrating as intended. Thus, when innocent citizens at the notorious Toronto G20 protests were rounded up, incarcerated without being allowed to telephone their loved ones, left without food or drink for twelve hours at a stretch, and so on, their complaints go well beyond that they weren't allowed to demonstrate. The libertarian says: these other complaints are perfectly legitimate, and for the same reason: they are acts against this person's efforts to live his life as he sees fit, given his resources.

Nevertheless, it would be possible for someone, A, to claim that Jones is being harmed when he is not subjected to the particular kind of harangue that A thinks would be good for Jones's soul to be exposed to, and so he would object that an authority who prevented him from engaging in this haranguing, supposing that it is unwanted by Jones, was "interfering with his (A's) liberty." Now, I regard A's complaint as totally unacceptable, and Jones's as perfectly acceptable. A's harangue is an attack on Jones, whether someone else wants to say it "harms" him or not.

Now let's take up the expression 'worse off'—which I agree is a very important notion in all this. That's because life is, as Hobbes says, motion: things are always changing in various ways. Given that they are, some of those changes will be morally unobjectionable even if they are awful—if I get cancer, it may be no one's fault, but it's still awful. But other things may be morally objectionable: if you do things to me that make me worse off than I was in the status quo, then you have done what is objectionable from the libertarian point of view, whether it was to move me from a state of pain to a state of even more pain, or from a state of pleasure to a state of less pleasure. Or, a state in which I had use of two cars to a state in which I now have use of only one, you having smashed up the other.

Alistair rightly accuses the libertarians, such as John Stuart Mill and myself, of objecting to paternalism, even though "The view that all acts that restrict someone's liberty or freedom are acts that harm that person or render that person 'worse off' would rule out the very possibility of defensible paternalistic acts." But that way of putting it is not quite right, since literal paternalism has to do with the treatment of children, and I certainly think Mill was right in holding that children are not eligible for the full protection of their liberty in the way that (we think) adults are—which I take it Alistair would agree with. But, since the only examples of paternalism he brings in to support his claim that our anti-paternalism is objectionable are about children, he doesn't yet have a point. Now, he would have a point if he thinks that the state (for example) may legitimately intervene to prevent citizens from "harming themselves" by, for example, taking "recreational" drugs. That, however, is in our view objectionably paternalistic, in the relevant sense in which paternalism is objectionable on the score of treating adults as if they were children. I don't know exactly where Alistair stands on that score, but it is quite possible that we really do differ there. But if we do, at least he can hardly complain that libertarianism is not consistent in its stand. Nor, I hope, will he say that just because our view differs, probably very sharply, with that of the man on the Clapham Omnibus, that therefore our view is wrong!

(3) Alistair raises this interesting matter: "This is the distinction between (i) the question whether negative liberty has value (and is therefore worth protecting) and (ii) the question whether there's a right to negative liberty." Since I spent the first many pages of *The Libertarian Idea* insisting on such a distinction, I don't feel properly accused when he says that I've ignored it! But anyway: when we are talking about the "value of liberty" we are, as he rightly notes, talking about our ability to pursue the things we value—not 'we' in the collective sense, but individual people, each with their own interests and projects. The reason why any given person wants liberty for himself is that he wants the things to do things—the things he wants to do, and therefore wants that he not be prevented from doing them, and therefore

that he not be prevented by other people from doing them. Of course all sorts of other things prevent us doing what we want—notably our sheer inability to do them. But those are not what we address in social philosophy, where we are concerned with addressing directives to other people, rather than to the weather or the gods.

Now, having correctly seen why I think liberty "is valuable" in the way relevant to this discussion, Alistair goes on to say: "But if freedom from interference by others (that is, negative liberty, conceived as consisting in absence of interference by others) gets its value from the role it plays in facilitating freedom to pursue our own projects and implement our own plans, it's natural to wonder whether negative liberty (as defined) is unique in having this sort of instrumental value. What if—in addition to negative liberty (conceived as freedom from interference by others)—importance or value of precisely the same sort attaches also to the fulfillment of certain further conditions? What if there are other conditions—that is, conditions other than 'noninterference by others'—of our being in a position to give effect to our own conceptions of the good life through pursuit of valued projects and through implementation of valued plans?"

In response to this, the first thing to point out is that indeed it is absolutely obvious that liberty from other people is not unique in importance to any individual. My ability to play tennis, say (I use the example because I am completely uninterested in tennis, but lots of people are) is obviously interfered with by the onset of arthritis or cancer or, say, lack of funds to join the adjacent Tennis Club. Now, Alistair lists as his examples "opportunities to develop skills and competences" and "the economic resources needed for implementation." Absolutely right: these can be and often are impediments to us. So what? For the question is whether one means of achieving these in various cases, namely by compelling others to help supply the needed opportunities or funds, should be politically open to us. My answer is: no, it should not. That's just what libertarianism holds.

Now, Alistair's take on this is that we need to find out two things: "First, the obstacles must be comparable. Second, the obstacles must be comparably important." But notice at this point that he does not raise the questions, comparable to whom and important for what? He just assumes that we can raise these questions, just like that, in the legislature. Politicians will do the comparing and the estimating of importance. This is a fundamental point of disagreement between us. Those politicians would be judging these issues for their constituents. If Bill thinks that a certain possible impediment either to his own or some other person's, or maybe every other person's, freedom of action is worth paying $x to remove or help removing, then he will pay. But if not? On Alistair's view, somebody else gets to judge this, and decide for Bill to charge Bill the $X that Bill does not think are worth paying. Of course he'll charge Sam and Audrey and so on, too. Possibly he thinks that if a majority of Bill's fellows think that Bill will "do better" if he gets or is allowed to do x, then that's what is better for him. I deny both that other persons' judgements are to be accounted superior to Bill's, and that we should be talking this way at all. Interpersonal comparisons of values are not to be allowed to enter into social decision-making in this way.

Alistair is far from the first to suppose that governments, somehow, are allowed to make interpersonal comparisons of utility and to use them as the basis of action that is then supported, involuntarily, by members of the community. But if he's asking, "why shouldn't the members in question go along with this?," the answer is that they don't want to do it. Why isn't that sufficient? Claiming that the claims of others are "more important" will get you nowhere with an individual who has his or her own goals to pursue. That individual is happy to trade in some of his liberties in order to get certain kinds of obstacles to certain pursuits on the part of certain persons removed. That's the response to Alistair's point that other things may be "more important" than liberty. Of course they might—more important to a certain individual, who will thereby be motivated to trade in some of his liberty to achieve that. Everyone, in our view, should have the right to make such decisions for himself.

Now, the social contract idea is that the fundamental principles in this area are to be objects of unanimous agreement—not subject to majority vote, unless, somehow, the unanimous agreement is that we should decide this by majority vote. That isn't going to happen, I should think, with proposals to leave people subject to imposition for things they don't desire. On the other hand, for things they do desire, and to achieve which they need the help of others—what they have to do is persuade those others that it is worth doing, usually by making them an offer of services they find valuable; and they've got a deal. That's the free market way of getting things done. But Alistair wants to dwell in a sort of person-neutral realm of political value, where somehow judgments about what to do can be made without reference to the wills of those who are to do it, unless perhaps in the sense provided by a democratic vote. But that's all fake. There are only the values and judgments of individual people, and if you want to insist on using some of the values and judgments of other people for political purposes, thus to decide what's going to happen to me, or Bill, or whoever, then you are into a very different moral and political outlook than the libertarian one.

I should note, too, that the claim to know which of the innumerable possible obstacles to which of the innumerable possible interests and values people do have are "worth more" than the liberty of those who would be coerced into helping remove them, would be pretty well impossible. As innumerable socialist experiments have shown, when it comes to matching individual desires to individual means of satisfying those desires, the market does best—not surprisingly. When we appreciate that it is individuals' actions that are the subjects of all these disquisitions, it's not hard to understand why that's the way to do things: viz., by the decisions and voluntary actions of those individuals.

So his claim that "The upshot is that Narveson's account of the rationale for the negative liberty ideal seems to undermine the claim he would like to be able to make about libertarianism in the version he favors being a corollary of endorsement of the ideal" is seen to be a huge misunderstanding. We "endorse the ideal of liberty" when we understand that our actions are motivated by our interests—not somebody else's—and thus that any individual ipso facto must decide which of his various liberties to curtail in the interests of pursuing which objectives—not someone else, whether that someone was elected or not.

Alistair misunderstands my reasoning on behalf of the social contract for liberty, when he says "it looks as though the question of what it would cost a society to implement the needed measures is simply irrelevant. If it proved to be too costly to implement the needed welfare state measures, a social decision not to provide such measures might indeed have to be made." My point was not, just as such, about "what it would cost a society." It was about what it would cost an individual to accept a fundamental principle of one kind rather than another. There is no issue of "cost to society" in the social contract view. The libertarian program, I argue, gives each individual the best result in the sense that the benefits to a given individual outweigh the costs to that individual (the costs may or may not be monetary, of course). On the libertarian program, the only costs I must involuntarily endure are the costs that I would incur for imposing costs on others. For such things, I can't reasonably object to others trying to set matters right by compelling me to desist or to compensate those I have "invaded and despoiled." Beyond that, however, the question is why one would put in for a principle that imposed costs for the purpose of benefiting others in ways for which one would get no compensation at all. Voluntary insurance groups, after all, can be formed to guard against various possible maladies and emergencies, at prices accepted by all concerned. Involuntary ones, on the other hand, while they might possibly give benefits, will also impose costs that one would not, if one had one's choice, have been willing to buy at that price.

Alistair wants to impose a fundamentally socialist ideology on the social contract. But that's exactly what the social contract is out to avoid!

In his third section, Alistair undertakes to pursue further the question whether Sterba and I are really disagreeing, despite appearances. He reiterates, "despite the lip-service they both give to a merely 'negative' construal of the content of the liberty ideal, they disagree about which the 'negative liberties' are that the ideal should be taken to protect." The question is, however, why we disagree about this. For the libertarian principle allows only one consideration here: does the thing in question interfere with—that is, impose on—the liberty of others? Now, I claim that Sterba and I disagree in ways which imply that Sterba has gone beyond the bounds of the libertarian principle, which holds that the only justification for using force lies in the threat of force from others—that only defense justifies it. Sterba wants to add to this, "defense" from starvation, even where nobody else is imposing the starvation in question. I don't see how that cannot be an addition. It can certainly be a misunderstanding: Sterba continually insists that we have to assess the relative values of the two liberties in question (the liberty to use peaceably acquired resources as one wants vs. the liberty to take resources from other when one really "needs" them despite those others having peaceably acquired them). The ball is in his court on this one, so far as I can see.

Now, Alistair is correct in pointing out that I initially attributed to Jim a much narrower and, I should think, more plausible view than the one he turns out to be defending. The view I thought he had was that only the needs of others that are really basic to life—food, water, air (normally it's only the first that's in question) would justify the incursions he thinks they are entitled to. But then it turns out that he's upping the ante so that falling below contemporarily fashionable politically-enshrined "poverty lines" counts as well. Not only must I allow people to take from my peaceably made income to keep alive, but they also get to do so in the interests of that second color TV set, and all the other things that persons below the American poverty line are accustomed to. To take and take and take, then—leaving us with contemporary tax levels in the area of 50 percent of our incomes. Trying to defend that in the name of liberty seems to me quite an incredible undertaking.

At the end, Alistair, in an interesting and revealing paragraph, says that we are really asking two different questions: "To give content to the liberty ideal . . . is to be committed to asking about which the liberties or freedoms are that individuals ought to have if they are to live satisfactory (fulfilling, etc.) lives. . . . To give content to the equality ideal, by contrast, is to be committed to asking how a society's institutions—social, economic, legal, political, etc.—ought to be structured if all the members of a society are to be afforded an equal opportunity to live their lives in a satisfactory and fulfilling way."

Well, that is not the question that libertarianism answers. To put it that way is, as I say, to cloak the whole thing in socialist premises entirely alien to the individualism that is the fundamental source of the liberalism of the West. We are not out to say what your life would be best having. We are out to say that if we are dealing with each other, the best principle by which to do so is the one that allows each the maximum liberty compatible with the extension of a like liberty to others. You want this, no doubt, because you think that the things you will thus be permitted to do are the ones that will give you your best life. I may or may not agree with you on that point; but whether I do is not what this is all about, because it's beside the point. Those judgments are yours to make, not mine.

And as to egalitarianism—well, Jim or anyone is entitled to take equality to be a fundamental normative commitment, no doubt—but not under the banner of liberty. I am not asking Alistair's other question because I reject the egalitarianism it (without argument) invokes. Alistair is right to say, I think, that if someone is going to be an egalitarian by the libertarian route, he would have to proceed by trying to show that somehow the liberty principle itself, in the "negative" form in which both Jim and I (claim to) understand it, entails this. I frankly don't see how this could be done, and I certainly don't think he has succeeded—but I think we both agree that he's got his work cut out for him if that's what he's trying to do!

It might seem a little more promising to hold that we all ought to accept as a requirement of justice that we at least keep each other alive when the actions of others are required to do this. A little more promising, yes—but not enough to do the job. For I am clearly not, in any sense, invading you when I fail to feed you, no matter how much you need it. The claim that, as a member of the human race in good standing, I would subscribe to a principle that would impose on us all the enforceable duty to help our fellow man when in need may look a lot more promising than the huge, across-the-board egalitarianism that Sterba has now put in for. But in the end, I claim it is not acceptable either. For everybody, which includes me, to subscribe to that principle is still to call for more than a rational individual would find acceptable in many circumstances. I'll do better to accept a principle that leaves even those decisions up to me rather than permitting "society" to impose their version on me instead.

I continue to insist, then, that (a) the liberty principle is univocal, and what it says cannot really be stretched to accommodate even Jim's minimal level of welfarism; (b) that the social contract yields the liberty principle and nothing more; and (c) that we shouldn't distort the social contract idea which, I claim, underwrites libertarianism by seeing it through socialist lenses from the start.

Jan Narveson, University of Waterloo

Notes

1.   Immanuel Kant, *The Metaphysical Principles of Justice*, trans. John Ladd (Indianapolis, IN: Bobbs-Merrill Co., Library of Liberal Arts, 1965), 35. From Kant's *Doctrine of Right* [Intro] "C. Universal Principle of Right: 'Every action is right which in itself, or in the maxim on which it proceeds, is such that it can coexist along with the freedom of the will of each and all in action, according to a universal law.'"

2.   Anthony de Jasay, "Self-Contradictory Contractariansm," in *For and Against the State*, ed. Jan Narveson and John T. Sanders (Lanham, MD: Rowman & Littlefield, 1996), 137–70.

3.   Frederic Bastiat, *The Law* (Foundation of Economic Education), http://fee.org/library/books/the-law-by-frederic-bastiat-free-download/. See also Jan Narveson, "What, Then, Is Law? It Is the Collective Organization of the Individual Right to Lawful Defense," *Classics of Political Philosophy* 2010, 159.

4.   Jan Narveson, *The Libertarian Idea* (Peterborough, Ontario: Broadview Press, 2001), 32–40.

Part V:
NASSP Book Award:
Amartya Sen, *The Idea of Justice*

Reciprocity, Closed-Impartiality, and National Borders: Framing (and Extending) the Debate on Global Justice

DEEN CHATTERJEE

Abstract: Liberal nationalists have been hard pressed to respond to the normative demands of human rights and global impartiality in justifying special redistributive requirements for fellow citizens in a democratic polity. In general, they tend to support disparate standards of distributive justice for insiders and outsiders by favoring a relational approach to justice that affirms co-national preferences while not denying the importance of global impartiality. Following Sen and critiquing Rawls, I re-frame the debate by re-configuring the notion of relationality with a globalist tilt, with the hope of rescuing the discourse on global justice from its current stalemate.

L iberal nationalists have been hard pressed to respond to the normative demands of human rights and global impartiality in justifying special redistributive require-ments toward co-nationals. In general, they tend to support disparate standards of distributive justice for insiders and outsiders by favoring a relational approach to justice that affirms co-national preferences while not denying the importance of global impartiality. Some of them hold that ties of community create special duties of obligation toward co-nationals. For them, unless the imperative of global impartiality is circumscribed within the claims of culture, it would run counter to this commonly held bias toward moral closeness.

Though the idea of a normative theory is to go beyond existing bias and not be based on it, these liberal nationalists who cite claims of culture to justify compatriot partiality seem to fall prey to this trap. Normative theories of justice should rise beyond the everyday bias of the vast majority of people. The claim that obligations of distributive justice are shaped by shared cultural practices and apply primarily within communities is to conflate justice with the socio-political status quo. Michael Walzer (1984), Yael Tamir (1993), and David Miller (1995) are three such theorists who espouse the theme, in their own ways, that distributive justice is local—not global—because its viability is determined by the standards internal to the community. However, community consensus, shared social history, or felt cultural identities are contingent matters; they do not provide an inherently normative justification for principled discrimination between insiders and outsiders. If normative obligations were based on existing biases and social sentiments, then that would make morality easy and convenient. To properly construe egalitarian impartiality in the liberal theory of justice, one has to go beyond the contingency of prevailing social and cultural norms, practices, and expectations that can change over time. Otherwise, the contingency of the prevailing norm, when changed, can support a very different conclusion, making the criterion useless in deciding between the viability of local and global justice. One can point out, for instance, that the reason cosmopolitan norm is not yet a felt reality is because it does not correspond to people's desire to connect themselves beyond their small units, but if and when people's felt identities and their objects of loyalty expand to coincide with the global domain, political globalization may go hand in hand with economic globalization. (see Richard Arneson 2003 and 2004; Andrew Oldenquist 2007. See also Gillian Brock 2009, 262). In other words, shared social meaning or collective practices can change depending on contingent factors and should not be the criterion for moral justification.

The majority of liberal nationalists approach the topic of compatriot preference from a different angle. Their rejection of cosmopolitanism is not based on claims of culture; for them, disparate standards of justice in the name of moral equality of persons is justified on the basis of duties generated due to citizenship in a political community. Richard Miller (2010), Michael Blake (2002), and Thomas Nagel (2005) are three such theorists. Despite their differences on some of the details, their views are sufficiently similar. For them, citizens in a liberal democratic polity collectively participate in the political project of coercively imposing rules of self-development and loyalty on one another, thereby creating institutions of political trust and mutuality. Self-governance in a democratic polity creates shared obligations that are collectively binding, unlike that with outsiders with whom we do not have such binding contracts.

Blake, Richard Miller, and Nagel—like Walzer, Tamir, and David Miller—can also be faulted for not providing a principled moral defense of a distinct idea of equality for fellow citizens in a liberal polity. After all, why should the absence of mutually binding coercive laws to individuals outside of national boundaries be normatively relevant for distributive equality within state borders when such borders and the exclusionary scheme they project are themselves contingent and can be viewed as morally arbitrary? Blake, Richard Miller, and Nagel take for granted the existence of states and build their normative justification based on that empirical premise. However, the premise itself needs to be normatively justified. The burden of proof seems to rest on those who would offer a statist justification for a distinct principle of moral equality based on boundaries. The locus of the concern is the justifiability of the connection between the normative reasons the three theorists provide for distributive equality amongst citizens and the contingency of common coercive laws. In a different world void of the modern state system, they would lack the needed empirical basis for their normative claim; in fact, in such a world, their claim for a distinct egalitarian principle for co-nationals would be redundant. As A. J. Julius has observed: "The ground for justice cannot be decided by speculating on its scope" (Julius 2006, 178). If the contingency of the political arrangements is allowed to reflect the normative scope of equality in a manner that favors special equality amongst fellow citizens, then the statist tilt enters at the outset of the debate, making the burden of proof rest on the side of the globalists. But if liberal egalitarianism is to be taken seriously, then it seems that the burden of proof should be the other way around.[1]

In a recent article, Andrea Sangiovanni claims that the normative ideal of a demanding equality for co-nationals is a requirement of reciprocity, not state coercion. Noting that reciprocity presupposes a relational view of distributive justice, he finds cosmopolitan global justice unacceptable because he sees it as non-relational and is based on the demand of moral personhood independent of institutional and cooperative affiliations. He admits that though there is a system of reciprocity and shared participation in the global order, and though there is no meaningful exit option among the states in the global order, inequality among fellow citizens is more troubling than inequality between residents of different states because fellow citizens "depend on, contribute, and are subject to the same system of legal and political institutions" that make up their own state (Sangiovanni 2007, 32). Accordingly, he too predicates the idea of reciprocity on appropriate institutional arrangements operative within a state. For a substantive principle of relational justice, based on the concept of reciprocity among fellow citizens in a liberal polity, Sangiovanni turns to the Rawlsian notion of justice as fairness.

Sangiovanni concedes that a reciprocity-based institutional arrangement need not presuppose the need for state boundaries. Reciprocity is open to other institutional arrangements that may eventually evolve. Accordingly, Sangiovanni's anti-globalism, though more nuanced, is still vulnerable to the same critique of being contingent and arbitrary that I labeled against the other liberal nationalists. He is against abstract non-relational globalism, but not necessarily against a relational global justice if the world institutional order would permit it. In that sense, he is not that far off from Nagel who, more than other liberal nationalists, insists on the imperatives of a global government for global justice to be viable. Accordingly, my critique of Nagel and other liberal nationalists would seem to apply to Sangiovanni as well.

Interestingly, nearly three decades ago, Richard Dagger made similar points that are so prominently featured in today's debate on the ground and scope of distributive justice.[2] In defending a qualified version of "moral parochialism," he observes: "Compatriots take priority because we owe it to them as a matter of reciprocity" (Dagger 1985, 446). For him, "the adoption of a human rights perspective does not force one to hold that the bonds of political community count for little or nothing" (Dagger 1985, 437). A broad variation of this position is held today by almost all liberal egalitarians regardless of whether they are statists or globalists. In that sense, Dagger not only predates and anticipates Sangiovanni and other liberal nationalists cited above but also the (non-cosmopolitan) later Rawls and most of the "Rawlsian" globalists such as Charles Beitz and Thomas Pogge.[3] All of them rely on Rawls for their substantive principles of justice but use their own grounding principles to modify and direct them accordingly. Beitz's "functional" approach to human rights is a veiled tribute to later Rawls (Beitz 2009) whereas Pogge's "situated" cosmopolitanism calling for global redistribution "as an obligation incurred in institutionally routinized interaction and not as the pre-institutional requirement of equal concern or fairness" (Julius 2006, 178) is an attempt to set Rawls right (Pogge 2002).

For all these reasons, it is important to take a critical look at Rawls on some of these issues (Rawls 1993, 1999, 2001). The fact that for well over these thirty years many of the same topics are being revived and debated on a predictable line among the cosmopolitan liberals and liberal nationalists seems to tell us that there's an impasse in the debate over these issues. Much of that has to do with the contractarian approach prevalent in today's political philosophy. The statism/globalism debate is an example, owing much of its rhetoric to Rawls's construal of public reason to justify state coercion in a system of reasonable pluralism. Rawls's idea of overlapping consensus predicated on the institutionally mediated relations holding within political communities has been critiqued for falling short of the demands of both egalitarian justice and democratic legitimacy. Critics point out his inadequate response to the demands of multiculturalism and his rejection of global justice in this context.

Multiculturalism and global justice have been two Achilles heels for the liberals, and Rawls is no exception. As I flesh out a few pertinent ideas from Rawls, we will see why the Rawlsian approach has led us to an impasse on some of the important issues of justice. It will also help us decide whether the debate could be fruitfully extended to and framed in a different setting. We will see why Amartya Sen's idea of justice, along with his critique of the Rawlsian contractarian approach, elevates the discourse to a new height. Below I focus on Rawls and Sen to show how the twin issues of multiculturalism and global justice relate to the debate on co-national partiality and global impartiality with regard to distributive justice.

The multiculturalist challenge to the liberal ideal of a just society that professes to be secular, inclusive, and egalitarian is a powerful reminder, echoed by Rawls himself in his later writings, that a viable liberal theory of justice must adequately articulate its professed claims of tolerance, pluralism, and impartiality. Liberal society's commitment to equality entails democratic pluralism, which means mainstream equality of even illiberal groups and cultures. But this requires a nuanced balancing of several competing claims on several fronts, which poses a dilemma for liberalism. Critics point out that multicultural accommodation in a pluralistic society may require giving minority cultures greater protection and more autonomy, especially in areas where their religious and cultural commitments pertaining to their identity may seem to be at stake, regardless of whether or not those commitments are compatible with liberal egalitarian values. In fact, Rawls himself has pointed out that an impartial liberal theory is not incompatible with distinct principles of affirmative equality with regard to illiberal groups—within reason, of course.

However, multicultural and democratic theorists alike have pointed out that despite the seeming commitment to neutrality, Rawls's idea of what counts as reasonable has a liberal tilt at the outset of the debate. They point out that liberalism needs to recognize the minority groups' reason on its own terms to give it validation; otherwise, the concept of public reason between reasonable parties would be a hollow idea. In fact, though Rawls's transition from robust egalitarianism to his political liberalism took place partly in response to some of these concerns, democratic theorists have challenged Rawls for not working at the grassroots level due to his liberal pre-commitments. Though Rawls himself has championed the connection between liberal justice and the practice of democracy, critics contend that the Rawlsian reasonable pluralism is not democratic enough. As Habermas has noted, Rawls's theory "generates a priority of liberal rights which demotes the democratic process to an inferior status" (Habermas 1995, 127, cited by Sen 2009, 325). Seyla Benhabib has aptly described this liberal conundrum as "the paradox of democratic legitimacy" (Benhabib 2005; see also Benhabib 2006; Bohman 2000; Cohen 1997; Deveaux 2006; Swaine 2006; and Young 2002).

Cosmopolitan liberals, on the other hand, have critiqued Rawls's political liberalism for being much too negotiable and not sufficiently committed to substantive liberalism (Buchanan 2004; Kuper 2004; Pogge 2002; Singer 2002). Thus, claims of conflicting equalities have posed a formidable dilemma for Rawls—a dilemma that seems to be endemic to the contractarian approach in general. Sen's "comparative" approach is set to go beyond the Rawlsian limitations by effectively responding to the twin challenges of grassroots democracy and substantive liberalism. Let me explain.

In his *The Idea of Justice* (2009), Sen calls the Rawlsian contractarian approach "transcendental institutionalism," focused on the idea of perfect justice via ideal institutional arrangements, not on actual societies and actual lives of people. The Rawlsian theory of justice, following the terminology made famous by Rawls himself, is about an ideal theory. In contrast, Sen proposes a comparative and pluralistic approach that is primarily about rectifying injustice than locating ideal justice. Though institutions play a crucial role in Sen's idea of justice, Sen's focus is not on ideal arrangements. Rather, his concern is more practical, guided by the realities of people's lives and capabilities. It is also more inclusive in its enunciation of what counts as reasonable, putting more emphasis on open public deliberation in the democratic process than the direction taken and typified by Rawls.

With this broad sketch of the two contrasting approaches, I now focus on some of the details.

The Rawlsian conception of reciprocity under reasonable pluralism is the idea of reasonable agreement—endorsing an arrangement that all can allegedly agree with. This is the civic face of prudential rationality of self-interested free people in the original position that was meant to produce, for Rawls, a unique set of principles of justice, yielding the Rawlsian basic structure of a just society (Rawls 1971). Rawls himself has raised doubts in his restatement of justice as fairness about whether his matrix of impartiality is poised to yield only one set of principles uniquely suited to his ideally just institutional arrangements (Rawls 2001, 132–4, cited by Sen 2009, 12). Early on, Sen himself, along with Kenneth Arrow and other economists, has raised this same concern. In his *The Idea of Justice*, Sen goes beyond Rawls on the idea of impartiality, calling his own idea "open impartiality," compatible with a multiplicity of competing principles, in contrast to Rawls's "closed impartiality." Citing Scanlon's non-rejectibility thesis—not what all can agree with but what nobody can reasonably reject—Sen makes the case for a "plurality of unbiased principles" that would meaningfully relate to the idea of democracy as public reasoning, or what he calls "government by discussion" (Sen 2009, 408–10). This is meant to be an inclusive and non-parochial idea of reasonable pluralism that is set to accommodate public discussion among disparate groups in a diverse world, thus catering to the democratic challenges of deliberation and difference.[4]

Sen shows us the need to recognize the existence of different approaches to the pursuit of reasonable behavior, not all of which need to be based on the reciprocity-based reasoning of mutually beneficial acts. He would like us to go beyond the Rawlsian limits of reasonable pluralism to the plurality of impartial reasons embedded in today's expanding circle of global democratic human-rights approach. Because the notion of human rights is predicated on our shared humanity, Sen's version of public reason is meant to take us not only beyond reasoning among fellow citizens across cultural divides but also beyond the limitations of national or state boundaries.

Sen's capabilities approach highlights his idea that the demands of a shared humanity require a broadening of the human-rights model from its state-centric institutional limitations. Along with this global tilt, the neutral capabilities agenda gives the rights discourse the substance it needs, thus providing a broad appeal across cultures and political boundaries. However, Sen points out that because capabilities are certain indicators of individual functioning and opportunities only, they by themselves cannot adequately account for the fairness or equity of the process involved in justice. For Sen, equality has multiple dimensions, including equality of capabilities, so equality is a concern in distributional equations, and enhancement of equality is an important consideration in promoting justice. But pursuit of justice for him is a nuanced and complex procedure where the focus on equality cannot trump the demand for procedural equity (Sen 2009, 295–8; see also 2005).

Thus, Sen's theory of justice caters to both the fairness of the process and the enhancement of freedom and opportunities. For Sen, these two demands are to be understood and realized in their comprehensive outcomes through the matrix of social choice. Though Sen appreciates the republican idea of freedom as non-domination, i.e., freedom from interference, direct or indirect, and would agree to the need for guaranteed and realistic provisions for ensuring such freedom wherever possible, he realizes that in the real world of interdependence and injustice, we cannot exercise control over every aspect of our life. Hence, he would emphasize the importance of understanding freedom as "substantive opportunity"—opportunities that we can actually have "to lead the kind of life we want and value" (Gotoh and Dumauchel 2009, 302–3; see also, Sen 2009, 304–9). Thus, the capabilities approach, though not inconsistent with the republican idea of freedom as non-domination, is more nuanced and realistic, opening up a wider dimension in our understanding of freedom. Sen's comparative methodology, conjoined with his capabilities approach, tells us that even when we cannot have freedom as an available option in the republican sense, some option can still give us more freedom than other options, thus helping us in the pursuit of the idea of justice as Sen understands it. Social choice mechanism decides how this expanded idea of freedom fares in relation to other competing ideas of equality, and how the idea of equality measures in the matrix of justice where equity of the process is the other important consideration.

Sen doesn't take illiberal communities to be uniformly insular and homogeneous. He understands that, like all groups, there are minorities within minority groups. Accordingly, Sen is hopeful that the universal mandates of human rights would trump the claims of oppressive practices in the name of religious or cultural autonomy by the leaders claiming to be speaking for the group (Sen 1997). The global forces of exposure and interaction are at work in all societies, making it difficult for societies to remain insular and for groups to be unexposed to evolving global human rights culture. Liberal democracy can use its own tool of grassroots democratic discourse to win over the hearts and minds of a moderate majority unable to find an exit option due to the vocal leadership of the extreme minorities. Sen's idea of open impartiality in the process of public reasoning is that the interests and needs of all affected persons, irrespective of their cultural or political membership, are given due and impartial considerations, thus connecting with them on issues that they value.

By re-framing and reinforcing certain ideas in Sen's capabilities approach, one can show how this idea of internal reasoning can be effectively deployed to reach out to those members of the illiberal communities (who could be the majority in the community) who are disenchanted by the rigidity of the groups' beliefs and practices. Sen's idea of public reasoning within and among groups can be utilized as a strategic device without filtering liberalism of its normative substance as a precondition for public deliberation.

Ingrained in Sen's idea of open impartiality is the universal mandate of broader humanity that makes room for multi-faceted and overlapping identities of individuals and groups. Sen has shown us how the exclusivity of any singular identity can lead to confrontation and violence (Sen 2006). Because the notion of human rights is predicated on our shared humanity, Sen's brand of public reason can take us beyond the Rawlsian dilemma of multiculturalism. Public reason, qua public, responds well in cutting through the rigidity of exclusive identities because it is predicated on open impartiality.

Contractarian theory of justice is also limited on another front. Such a theory is not overtly conducive to the philosophical debate that is embedded enough in empirical research.[5] Indeed, increasing attention to the empirical details has been boosting the efforts of the theorists to prescribe realistic and achievable directives, thus narrowing the gap between theoretical pronouncements and practical impediments. In fact, Sen's own studies have shown that the claim that there are unjudgeable differences across cultures on such issues as human rights is in fact overblown, thus making it easier for human rights theorists, including Sen, to claim that any undue restriction of rights in the name of local culture would be difficult to sustain in a globally vigilant and interconnected world (Sen 1997 and 2004). The social choice mechanism in Sen's comparative approach can help us toward mitigating many of these conundrums by making the social decision-procedure more "informationally sensitive" (Sen 2009, 93).

Sen's idea of justice makes it clear that though the issues of justice should not be defined or determined by cultural claims or group imperatives, they ought to be contextually sensitive if they are meant to have any sway over people's lives and imaginations. Thus, claims of justice ought to be understood and evaluated against the backdrop of a variety of cultural, social, historical, and other considerations that may often be unique to the groups or nations concerned. Accordingly, one need not be unduly deferential toward cultural demands by making liberalism a vacuous doctrine, as Rawls has been accused of doing in his political liberalism, nor should liberalism's pursuit of fairness and impartiality ignore cultural identities and variations. Thus, Sen shows us that liberalism can be both substantive and negotiable.

Rawls's limitations in responding to the demands of democratic pluralism in his political liberalism are reflected in his law of peoples. Rawls sees a rather limited scope for international obligation, comprising only a duty of assistance to burdened societies. As Sen notes, the Rawlsian closed impartiality generates "exclusionary neglect," leaving open the possibility of parochialism in neglecting "all voices from everywhere." In contrast to this Rawlsian "international justice" that relies on partitioning of the global population into distinct "nations" or "peoples," Sen is looking for "global justice," which, for him, caters primarily to actual lives of peoples and less on peoples as a political unit (Sen, 2009, 388–415). Indeed, Sen has been instrumental in drawing attention to the multiple identities of human beings across the world, and he sees no reason why national divisions should have any automatic, and hence undue, priority over other categorizations.

So, for Sen, a statist paradigm of justice would be arbitrary, especially in today's world where human associations breach political boundaries. The inability of the liberal nationalists to make the reach of liberal justice extend beyond state boundaries is rooted in their perceived non-feasibility of a cosmopolitan social contract because of the lack of relevant institutional arrangements of a shared and participatory global governance. Sen cites Nagel for his (Nagel's) skepticism of global justice based on this reason (Sen 2009, 25). In contrast, Sen believes in the search for global justice and mitigation of global injustices through his Adam Smithian route of open impartiality that is more practical and that is less dependent on ideal global institutional arrangements. Sen's approach would call for relieving suffering and injustices as practicable in the real world through a combination of institutional propriety as well as through what he calls "social realization" that would reflect people's functioning and capabilities in their social interactions. His carefully worked out social-choice matrix offers the needed empirical guidance and the grounding principles.

Predictably, Nagel and other liberal nationalists would be skeptical of Sen's "looser" Smithian approach toward global justice. However, I submit that Sen's re-configured notion of relationality, construed not necessarily in terms of the Rawlsian reciprocity between equals but with a more careful look at the empirical details of the actual global realities of entrenched inequalities, could direct Nagel, Sangiovanni, and others to proceed from contingent statism to principled globalism.

Sen draws our attention to a diverse world not necessarily of sterile reasonable pluralism but of fundamental value pluralism and of radical gap in terms of power and resources. He argues that we have responsibility to the global poor precisely because of the asymmetry between us—our power and their vulnerability—and not necessarily because of any symmetry that takes us to the need for cooperation and reciprocity. This turn in approach makes Sen's idea of justice open to the world. Drawing from the story of the Good Samaritan in the Gospel of Luke, where Jesus questions the idea of fixed neighborhood, Sen concludes that "there are few non-neighborhoods left in the world today" (Sen 2009, 173). If our neighborhood is our wide open world, then, for Sen, the entire debate on justice and injustice needs to be cast in the actual world, with recognition of need, vulnerabilities, and dependencies, as well as overlapping spheres of engagement and interaction all around.

The social choice matrix in Sen's theory is a measured response to the demandingness of justice predicated on the global world. Unlike Peter Singer's principle of beneficence in his demanding cosmopolitanism that was roundly critiqued for its moral rigorism (Singer 1972), Sen's idea of justice is based on social realization which, unlike Singer's utilitarianism, is broad, situated, and agent-sensitive. It is a theory of justice "as practical reason," as Sen calls it (Gotoh and Dumouchel 2009, 299), relying on consequential evaluation of need, ability, choice, responsibility, and other features in a comprehensive scheme (cf. Sen, 2000). As a non-ideal theory, it does not need an ideal counterpart or a notion of perfect justice. Likewise, as a theory of justice, it distinguishes between beneficence and justice. Though beneficence is an important consideration in promoting justice, pursuit of justice for Sen is based on social choice mechanism where the focus on beneficence needs to be integrated with the fairness of the process.

Sen's approach helps us understand that the narrow conundrum of statism versus globalism that has led to so much debate in the justice literature need not be an irreconcilable dilemma within liberalism. If a pluralistic theory of justice for Sen has several dimensions based on the demands of social realization, then statist claims may indeed play their part in deciding on justice, but they need not by themselves be decisive. Indeed, attention to claims of political or cultural community would be no different from taking note of other relevant claims in responding to the comparative merits of available alternatives. Accordingly, the two camps of statism and globalism should not pose a case of conflicting loyalties but that of multiple loyalties. Claims of statism may sometimes compete with wider objects of loyalty such as globalism, but nested multiple loyalties, like our plurality of identities, is a challenge that we negotiate all the time. Consequently, Sen's idea of justice is nuanced enough to resist fixed labels. Though justice for Sen is predicated on the global world, he is not a globalist or a cosmopolitan if this is understood to require a single global standard of distributive equality or a global application of principles of domestic justice.

Critics have questioned the feasibility of what they take to be Sen's rejection of an ideal theory of justice (Freeman 2010; Simmons 2010; Swift 2008). They claim that a non-ideal theory needs an ideal counterpart. It seems to me that the best defense on Sen's behalf is to restate the pertinent details of his theory that would suitably respond to this concern.

Sen calls his own idea of justice a theory "in a very broad sense," not aimed at determining the nature of perfect justice at an ideal level, but an exercise "that aims at guiding practical reasoning about what should be done" (Sen 2009, ix). For Sen, to be focused on identifying the demands of perfect justice is an exercise in futility. Perfect justice in theory is a difficult if not an impossible pursuit due to the possibly divergent priorities over of competing demands such as the utilitarian, the egalitarian, and the libertarian, none of which stands out as more reasonable than the others from the perspective of reason and open impartiality. Even if we can determine what perfect justice demands, remedying existing injustices by aspiring toward perfect justice via ideal arrangements is by no means guaranteed. Accordingly, instead of offering yet another grand theory of justice at an ideal level, Sen's approach focuses on assessing the comparative merits of available states of affairs. For him, we do not need to know—or agree on—what perfect justice is in order to be able to identify a particular state of affairs as unjust and how it stands in relation to some other state of affairs. This comparative approach can guide us in assessing and ranking available alternatives without the need to speculate on all possible outcomes. Even if this procedure cannot resolve all competing claims at times, "valuational plurality" makes public reasoning challenging, to be celebrated than shunned in a democracy. Too strict a commitment to definitive terms of justice risks neglecting injustices that fall outside of the preconfigured ideal and crowds out potential resolutions to injustice that do not fall under the ideal model yet may nevertheless prove valuable to the pursuit of a more just state of affairs.

Sen's approach calls for empowerment of existing institutions, both global and domestic, that are democratically responsive and open to unconstrained public scrutiny through global public reasoning. Sen's theory of justice is "a theory of normative social choice" (Sen 2009, 410), catering to both the equity of the process and enhancement of freedom, leading to comprehensive outcomes. In fact, over the decades Sen has been instrumental in drawing the world's attention to the limitations of rational choice and the virtues of social choice. Though Rawls made a strong case for including moral constraints in rational choice, Sen takes us beyond Rawls. Sen's theory of justice is a prime example of this.

Thus, though Sen does not focus on an ideal theory in the Rawlsian sense and on an ideal set of institutional arrangements, he in no way disregards the importance of institutions or the need for an appropriate normative theory. But instead of going top down with ideals first, his approach is to provide a comprehensive method that is pluralistic. Like the just-war doctrine where no single component decides for the entire set or for an ideal resolution, and where the push is for a comparative, comprehensive, and practical approach that responds to the need for deciding when it is okay to resort to war and how to go about it in the real world, Sen's idea of justice calls for a nuanced balancing—led by public reasoning—of several vital components none of which by itself is meant to be decisive.

In today's interdependent world, cosmopolitan liberals would be quite at home with the idea of a relational interpretation of justice, not exclusively in terms of reciprocity but broadly construed in terms of human encounters and relations. They would find Sen's approach appealing. Though some of these cosmopolitan liberals were early Rawlsians, now they have suitably modified their own approach.

Beitz utilizes the "practical/political" aspect of Rawls's later ideas in carving out a "functional" account of human rights meant for the real world. Pogge is focused on the idea of a global re-distribution of resources, a decidedly non-Rawlsian approach. Both Pogge and Beitz emphasize the need for an egalitarian democratic global order. Sen cites both of them with approval.[6]

The idea of a democratic world order is not that premature. Global trends indicate that the process of moving in that direction is already under way. The global recognition of endemic poverty and systemic inequity as serious human rights concerns has put pressure on individual countries for internal democratic reforms and made vivid the need for more just and effective international institutional directives. The demands of the developing countries in various world summits for democratic reform of the international global order are getting progressively vocal. Likewise, global socio-economic issues are increasingly dominating the agenda of the rich countries in their G-8 meetings, paving the way to the recent G-20 summits.

Today's entrenched global order affects all nations, especially the poor ones, and thus indirectly their citizens. It is well documented that the pervasive state-failure to respond to its citizens' broader human needs is linked to the inequity in the global order itself. Sen's justice project is centrally tied to the viability of democracy in a global world—both in the global order itself and in individual nations. He and Joseph Stiglitz (2002), among others, have been providing the conceptual framework for the slowly emerging trend of democratization of globalization. Indeed, one great achievement of development ethicists like Sen, Stiglitz, and Martha Nussbaum (2006) is that they have shown a viable way to shift the focus of global development from things to people. Accordingly, it is the task of an empirically informed liberal theory to conceptualize how to promote the democratic norms of equality and fair political participation on the domestic front and in the global system. At the least, it would call for an institutional rearrangement in the international order that would be democratically responsive and reflect the fluid dynamics of collaboration and interdependence in today's global world. For that, according to Sen, one need not be focused on ideal justice and ideal institutional arrangements, but on the need for *enabling* institutions. An ancient Chinese proverb is relevant here: Hope is like a road on the earth—at first, there is no road, but when more and more people try it, a road is formed.

Normative pronouncements, empirical analysis, and strategies of enforcements must go together to make viable the theories of global justice and human rights. Cross-disciplinary dialogue and cross-fertilization of ideas are also needed for introducing an enriched and substantive vocabulary in the debate. Sen and Nussbaum are good examples. Another good example of this strategy is Ayelet Sacher's recent focus on the citizenship-as-inherited-property thesis. Sacher's work argues for enhancing citizenship's enabling dimension domestically and extending its redistributive obligations globally to mitigate the moral luck of "birthright lottery" (Sacher 2009).

Moral luck is a thorny issue for the liberal egalitarians. Mathias Risse conducts a thought experiment to demonstrate the initial plausibility that the "earth belongs to humanity in common." He writes: "Let us suppose for the sake of argument that the population of the United States shrinks to two, but that these two can control access into the country through sophisticated electronic border-surveillance mechanisms. Suppose, too, that nothing changes in the rest of the world. I would argue (and I think most would agree) that under such conditions these two citizens should allow for immigration based on the fact that they are grossly underusing the territory under their control" (Risse 2008). Risse concludes that the burden of proof is on those who would wish to override implications of the common-ownership standpoint.

However, for Sangiovanni and other liberal nationalists, moral arbitrariness, by itself, is not "sufficient to generate a prima facie claim against anyone, anywhere to compensation" (Sangiovanni 2007, 25). Special provisions against such inequalities apply only "among those who share in the maintenance and reproduction of the state" (Sangiovanni 2007, 29). Accordingly, a globalist, non-institutional demand of egalitarian justice would not do; for them, such a demand would be "question-begging" (Sangiovanni: 2007, 37). For the globalists, on the other hand, to leave the claims of justice on the existing arrangements of inequitable state system is also question-begging. For them, the burden of proof would fall on a relational view of justice based on the claims of sufficiency of reciprocity predicated on the contingency of national boundaries in generating a distinct principle of egalitarian justice only among fellow citizens, especially in a densely populated, interconnected, and interdependent world.

It would be instructive to go back to Dagger's earlier article where he defends compatriot partiality as a matter of reciprocity while holding on to the universal mandates of human rights claims (Dagger 1985). Dagger acknowledges that there are cases where compatriots simply have no moral claim to priority where, for instance, the relationships are marked not by reciprocity but by exploitation, as in a dictatorial regime. This is a telling point against liberal nationalism! People who are citizens of these unjust states are especially the ones who need special recognition from their capable fellow citizens and from everybody else due to their special needs and vulnerabilities. If reciprocity creates mandates for a demanding egalitarian justice, it is not clear what would generate equally strong obligations of justice and human rights for those with whom we do not have such reciprocity but who could be victims of oppression and bad, brute luck. Rawls, Sangiovanni, and others are mistaken in carving out the domain of demanding equality only among citizens in a democratic polity. Indeed, Rawls's exclusion of citizens of outlaw states from the global community would be unjust because it is not the fault of these citizens that their states won't accept the law of peoples (cf. Jason Breen 2010).

Contractarian justice has difficulties in accommodating luck egalitarianism. The idea of relational justice needs to be expanded to make room not only for reciprocity but solidarity as well. Solidarity turns vulnerability into empowerment in a way that social contract cannot. Rousseau is a good example of both social contract and solidarity, and Sen should have counted Rousseau on his side than lumping him with other contractarians.[7]

Notes

Portions of this article, in earlier versions, were presented at the British Academy, Yale Political Theory Workshop, and at the meetings of the North American Society for Social Philosophy (NASSP) and American Section of the International Association for Philosophy of Law and Social Philosophy (AMINTAPHIL). I thank the attendees of these meetings, especially Seyla Benhabib, Frank Cunningham, Win-Chiat Lee, Jan Narveson, Onora O'Neill, and Sally Scholz for their valuable comments. One portion of this article draws on a collaborative entry on Amartya Sen, done with Lynette Sieger of NYU and published in *Encyclopedia of Global Justice* ed. Deen K. Chatterjee (Springer, 2011).

1. This point will find support in Kok-Chor Tan's defense of global egalitarianism. (Tan 2004) However, Tan's liberal internationalism seems to be in tension with his statist thesis—if cultural and linguistic solidarity is needed for a viable democratic polity, then it is not clear how this requirement can be overcome in an international democratic setting. Similarly, though Richard Miller advocates a form of "quasi-cosmopolitanism" for his account of global justice in transnational responsibilities, his liberal nationalist thesis seems to override (or be in tension with) his principle of "quasi-cosmopolitan" beneficence (Miller 2010).

2. I thank Michael Morrell for bringing Dagger's article to my notice at a Yale political theory workshop.

3. Beitz and Pogge would agree with Dagger's broad premise that bonds of political communities are compatible with the demands of human rights, but would not agree with Dagger's specific idea of compatriot priority except in a severely truncated and benign version.

4. In an excellent article, David Reidy elaborates on the distinction between reasonable agreement and reasonable disagreement with regard to the liberal principle of legitimacy. Reidy opines that reasonable disagreement is a more challenging requirement for liberal legitimacy than reasonable agreement, catering to more diverse and competing points of views, thus proving to be more suitable for *democratic* legitimacy that is missing in the Rawlsian formulation of reasonable pluralism (Reidy 2007).

5. For instance, both Sangiovanni and Darrel Moellendorf use the idea of reciprocity to arrive at their two competing conclusions—Moellendorf for cosmopolitnism and Sangiovanni for co-national preference—yet both of them cite the same empirical evidence of global governance and domestic institutions. Obviously, more empirical research is needed to decide which evidence is more conducive in supporting what conclusions. (Sangiovanni 2007; Moellendorf 2002 and 2009).

6.   James Sterba has pressed me for providing an account of the Rawlsians in Sen's theory of justice. As he has put it, there is Rawls and then there are the Rawlsians; Sen cannot simply focus on Rawls and ignore the Rawlsians. Well, Sen doesn't. Sen takes note of Nagel, Beitz, Pogge, Barbara Herman and others, but perhaps not to Sterba's satisfaction. In any case, Sen would find Sterba's point challenging.

7.   I am grateful to Sally Scholz for this point on Rousseau at a recent meeting. For an excellent account of political solidarity, see Scholz (2008). See also Scholz's chapter, "Rousseau," in *Encyclopedia of Global Justice*, ed. Deen K. Chatterjee (Dordrecht: Springer, 2011).

References

Arneson, Richard. 2003. "Consequentialism vs. Special-Ties Partiality." *Monist* 86 (July).

————. 2004. "Moral Limits on the Demands of Beneficence?" In *The Ethics of Assistance: Morality and the Distant Needy*, ed. Deen Chatterjee. Cambridge: Cambridge University Press.

Beitz, Charles. 2009. *The Idea of Human Rights*. Oxford: Oxford University Press.

Benhabib, Seyla. 2002. *The Claims of Culture: Equality and Diversity in the Global Era*. Princeton, NJ: Princeton University Press.

————. 2005 . "On the Alleged Conflict Between Democracy and International Law." *Ethics and International Affairs* 19.

————. 2006. *Another Cosmopolitanism*. Oxford: Oxford University Press.

Blake, Michael. 2002. "Distributive Justice, State Coercion, and Autonomy." *Philosophy and Public Affairs* 31.

Bohman, James. 2000. *Public Deliberation: Pluralism, Complexity, and Democracy*. Cambridge, MA: MIT Press.

Breen, Jason. 2010. "It's Not My Fault that My State Won't Accept the Law of Peoples: Why Rawls' Exclusion of Citizens of Outlaw Sates from the Global Community is Unjust." Presented at the annual conference of NASSP, Toronto, July 2010.

Brock, Gillian. 2009. *Global Justice: A Cosmopolitan Account*. Oxford: Oxford University Press.

Buchanan, Allen. 2004. *Justice, Legitimacy, and Self-Determination: Moral Foundations for International Law*. New York: Oxford University Press.

Cohen, Joshua. 1997. "Procedure and Substance in Deliberative Democracy." In *Deliberative Democracy: Essays on Reason and Politics*, ed. James Bohman and William Rehg. Cambridge, MA: MIT Press.

Crocker, David. 2008. *Ethics of Global Development*. Cambridge: Cambridge University Press.

Dagger, Richard. 1985. "Rights, Boundaries, and the Bonds of Community: A Qualified Defense of Moral parochialism." *The American Political Science Review* 79.2.

Deveaux, Monique. 2006. *Gender and Justice in Multicultural Liberal States* (Oxford: Oxford University Press.

Freeman, Samuel. 2010. "A New Theory of Justice." In *New York Review of Books*, October 14, 2010.

Gotoh, Reiko, and Paul Dumouchel, eds. 2009. *Against Injustice: The New Economics of Amartya Sen* (Cambridge: Cambridge University Press.

Julius, A. J. 2006. "Nagel's Atlas." *Philosophy and Public Affairs* 34 (Spring).

Kuper, Andrew. 2004. *Democracy Beyond Borders: Justice and Representation in Global Institutions.* New York: Oxford University Press.

Macedo, Stephen. 2007. "The Moral Dilemma of U.S. Immigration Policy: Open Borders Versus Social Justice?" In *Debating Immigration*, ed. Carol M. Swaine. Cambridge: Cambridge University Press.

Macleod, Alistair. 2005 "The Structure of Arguments for Human Rights." In *Universal Human Rights*, ed. David Reidy and Mortimer Sellers. Lanham, MD: Rowman and Littlefield.

Miller, David. 1995. *On Nationality.* Oxford: Clarendon Press.

Miller, Richard W. 2010. *Globalizing Justice: The Ethics of Poverty and Power.* Oxford: Oxford University Press.

Moellendorf, Darrel. 2002. *Cosmopolitan Justice.* Boulder, CO: Westview Press.

———. 2009. *Global Inequality Matters.* New York: Palgrave MacMillan.

Nagel, Thomas. 2005. "The Problem of Global Justice." *Philosophy and Public Affairs* 33.

Nussbaum, Martha. 2006. *Frontiers of Justice: Disability, Nationality, Species Membership.* Cambridge, MA: Harvard University Press.

Oldenquist, Andrew. 2007. "Varieties of Nationalism." In *Democracy in a Global World*, ed. Deen Chatterjee. Lanham, MD: Rowman and Littlefield.

Pogge, Thomas. 2002. *World Poverty and Human Rights.* Malden, MA: Polity Press.

Rawls, John. 1971. *A Theory of Justice.* Cambridge, MA: Harvard University Press

———. 1993. *Political Liberalism.* New York: Columbia University.

———. 1999. *The Law of Peoples.* Cambridge, MA: Harvard University Press.

———. 2001. *Justice as Fairness: A Restatement.* Cambridge, MA: Harvard University Press.

Reidy, David. 2007. "Reciprocity and Reasonable Disagreement: From Liberal to Democratic Legitimacy." *Philosophical Studies* 132.

Risse, Mathias. 2008. "On the Morality of Immigration." *Ethics and International Affairs* 22.

Sacher, Ayelet. 2009. *The Birthright Lottery: Citizenship and Global Inequality.* Cambridge, MA: Harvard University Press.

Sangiovanni, Andrea. 2007. "Global Justice, Reciprocity, and the State." *Philosophy and Public Affairs* 35.

Scholz, Sally. 2008. *Political Solidarity.* University Park, PA: Penn State University Press.

Sen, Amartya. 1997. "Human Rights and Asian Values." *The New Republic* 10.

———. 1999. *Development as Freedom.* New York: Anchor Books.

———. 2000. "Consequential Evaluation and Practical Reason." *The Journal of Philosophy* 97.9.

————. 2004. "Elements of a Theory of Human Rights," *Philosophy and Public Affairs* 32.

————. 2005. "Human Rights and Capabilities," *Journal of Human Development* 6

————. 2006. *Identity and Violence: The Illusion of Destiny*. New York: W.W. Norton.

————. 2009. *The Idea of Justice*. Cambridge, MA: Harvard University Press.

Simmons, A. John. 2010. "Ideal and Nonideal Theory." *Philosophy and Public Affairs* 38.

Singer, Peter. 1972. "Famine, Affluence, and Morality." *Philosophy and Public Affairs* 1.2.

————. 2002. *One World: The Ethics of Globalization*. New Haven, CT: Yale University Press.

Stiglitz, Joseph. 2002. *Globalization and Its Discontents*. New York: W.W. Norton.

Swaine, Lucas. 2006. *The Liberal Conscience*. New York: Columbia University Press.

Swift, Adam. 2008. "The Value of Philosophy in Nonideal Circumstances." *Social Theory and Practice* 34.

Tamir, Yael. 1993. *Liberal Nationalism*. Princeton, NJ: Princeton University Press.

Tan, Kok-Chor. 2004. *Justice Without Borders*. Cambridge, UK: Cambridge University Press. Walzer, Michael. 1984. *Spheres of Justice: A Defense of Pluralism and Equality*. New York: Basic Books.

Young, Iris. 2000. *Inclusion and Democracy*. New York: Oxford University Press.

Amartya Sen's *The Idea of Justice*–
Some Kantian Rejoinders

HELGA VARDEN

In an American Philosophical Association (APA) session in her honor, Barbara Herman responded to those praising her by saying that she didn't quite recognize herself in some of the very favorable descriptions of her work given that she had been walking among true giants.[1] Evecn if Herman does not feel like a true giant, she certainly is one. But more importantly here, one of the giants Herman was referring to was, I believe, Amartya Sen. Sen's influence in the world—and not only in the academic world or the world of philosophy—has been and continues to be tremendous. And like other true giants, some of his impressiveness resides in his ability to engage difficult and charged questions in a way that helps the world move in a better direction. As a woman living in a world dominated by men, I am very glad and deeply grateful that I have not only Herman as my friend and advocate, but also Amartya Sen. Sen's commitment to the advancement of women's conditions everywhere is unwavering. Another, often overlapping, group that Sen consistently fights for is the poor. Since I won one of the largest lotteries in the world, that is, I was lucky enough to be born in a wealthy country genuinely committed to the rights of its citizens, I have no firsthand knowledge of what it is like to be truly poor. Yet I believe it is reasonable to think that those who do know would join me in thanking Sen for going to bat for them time and time again, and now once more in his new book—*The Idea of Justice*. Moral, political, and social evolution is a slow and non-necessary process, and it requires, among other things, that those with power exercise it wisely. Fortunately, Sen is one of those wise people.

In philosophy, one great sign of respect is serious engagement with your colleagues' arguments. One of the most important colleagues in Sen's life has been John Rawls, another true giant and *The Idea of Justice* reflects this; not only is it dedicated to Rawls, but throughout the book Sen's admiration and affection for Rawls are impossible to miss. Which is not to say that Sen agrees with Rawls. Quite the contrary. Sen believes that the kind of contractarian position Rawls defends, which Sen calls "transcendental institutionalism" (5), has some serious problems—problems that can best be overcome by adopting Sen's "comparative" or "realization-focused," capabilities approach. According to Sen, Rawls's theory shares two main features with other contractarian theories. On the one hand, Rawls's theory "concentrates its attention on what it identifies as perfect justice, rather than on relative comparisons between justice and injustice" (5ff.). On the other hand, "in searching for perfection, transcendental institutionalism concentrates primarily on getting the institutions right, and it is not directly focused on the actual societies that would ultimately emerge" (6). Sen argues that a major reason why these transcendental theories have problems when it comes to actual societies is that when reflecting on whether or not the theory is realizable, they engage only arguments concerning persons' ideal behavior. He also proposes that because contractarian theories—whether Rawlsian, Kantian, Hobbesian, Rousseauan, or Lockean—focus on institutions and ideal behavior, we can describe them by referring to a corresponding concept, "niti," utilized in Sanskrit writings on ethics and jurisprudence (20). I will return to the concept of *niti* as well as its contrary, *niyaya*, shortly.

The two main problems with contractarian theories with respect to actual societies, Sen continues, are that they are not "feasible" and that they are "redundant" (9ff.). The first problem, that contractarian theories are not feasible, is seen as issuing from their commitment to transcendental institutionalism. This commitment requires that they demonstrate the possibility of "reasoned agreement"—or what is often referred to as 'hypothetical consent'—regarding "the nature of the 'just society'" (9). And demonstrating "reasoned agreement" requires these theories to determine the institutional structure of the just society as well as the associated ideal behavior of persons. In these ways, Sen argues, contractarian theories "seem determined to take us straightaway to some fairly detailed formula for social justice and to firm identification, with no indeterminacy, of the nature of just social institutions" (89). Sen reflects that the problem, however, is that there is no such determinacy in detailing the ideal structure of society. He maintains that there is indeterminacy regarding both what the fundamental principles of justice are and how to apply "otherwise significant concept[s]," or principles, in particular circumstances, such as those that determine exactly which tax rate should regulate economic redistribution in a society (374). Also, in relation to Rawls's principles of justice as fairness (or, alternatively, his lexical ordering of principles of liberty and equality), Sen proposes that there is too much "decisiveness" (ibid.). Even though liberty is essential and most of the time should override concerns of equality, sometimes concerns of equality should override liberty. Sen thinks that Rawls is starting to realize these problems of indeterminacy in his later philosophy, as evidenced by his introduction of the notion of a family of liberal, political conceptions of justice, of which justice as fairness with the original position is but one. The problem however is that Rawls never clarifies the implications of this concession. Indeed, Sen concludes, "Once the claim to uniqueness of the Rawlsian principles of justice is dropped (the case for which is outlined in Rawls's later works), the institutional programme would clearly have serious indeterminacy, and Rawls does not tell us much about how a particular set of institutions would be chosen on the basis of a set of competing principles of justice that would demand different institutional combinations for the basic structure of the society" (12). One option "forcefully raised" by Rawls's later philosophy, Sen suggests, is to abandon transcendental institutionalism altogether, but, Sen says "I am afraid I am not able to claim that this was the direction in which Rawls himself was definitely heading" (ibid.).

Regardless of the possible complexities Rawls's later philosophy raises in relation to the issues of indeterminacy, Sen proposes that Rawls's decisiveness at least in earlier work regarding the institutional structure of the just society entails that Rawls excludes considerations he ought not to exclude. These unfortunate exclusions include considerations such as investigating "comparative questions about justice;" incorporating "broader perspectives of social realizations;" integrating "adverse effects on people beyond the borders of each country;" developing a "systematic procedure for correcting the influence of parochial values;" ignoring "the possibility that even in the original position different persons could continue to take, even after much public discussion, some very different principles as appropriate for justice;" and, finally, "giving no room to the possibility that some people may not always behave 'reasonably' despite the hypothetical social contract, and this could affect the appropriateness of all social arrangements" (90). These deficiencies of analysis, or derivatives thereof, are those that Rawls is seen as sharing with most contractarian theories, and they are deficiencies that make these theories unfeasible. They are unfortunate results of assuming determinacy where there is none to be found, and of assuming ideal behavior that does not exist in the real world. Indeed, the problem of indeterminacy is seen as intensified by the somewhat "tyrannical" commitment of so many of these theories to states "as being, in some way, fundamental, and in seeing them not only as practical constraints to be addressed, but as divisions of basic significance in ethics and political philosophy," including for dealing with issues of poverty (143). And since the global state is likely to be a practical impossibility in the foreseeable future, this entails, Sen thinks, that most of these theories are much too toothless regarding the gross injustices in the distribution of the world's material resources.

The only way to avoid these problems, Sen argues throughout *The Idea of Justice*, involves accepting that "the identification and pursuit of the demands of justice may have to take a much broader and more contingent form" (91). And this connects up with the second main problem Sen sees as associated with contractarian problems, namely the "redundancy of the search for a transcendental solution" (9). Not only are contractarian theories not "feasible," Sen maintains, but they are also redundant or unnecessary. In fact, all we need for a theory of justice in the actual world is "a framework for comparison of justice for choosing among the feasible alternatives and not an identification of a possibly unavailable perfect situation that could not be transcended" (9). The alternative to unfeasible and redundant contractarian theories is, Sen continues, the "comparative," "realization-focused," or "*nyaya*" (Sanskrit) theories of justice, which share a commitment to "social choice" theory. In the Western tradition, social choice theory is taken to include thinkers from Jean-Charles de Borda and Marquis de Condorcet to Adam Smith, Mary Wollstonecraft, J. S. Mill, and Karl Marx. In the Indian ethical and jurisprudential tradition, *nyaya* is a prevalent idea throughout, but captured most famously in Krishna's position against Arjuna (who is defending *niti*) in the *Bhagavadgita* (22–23). The common thread among the Indian thinkers is that they were "all involved in comparisons of societies that already existed or could feasibly emerge, rather than confining their analyses to transcendental searches for a perfectly just society. Those focusing on realization-focused comparisons were often interested primarily in the removal of manifest injustice from the world that they saw" (7). In like fashion, Sen proposes that justice requires us to look not at how various social choices and institutions affect average utilities or happiness—or for that matter, Rawls's 'primary goods'—but instead at capabilities understood as "the substantial freedoms that people enjoy" (19) or "the *actual opportunities* for living" (233). In addition to avoiding some of the problems haunting much utilitarian and happiness-based accounts (including those of prominent economic theories), this perspective, Sen maintains, has a particular advantage in its ability to give proper voice to the freedoms of the vulnerable—whether as victims of historical oppression, such as women and the poor, or of some misfortune, such as the disabled and the sick. He argues that by insisting on a focus that pays attention to what persons actually can do, one avoids building theories that fail to pay proper attention to the actual hindrances to freedom with which real people struggle. These hindrances—whether natural or human-made—are front and center in Sen's own conception of freedom, given that its focus on capabilities requires one explicitly to identify and deal with them.

At the heart of Sen's approach lies a commitment to fighting "blatant injustices," such as eradicating starvation and providing basic medicines for vast populations of the world. To do this, as noted already, Sen argues that we do not need the comparison case of the perfectly just society. Assuming that the Mona Lisa is the perfect painting, we do not, he suggests, need Mona Lisa to determine whether a painting by Van Gogh is better than a paining by Rembrandt (16). Similarly, to identify starvation in the world as a crisis of injustice and to search for ways to alleviate it we do not also need the standard provided by a perfectly just society. That is, finding ways to alleviate the blatant starvation and thereby make the world a more just place doesn't require such a grand standard. In addition, an extension of Sen's indeterminacy argument concludes that it is not possible to say in the abstract what weight should be given to which important concerns of justice when it comes to developing and implementing solutions. For example, when comparing which of three children should be given the flute that one of them has made, Sen argues, along with much libertarian theory, that the child who made it presumably has a stronger claim on it than either the child who can actually play it or the child who has no toys. But he also argues, against libertarian theories, that some considerations may override all other concerns (297ff.). For example, if the flute is the only way to provide a poor child with a means of survival, perhaps by busking, that child's claim could override the others', including the claim from the child who made the flute.

Sen's emphasis on the importance of freedom as capability in a just world does not, however, entail that he thinks everything in the world can be coercively redistributed so as to secure equality for all in respect to capabilities (231ff.). Several other considerations, including liberty and labor, are also seen as important. More generally, Sen emphasizes that the *process* by which a person's capability is enabled and secured cannot be ignored when determining which capabilities a person can be seen as having a right to. And although Sen doesn't think there are exact, determinate answers regarding the appropriate balance between "opportunity aspects" and "process aspects" of freedom-as-capability in the absence of actual cases (228), he does make two further, important clarifications regarding freedom. First, he argues that even if one's actual choices coincide with the coercive restrictions imposed on one's choices, this does not entail that the choice is unrestrained. For example, if there is a law preventing me from going outside in the evening, then my choices are coercively restrained even if it happens to be the case that I prefer to stay inside in the evenings (225ff.).

Second, Sen takes issue with Philip Pettit's republican conception of freedom, according to which "a person's liberty may be compromised even in the absence of any interference, simply by the existence of the arbitrary power of another which *could* hinder the freedom of the person to act as they like, even if that intervening power is not actually exercised" (305). Sen responds to this view by saying that

> Certainly being free to do something independently of others (so that it does not matter what they want) gives one's substantive freedom a robustness that is absent when the freedom to do that thing is conditional either on the help—or on the tolerance—of others, or dependent on a coincidence ('it so happens') between what the person wants to do and what the other people who could have stopped it happen to want. (305)

To illustrate this point, Sen reflects upon three different cases involving a disabled person. In the first case, "Person A is not helped by others, and she is thus unable to go out of her house;" in the second case, "Person A is always helped by helpers arranged either by a social security system in operation in her locality (or, alternatively, by volunteers with goodwill), and she is, as a result, fully able to go out of her house whenever she wants and to move around freely"; and in the final, third case, "Person A has well-remunerated servants who obey—and have to obey—her command, and she is fully able to go out of her house whenever she wants and to move around freely" (306). Sen then maintains that in terms of capability, both the second case (disabled person supported by a social security system or by volunteers) and third case (disabled person with servants) are equal. The main contrast in terms of capability concerns only the contrast between these two cases and the first case, where the disabled person is not helped to go out of the house. Sen argues that Pettit, however, wrongly concludes that only the person in the third case (disabled + servants) is free. Sen reasons that although the republican approach has a "discriminating power that the capability approach lacks," which is the ability to focus in on a person's dependence on others or on a system (as exemplified by the person in the second scenario), it lacks a discriminating power of the capability approach, namely to identify whether or not a person has "the capability and freedom to go out of her house whenever she wants" (307). Hence, the main problem with the republican approach, Sen maintains, is that "Placing Cases 1 and 2 in the same box of non-freedom, without further distinction, would steer us towards the view that instituting social security provisions, or having a supportive society, cannot make any difference to anyone's freedom, when dealing with disabilities or handicaps. For a theory of justice that would be a huge lacuna" (307). On the basis of these reflections, Sen concludes that although the republican concept of freedom as independence can complement or "add to" the idea of freedom as capability (308), it cannot "*replace* the perspective of freedom as capability" (306, 308). Then again, he points out, the view that seeing freedom as capability and freedom as independence are necessarily in tension "arises if and only if we have room for 'at most one idea.' It arises when looking for a single-focus understanding of freedom, despite the fact that freedom as an idea has irreducibly multiple elements" (308).

One final point concerning the complexity of the idea of freedom as it relates to justice should be mentioned. For Sen, human rights are not limited to what can be enforced. Human rights also require the efforts of, and can be established by, at least to some degree, the voluntary activities of non-governmental organizations, activists, global agencies (including the news media), and heroic visionaries. To what extent states—including a world state—and their institutions are necessary for justice on our planet is a contingent question. These public institutions are not in principle necessary for justice; it is a contingent issue to what extent they are useful or not for bringing justice about. Sometimes they further global justice, sometimes not. Moreover, Sen emphasizes democracy and, in particular, free speech and a free responsible media as essential to the possibility of justice. Without the free flow of information that free speech and a reliable media enables, good decisions concerning any specific issues in any actual society are simply impossible. Indeed, though Sen thinks the global state as a prudent solution to issues of global justice is far off in the future, he thinks that a well functioning media in combination with other organizations that can provide conditions of global democracy in the context of information is a first step in the right direction (408ff.).

Naturally, the above summary of Sen's 400 plus page book does not do justice to all of its insights. Still, I trust it is sufficient to provide a basis against which I can raise some, I hope, fruitful questions concerning Sen's view that liberal theories' typical focus on states and institutions is misplaced. Contrary to Sen, I will argue that justice requires enforceable rights, including for the disabled, and that states have an in principle necessary role to play here. Second, I will try to boost my argument for the necessity of states by arguing that rightful resolutions of many of the indeterminacies Sen points to require the establishment of public authorities, including states. Third, I will argue with Kant that close attention should be paid to the distinction between private and public right, and that such a distinction may equip a republican theory with the framework within which indeterminacies, capabilities, and public reason get the importance Sen wants them to have. Hence, Kant's republicanism, one of a few important philosophical theories of justice Sen barely engages, and one that Pettit doesn't engage at all in his book on republicanism, may turn out to be a significant defense of much of what Sen wants to argue for. Therefore, Kant's suggestion that justice—for ideal, rather than merely prudential reasons—requires the establishment of public authorities constituted by a certain set of institutions is not, I propose, a drawback for a theory of justice. Quite the contrary, it is a significant strength. Fourth, I will argue that Sen's employment of the concept 'transcendental' does not agree with Kant's own, as it seems closer to Kant's use of 'transcendent.' Moreover, when we understand how Kant uses these two concepts, some of the worries Sen raises may be quieted. In the final section, I will argue that although I find Sen's proposal that ideal theories should spend more time taking people's bad or non-ideal behavior into account a compelling one, questions concerning non-ideal behavior are primarily important for the institutional design for a theory of justice. In an attempt to be space-efficient, I will utilize an example employing Thomas Pogge's recent suggestion for a "Health Impact Fund" to help address these issues.

I believe Sen would agree that one prominent current example of academic initiative and engagement that furthers the cause of justice is the Incentives for Global Health's (IGH) "Health Impact Fund" (HIF), a non-governmental organization (NGO) led by Thomas Pogge.[2] The idea behind the HIF is, in brief, that the IGH will raise money—mainly from governments—to finance rewards to pharmaceutical companies for innovations in medicines having great health impact for the world's poor. The pharmaceutical companies must agree to sell the medicines to the poor at cost, but in return they will be rewarded for the actual positive impact the medicines have on the health of the poor. This, the hope is, will give the pharmaceutical industry an apparently much needed incentive to focus research where the impact on health is likely to be the greatest, and from where the biggest threat to human survival is likely to come, and so should be addressed first.[3] I believe that Sen will say that for each penny that is thereby transferred from the powerful to the powerless, and thereby increases the powerless persons' capabilities, the world becomes a more just place.

I have no doubt that if successful, such a system will make the world a better place, and I also believe that if successful, it will create pragmatic preconditions for a more just world. Indeed, it may be one of the more prudent and effective means of bringing about such preconditions for a more just world, given the horrible state the world is in. I'm not so sure, however, that private initiatives (such as the HIF) falling under the umbrella of an NGO are constitutive of a just world, or can make the world just. The reason for my skepticism is that the 'rights' of the poor to medicines in this system are still dependent upon the choices of the rich, since such a privately constituted system does not, by itself, secure poor persons' rights to healthcare. Securing poor persons' rights to healthcare requires, I believe, creating public institutions in relation to which the poor have in principle enforceable health care claims.

To illustrate this point, let me draw on Lucy Allais's powerful Kantian analysis of whether or not to give money to beggars.[4] Allais argues that giving money to beggars should not fill us with moral feelings of satisfaction, but conflicted feelings. The reason for the conflict is twofold. On the one hand, we recognize that it's the best we can do under current conditions. On the other hand, we recognize that having such private power over other human beings is unjustifiable, and that private responses are not a proper solution to a rights issue. The source of the problem is that giving to beggars amounts to trying to solve a public, systemic problem by individual private means. Yet private responses are in principle inadequate, since they are irreconcilable with persons' rights to freedom or to independence from being so subject to other private persons' power or choices. Hence, finding ourselves in a situation where some have to beg for money in order to legally access means is not only to find ourselves in a relation of unjustifiable power over other human beings that no person has a right to be in, but also to recognize that the only response within our own means is one that is insufficient to solve the problem. Consequently, moral feelings of gratitude (on the part of the poor) and of beneficence (on the part of the rich) are inappropriate moral feelings. Instead, the appropriate feelings on behalf of the rich are those of inadequacy and inner conflict, as one recognizes that one is not rightfully interacting with others. Rightful interaction on the part of all parties requires independence from the type of private dependency relation begging involves. Therefore, even a world in which the rich continuously give money to beggars so that none of them starve still is not a just world. It is likely that generously donating to the poor may be the only available means of empowerment, and hence a first step towards enabling rightful or just relations in the future. But charity in itself does not establish justice or rightful relations among persons.

Applying this reasoning both to Pogge's example and to Sen's conception of justice creates the same worry. To start, it is true that if the Health Impact Fund is a wonderful success and hence increases the capabilities of all the poor persons in the world, then the world will be a much better place. It is also true that the poor will now be situated in conditions where advancing the establishment of their rights has become a much more feasible project. I do not, however, think it is true that it is now a more just world. The reason is that the possibility of capability for the vulnerable is still fundamentally dependent upon the powerful persons' choices. A just world requires that the poor are not so dependent upon the actual choices of the rich (private persons and countries) to continue to give money to the Health Impact Fund, and of the pharmaceutical companies to continue to support the IGF's efforts. So-called welfare rights require that persons are able to exercise joint control in relation to the total system of freedom-determining economic, financial, and technological systems upon which they are dependent for legal access to means. Welfare rights are systemic measures to secure all citizens' rights to independence from each other's arbitrary choices and their dependence on public law alone, which guarantees legal access to means for those who have none. Welfare rights are therefore not rights individuals have in relation to one another as private persons. Rather, they are rights citizens have in relation to their public institutions.[5]

At this point, one may object on behalf of Pogge and Sen that the HIF could assume sufficient coercive control in the world to ensure that everyone complies with its requirements concerning medicines. That is, one could argue that the only reason why the HIF is merely a voluntary adventure is pragmatic; it could, in principle, have coercive powers. But this response will not solve the underlying problem, since the poor are still subject to some private persons' arbitrary choices; it just so happens that the powerful private persons in charge (Pogge and the IGF) choose to act in the interest of the poor. But they could choose otherwise. Therefore, poor persons' rights to be independent of other persons' arbitrary choices are not secured by the adoption of coercive power by private institutions. The only way to overcome this problem of private dependence in a way consistent with persons' rights to be independent of the arbitrary choices of others, I suggest with Kant, is through the establishment of public institutions. A public institution represents all and yet no one in particular, and it is the means through which we choose together, as a unified, representative body. Public institutions, including states, are therefore ideal preconditions for justice—and not merely possible, instrumental means for securing justice.

This same point applies also to fiduciary relations. As we noted above, in his discussion of Pettit's conception of republicanism—or freedom as independence— Sen is quite sympathetic to the emphasis on independence, but Sen argues that republicanism fails to pay sufficient attention to the moral improvement of the world that comes with increased capability. The three earlier mentioned cases of a disabled person's ability to leave her house is paralleled by Sen's discussion of the distinction between "direct control" and "indirect control" as enabled by "effective power" (301ff.). Sen's examples of indirect control are the kind of effective power a patient has when a physician acts on his behalf and when civic authorities fight local epidemics on behalf of the affected people. In the physician-patient example, Sen argues that "there is no violation of the patient's freedom—indeed, there is an affirmation of that freedom in the sense of 'effective power' if the physician's choice is guided by what the patient would have wanted" if unconscious, and regardless of whether the patient is conscious or unconscious, if the physician's choice is guided by "how the patient would actually choose, given enough knowledge and understanding" (302). The important thing to note here—for the purposes of discussing the ideal role of public institutions—is that Sen is defending a fundamentally prudential view of public institutions. As long as the person who is in effective control acts in line with what the person incapable of acting would want (given consciousness, sufficient knowledge etc.) or would reasonably want, the resulting relation is just. Sen sees no ideal problem of freedom related to acting on another person's behalf, or, for that matter, to being dependent on another in order to exercise agency at all. Even though Sen is sympathetic to the view that it's better if the vulnerable are not dependent upon others' voluntary help and charity, justice as capability does not require such independence. Moreover, justice as capability also does not require anything but virtuous private persons acting on our behalf when our agency is for some reason impaired. For Sen, there is no principled need to establish public institutions to secure freedom also in this regard.

I am skeptical of this view of what we may call rightful fiduciary relations. As I argue elsewhere, I believe that the reason why we have laws governing professionals acting on our behalf—whether physicians, lawyers or social workers—is not merely in response to the harmful effects of vicious, incompetent, or unqualified professionals.[6] The ideal reason, I believe, is to make sure that the relationship itself is governed by public law rather than by the powerful person's arbitrary choices, that is, by right rather than might. This is so regardless of whether or not the professional action taken is beneficial for the patient. On the one hand, legal regulation of fiduciary relations is the way in which we give proper voice also to the vulnerable, namely to those who do not have the knowledge or expertise required to evaluate the wisdom of those acting on their behalf. On the other hand, legal regulation is the way in which we ensure that indeterminacies regarding how even sound principles of care are applied to particular cases are not merely solved by someone's (the powerful persons') arbitrary choices. That is to say, by establishing public, rule-governed institutions, we establish an artificial person through which we seek to exercise common agency, rather than relying on fiduciary relations in which only one of the persons in reality has agency. The public authority represents all interacting parties, and yet no one in particular—and in so doing it is able to give proper voice to those who do not have one. In addition, it enables us to solve indeterminacies concerning the application of sound principles to particular cases in a way that yields rightful relations. The establishment of public authorities—or the liberal state—is therefore not only a prudential response to the inconveniences involved in trying to establish justice without it, but more importantly it is the ideal way in which we go about establishing justice.

Making an ideal—or non-prudential—case for the necessity of public institutions, including the state, can be done also with respect to relations other than fiduciary ones. We can, still with Kant and in support of much of what Sen is arguing for in *The Idea of Justice*, show that the indeterminacies in the application of the principles of private property and contracts lead to the necessity of public institutions.[7] Similar to Sen's discussion under the heading of "Positional Perspectives" (155ff.), Kant argues that there are reasonable disagreements regarding the specifications of the application of principles of private right concerning property and contracts. The possible disagreements concerning, say, where your property ends and mine starts, and regarding what we actually agreed to when we signed the contract, are not all unreasonable. Because what we are disagreeing about is how normative principles apply to empirical circumstances, and because both sides in the disagreement can be reasonable, there is no single correct answer to many questions of justice. Moreover, Sen rightly, in my view, makes an analogous point in his discussion of Rawls. Sen notes that in Rawls's later writings, he admits that there can be a family of liberal political conceptions of justice, which raises the question of how to select the specific principles that will govern any actual interaction. Sen, it seems, falls on the side of saying that we must select the 'right' principle through informed, public reasoning, where by 'public' Sen means individuals reflecting together on the choices in public forums. Although Rawls and Sen, in my view, correctly identify the problem, I'm suggesting (with Kant) that appealing only to public reason so understood is an insufficient response, since we do not thereby solve the problem. For even when we have reasoned as well as Sen wants us to, still we end up with an informed private choice, not a public one. Or to put the point in Sen's language, the problem of the 'tyranny of the majority' is not thereby eliminated, since if we enforce one reasonable choice rather than some other reasonable choice, what we are enforcing is still an arbitrary reasonable choice.[8] That is to say, we are still enforcing a form of power that is inconsistent with each person's right to independence from being so subject to other persons' might. Thus there may be an alternative reason why Rawls (in his later philosophy) is increasingly concerned to show the role of public institutions as necessary for providing solutions to justice. And Kant can give Rawls what he needs to overcome Sen's worries. Kant, in his account of private right, explains what the principles of private right are and why a solution to the problems of indeterminacy regarding the application of principles of private right involves the establishment of a 'we' proper, namely a will the represents everyone's general or common will, or the establishment of common agency with the right impartial form. That is, the solution requires a public authority that acts on behalf of each of us and yet on behalf of no one in particular.

On the Kantian position I have outlined above, there are three different types of private right principles, understood as principles regulating relations between private persons. They are principles governing (1) private property appropriation,

(2) contract relations, and (3) fiduciary relations (or what Kant calls "status relations").[9] Given the empirical fact that each human being occupies a tiny amount of physical space relative to the size of the globe, our first attempts at rightful political interaction will be local. Therefore, we start with liberal states. By establishing liberal states we establish geographically limited monopolies on coercion. The liberal states, in turn, secure all of their citizens' rights to access protection under laws that in addition to securing their physical protection also enable rightful private relations with regard to property appropriation, contracts and fiduciary relations.[10] Naturally, if this were all that the liberal state accomplished, then it would look like a libertarian state. But Kant's insight is that the libertarian state is not enough to ensure justice. Because the state must secure each of its citizens' basic right to freedom as independence, it must also ensure that no one ends up in private dependency relations, in which a person's freedom and legal access to means is subject to some other private person's choice. In this way, Kant justifies the general claim that public right is not reducible to private right—or that the state must go beyond what is required to ensure private right by establishing basic public institutions, which secure everyone unconditional poverty relief as well as economic and financial conditions under which independent interaction is possible. It does this as a matter of public right, not private right.[11]

Although reasons of space hinder me from further detailing these aspects of Kant's conception of justice, notice that it follows from this Kantian position that understanding how the rights of the mentally disabled are secured in relation to their legal guardians, strangers, fellow citizens, and public institutions is not a 'single-lens' analysis of the kind Sen is so worried about. It is an analysis that requires the combination of several perspectives (principles of both private and public right) as well as sensitivity to the actual world in which a particular mentally disabled person lives.[12] Hence, Kant's theory of justice is able to overcome the difficulties associated with the problematic kind of power over others Sen attributes to private persons due to an asymmetry in knowledge, wealth or otherwise, and it is able to capture the important requirement of a multi-perspectival analysis of complex issues such as we find in the rights of the disabled. Moreover, in contrast to what Sen seems to imply, it is not the case that this kind of position defends an 'either-or' conception of the existence of justice with no room for nuance and partial progress. It does put the foot down when it comes to certain kinds of regimes, such as Nazi Germany or apartheid South Africa, and, in my view, this is a strength rather than a weakness of the theory.[13] But it does not maintain that there is no room for improvement within minimally just societies, or that some blatant injustices, such as denying same-sex marriages, must be approached in exactly the same way as others, such as sodomy laws.[14] Being denied the right to marry is to be denied entrance into civil society in relation to one's family, whereas sodomy laws deny citizens' rights to their own bodies and hence to their own persons. Consequently, people have a right to physically resist sodomy laws, whereas they must keep working towards establishing same-sex couples' right to marry. And, of course, none of this undermines the claim that if justice is not realizable, then perhaps the best we can do is to further conditions making the possibility of justice more likely—whether through private charity or such private initiatives such as the Human Development Fund. Neither does it deny that there are ways in which virtue may be a precondition for justice. Rather, all I have maintained is that it seems possible to argue both that Sen's '*niti*' provides necessary conditions for getting '*nyaya*' right and that justice is restricted to enforceable aspects of freedom without thereby saying that all there is to freedom is niti and enforceability.

Let me also include a brief note on Sen's use of the concept 'transcendental.' Sen views his understanding of this concept as one that captures Kant's philosophy, but Kant's own understanding of this concept is very different from Sen's. In fact, Sen's 'trancendental' is much closer to, even if not the same as, Kant's understanding of the concept 'transcendent.' According to Sen, remember, 'transcendental institutionalism' refers to theories that aim to outline ideal behavior and the ideal just society, and then to use these ideals as the standard against which actual societies are measured. But this understanding of 'transcendental' is quite different from Kant's own. In brief, in the theoretical philosophy, Kant uses the term 'transcendental' to refer to necessary *a priori* conditions for empirical knowledge. If we were to use this term in relation to his political philosophy, it would refer to necessary conditions for justice, or rightful relations. If we stay focused on political philosophy, then, transcendental conditions for right—such as the *a priori* principles of private and public right—are not an attempt to outline an ideal, perfect world beyond our own, but rather to describe the necessary conditions that make rightful interactions with regard to various empirical objects in the world possible. Now, if we move beyond trying to identify the necessary conditions for just private and public relations, to envisioning how the principles of private and public right would be systematically unified in an ideally just state, then we are trying to construct a 'trancendent' ideal. That is, we move beyond our world to imagine a perfect and unattainable world. The purpose of providing an analysis of a transcendent political ideal is to become increasing clear on what we are striving towards, even though we also know that we can never fully realize it. Given this way of reading the distinction between 'transcendental' and 'transcendent,' I see no reason for Sen's skepticism with respect to the project of 'transcendental institutionalism,' nor for his suggestion that we ought only employ 'contingent' distinctions. For all the transcendental institutionalist so understood wants to do is to provide an analysis of various principles necessary for rightful interactions in this world.[15] For example, the transcendental arguments can show why same-sex couples should have the right both to marry and to engage in consensual sexual relations. In contrast, the ideal transcendent society merely becomes a means of making the overall aim more vivid and clear to us.

I would like to finish by supporting Sen's claim that ideal theories of justice must spend more time incorporating the problems associated with bad or non-ideal behavior when they envision reliable paths to justice. Since I'm currently convinced by Kant's argument that public institutions are constitutive of rightful relations, I'd like to rephrase Sen's point slightly. I believe liberal theories, in their aim to envision both what constitutes a minimally just society and what constitutes the necessary institutional structure of the public authority, must take the time to ensure that the structure itself does not recreate arbitrary private power in its worst forms even if very bad people are in charge of public offices. The crises attending private organizations—for example, the Catholic Church and its institution of unchecked trust-based associations between its priests and children as well as other vulnerable persons—have unsurprisingly had their parallels in the history of public institutions. To give one example, the history of abuse in public orphanages around the world is at least as gruesome as the Catholic Church's history of its priests' abuses of children. The problem, it seems fair to say, is that much previous and current thinking—common sense or theoretical—around these institutions has been based, terribly naively, on a false assumption. That assumption is that, because these institutions are supposed to create an environment of trusting and caring relations for persons who have already been abused or who are particularly vulnerable, those entrusted with these jobs or vocations would themselves neither be tempted by, nor have sought jobs in these institutions precisely because of, the opportunity they provide for power over weak and vulnerable others. The assumption is that only virtuous or just people do the work of virtue or justice. Hence, whether religious, private, or public, the institutions set up to protect the weak and vulnerable had no required, enforceable institutional measures to ensure the absence of abuse. That is to say, although these institutions were envisioned to be regulated by rules of law and virtue—say, public or religious law constitutive of institutional authorities created to protect the rights of children and other vulnerable people—in reality the actual persons vested with this authority were unchecked in their exercise of this authority. Because of the way in which the rules permitted these authority figures to associate one-on-one with, and apply and enforce rules against the vulnerable for long periods of time, these institutions became havens for abuse rather than functioning as institutions for preventing it. In other words, the institutional design was disastrously flawed. In fact, although I agree with Sen that a properly functioning media and information system is one necessary safeguard for inhibiting persons from committing such abuses, I suspect that unless there is a sufficient public system for securing the oversight of the rights of each vulnerable person, there is still much too much dependence on the virtue of individuals to do the job.

Helga Varden, University of Illinois at Urbana-Champaign

Notes

Thanks to Lucy Allais, Michel DeMatteis, and Shelley Weinberg for very useful discussions of the ideas and their presentation in this paper.

1.   The annual conference of the Pacific Division of the American Philosophical Association, in Vancouver, Canada, April 2009.

2.   On page 263, Sen responds to Pogge's earlier criticisms that Sen fails to order the importance of various capabilities, by arguing that, "I would like to wish good luck to the builders of a transcendentally just set of institutions for the whole world, but for those who are ready to concentrate, at least for the moment, on reducing manifest injustices that so severely plague the world, the relevance of a 'merely' partial ranking for a theory of justice can actually be rather momentous." In light of this discussion, it seems fair to believe that Pogge's proposal of the Health Impact Fund is a step in the right, non-ideal direction according to Sen.

3.   This outcome is, I believe, also in line with Sen's view of asymmetrical, power obligations. At one point, Sen illustrates his objection to Rawls's mutual cooperation conception by drawing on Gautama Buddha's view of 'obligations of power.' Sen explains that on this view, obligations track asymmetry rather than the contractarian notion of symmetry. In addition to enabling explanation of obligations to animals, Sen argues with Buddha that it also enables us to explain an important aspect of parental obligations. In particular, "The mother's reason for helping the child, in this line of thinking, is not guided by the reward of cooperation, but precisely from her recognition that she can, asymmetrically, do things for the child that will make a huge difference to the child's life and which the child itself cannot do" (205ff.). A little later Sen adds this reflection: "Arguments that do not draw on the perspective of mutual benefit but concentrate instead on unilateral obligations because of asymmetry of power are not only plentifully used in contemporary human rights activism, but they can also be seen in the easy attempts to recognize the implications of valuing the freedoms—and correspondingly human rights—of all." He draws on examples of Tom Paine and Mary Wollstonecraft by arguing that "what Wollstonecraft called 'vindication' of the rights of women and men drew a great deal on this type of motivation, derived from reasoning about the obligation of effective power to help advance the freedoms of all" (206).

4.   Lucy Allais, "Should I Give To Beggars?" This paper was presented at the conference "Poverty; Charity; Justice," organized by The Wits Centre for Ethics and the Philosophy Department at the University of Witwatersrand, March 12–14, 2010. It is cited here with approval from the author.

5.   I develop this interpretation of Kant on poverty in "Kant and Dependency Relations: Kant on the State's Right to Redistribute Resources to Protect the Rights of Dependents," *Dialogue—Canadian Philosophical Review* 45 (2006): 257–84. In "Kant's Non-Absolutist Conception of Political Legitimacy: How Public Right 'Concludes' Private Right in 'The Doctrine of Right,'" *Kant-Studien* (forthcoming), I show this argument fits into Kant's overall account of public right.

6.   My main paper on this issue is "The Priority of Rightful Care to Virtuous Care: A Kantian Critique of the Care Tradition," which is under revision for *Kantian Review*. An outline of some core features of this argument is also found in "Kant's Non-Voluntarist Conception

of Political Obligations: Why Justice is Impossible in the State of Nature," *Kantian Review* 13.2 (2008): 1–45.

7.   Sen notes (325) that John Rawls never defends "a general right to property." In line with what I'm arguing in this paper, I believe this is correct. I believe however, that Rawls's lack of a private right account is a drawback for his position, as it deprives him of the possibility of explaining the necessity of a public authority, on which so much of his account relies. It also deprives him of the distinction between private and public right. Indeed, I believe that Rawls's account is best read as a public right account, to which a private right account needs to be added. I defend this reading of Rawls in both "G. A. Cohen's *Rescuing Justice and Equality*—a Critical Engagement," in *Social Philosophy Today* (forthcoming), and in "The Priority of Rightful Care to Virtuous Care." In my view, Arthur Ripstein, in "Private Order and Public Justice: Kant and Rawls" *Virginia Law Review* 92 (2006): 1391–1438, also argues consistently with these claims.

8.   See, for example, a related discussion by Sen in chap. 18, "Justice and the World," 388–415.

9.   See Immanuel Kant, *The Metaphysics of Morals*, ed. and trans. Mary Gregor (Cambridge: Cambridge University Press, 1996), 37–66.

10.   In the global context, corresponding indeterminacies arise in interstate relations as well as in cosmopolitan relations, which again give rise to the need for related public institutions. Given the space constraints of this paper, I cannot go into those issues here. I do, however, deal with some of them in "Diversity and Unity. An Attempt at Drawing a Justifiable Line," *Archiv für Rechts- und Sozialphilosophie/Archives for Philosophy of Law and Social Philosophy* (ARSP) 94 (2008), Heft 1: 1–25; and in "A Kantian Conception of Global Justice," *Review of International Studies* (forthcoming).

11.   I have written several papers on this distinction between private and public right as it relates to poverty, the economy and financial systems. For example, see my "Kant's Non-Absolutist Conception of Political Legitimacy," 257–84. In these papers, I also refute Onora O'Neill's take on Kant and poverty, which is the only Kantian approach Sen uses positively in *The Idea of Justice* (see 382ff.). In addition, I justify those statements by Barbara Herman concerning why states are primary loci for poverty relief that Sen finds so puzzling and unconvincing (see 413n). For a somewhat different interpretation of Kant and poverty relief that also emphasizes Kant's distinction between private and public right, see Sarah W. Holtman's "Kantian Justice and Poverty Relief," *Kant-Studien* 95: 86–106.

12.   I expand upon these kinds of issues in "The Priority of Rightful Care to Virtuous Care."

13.   I engage this issue in "Kant's Non-Absolutist Conception of Political Legitimacy."

14.   See my "A Feminist, Kantian Conception of the Right to Bodily Integrity: The Cases of Abortion and Homosexuality," in *Analytical Feminist Contributions to Traditional Philosophy*, ed. Anita M. Superson and Sharon Crasnow (New York: Oxford University Press, forthcoming), and in "A Kantian Conception of Rightful Sexual Relations: Sex, (Gay) Marriage and Prostitution," *Social Philosophy Today* 22 (2007): 199–218.

15.   I am very grateful to Lucy Allais for helping me understand this distinction between transcendental and transcendent in Kant's philosophy.

The Idea of Justice: A Reply

AMARTYA SEN

I must begin by expressing my deep appreciation of the illuminating comments on my book, *The Idea of Justice*, by Deen Chatterjee and Helga Varden. They have been kind and fair in their presentations, and have also raised really interesting questions. I am much stimulated by their arguments.

Response to Deen Chatterjee

Deen Chatterjee's comments clarify and extend the arguments I have tried to present, and he also connects my attempts with the arguments presented by other authors writing on political and moral subjects. What makes Chatterjee's essay particularly important is the way he weaves together different threads of arguments, from his own writings and those of others, to construct an alternative approach to "relationality" which, he shows, is able to accommodate and facilitate a globally inclusive understanding of the demands of ethics and justice—very different from what we get from the standard social contract approach, with its confinement within national borders through its invoking of the instruments of a sovereign state.

I have, of course, reason to be pleased by the fact that Chatterjee shows elegantly how particular concepts I have been occupied with, including the openness of impartiality, the multiplicity of individual identities, the relevance of processes along with substantive opportunities (reflected in capabilities), among other notions, link closely with his comprehensive notion of relationality. I also appreciate Chatterjee's supportive arguments and the kindness of his exposition in discussing my attempts in developing an alternative route to public reasoning about justice.

In commenting on Samuel Freeman's review essay ("A New Theory of Justice") on my book (*The Idea of Justice*),[1] Chatterjee has pointed out that "though Sen is not focused on an ideal theory and an ideal set of institutional arrangements, he in no way disregards the importance of institutions or the need for an appropriate normative theory" (179). I shall perhaps make here a few supplementary observations.

First, do I regard institutions to be unimportant, as has been alleged in some of the reviews? The focus of my work is on comparative assessment of social realizations (and this includes the lives of people as well as the fairness of processes), and as I have explained in my book, institutions figure in the social realizations both when they have intrinsic significance of their own (which may be rare but still quite important), and—indirectly but perhaps more extensively—through the impact that particular institutions (and their combinations) have on the lives of people. In fact, throughout my life I have worked on the importance of institutions, varying from public distribution systems (of food and famine relief, for example), to the organization of health care and of public education, and democratic and judicial institutions. There is, it should be obvious, a central place for institutions, including state institutions, in my exploration of the idea of justice.

What, however, I do resist is the tendency in the social contract tradition, which has been so dominant in mainstream theories of justice (as Chatterjee also discusses), to focus primarily, and sometimes exclusively, on "ideal institutions" and not directly on the lives of people—a tradition that is exemplified even by John Rawls's otherwise momentous analysis of justice (*A Theory of Justice*).[2] I do focus primarily on human lives (including what we—as thinking human beings—have reason to value, including the lives of animals and the survival of threatened species), and only secondarily on institutions, but that does not amount to ignoring the role of institutions—for they can be critically important for the lives and liberties of people and for guaranteeing the fairness of processes.

In addition to that departure towards a people-centred view, I have also argued for the importance of *comparative* engagements in assessing justice (will this change enhance justice and reduce injustice?), rather than being mainly confined to talking about "ideal situations," or—as is more common in the social contract tradition—about "ideal institutions." Our choices are almost always confined to comparisons of different non-ideal states, and we do need a theory for that, and that theory is not much helped, as I have shown, by any prior identification of ideal institutions, or even of ideal states.

None of this amounts to denying the inspirational—or motivational—role of talking about ideal states or about ideal institutions. I promise that if I were a part of the group that stormed the Bastille, I would have shouted "Liberty, Equality and Fraternity," and *not* "*more* liberty, *more* equality and *more* fraternity," even though the actual work to come should be better defined by the latter, rather than the former. Ideals are wonderfully important in arousing us, but we need also a theory of practical reason that can guide our actual choices and actions to be undertaken.

Where more clarification may be particularly needed is in the recognition that my rejection of focusing on "ideal institutions" does not amount to a rejection of the role of what are called "ideal theories" (as is presumed by Samuel Freeman's review essay on my book in *The New York Review*).[3] The two types of uses of the word "ideal" are completely different. An ideal theory abstracts from some real-life complications, and this can be very useful for the convenience of analyzing the central issues involved in an exercise—and sometimes even for tractability. But "ideal theories" are not confined to the analysis of "ideal institutions." They can be usefully employed also in clarifying some of the central issues involved in comparative assessments, without having to accommodate all the details of complications that would eventually have to be included—after the ideal theory has done its work. The rejection of the focus on *ideal states* (or on ideal institutions) has, ultimately, nothing much to do with the rejection of the contingent usefulness an *ideal theory*. My scepticism of focusing primarily on ideal states (or ideal institutions) does not, in any way, imply any scepticism of the usefulness of ideal theories.

There are many other issues of importance contained in—or related to—Chatterjee's discussion of my book. Since his exposition is very clear, there is no need for me to try to supplement what he says on these issues—other than, of course, expressing my appreciation of the reach of his wide-ranging review essay. I should, however, make a clarificatory remark, since Chatterjee comments, helped by his discussion with Sally Scholz, that I "should have counted Rousseau on [my] side than lumping him with other contractarians." I do, of course, count Rousseau as an ally in many respects, and have also noted that Rousseau's ideas have many features that distinguish him from other contractarians. The starting point of my first attempt at writing on justice (jointly with W. G. Runciman) in a 1965 essay called "Games, Justice and the General Will,"[4] was Rousseau's analysis of the general will. And Rousseau's concern about equality and solidarity was one of the inspiring motivations behind my analysis of inequality, as I noted at the beginning of my book, *On Economic Inequality*.[5]

In the book under discussion—*The Idea of Justice*—I have placed Rousseau with other contractarians to the extent that he too pursues a social contract approach. But as I have also noted in this book, despite the disagreement with the social contract approach in general, we have much to learn from the many contributions to our thinking that have come from the specific formulations of the contractarian approach (flawed as, I believe, the general approach is). Rousseau, along with Kant and Rawls, has lessons for us that surely go far beyond their use of the social contract approach. None of the great social contract theorists are *only* social contract theorists, and one would have to be oddly narrow-minded if one were to miss the richness of the ideas and analyses of Rousseau—or of Kant or Rawls—merely because of the reservations we may have about the social contract approach.

Response to Helga Varden

I am both touched by the generosity with which Helga Varden has described my work and much engaged by the interesting questions she has raised. Even though

I shall presently discuss why the points of disagreement between us that she has identified do not appear to me to be entirely compelling, I am delighted that she has directed our attention to really serious issues that need to be addressed both by social contract theorists and by those who, like me, are sceptical of that tradition.

There are five points of disagreement with me that Varden has clearly identified. First, she says: "Contrary to Sen, I will argue that justice requires enforceable rights, including for the disabled, and that states have in principle necessary role to play here" (193). My primary problem with this diagnosis lies in my attempt at understanding what Varden could mean by saying "contrary to Sen." Perhaps the problem arises from Varden's abstinence from considering fully the comparative approach and its demands. In a comparative approach, we are involved in a set of comparisons of justice and injustice, and in some of these comparisons (but not in all of them), the role of the state and that of enforceable rights would be absolutely central.

By liberating the assessment of justice from merely identifying (or trying to identify) a situation of perfect justice, a comparative approach gets involved in comparing different changes that can be brought about—or considered for being brought about—in terms of their contributions to the enhancement of justice and reduction of injustice. In the world that I know (and have written about), in overcoming the huge injustices from which many people, for example the disabled, presently suffer, extensive supportive arrangements are needed, provided by the state and the society. So that cannot be a point of division between Varden and me. For example, the grossness of the definitions of poverty that are typically used for state-supported relief, leading to insufficient state support for the capability-deprived disabled even in countries with a "welfare state" (for example, Britain), has been a particular subject of my critique of on-going social arrangements (particularly poverty relief programmes), in *The Idea of Justice* (258–60, 267–8).

There can, however, be a disagreement if Varden wishes to claim that no changes in anything other than state action, for example modification of social attitudes, of community activities, or of cooperative organizations, can possibly enhance justice in any way whatever: that is (according to this view), justice can be influenced only by state action and nothing else. That would be, I would argue, an odd necessity to insist on, and the removal of that constrained thought does not, in any way, compromise the understanding that a more fully functioning system of justice would require the state to get into the act.

The debate here, if there is one, is really about Varden's insistence, in line with what her transcendental institutional position, that nothing but ideal institutions matter in the discussion of justice.[6] The merit of a comparative approach is that we need not insist that the only changes that achieve perfection make any difference to justice. That transcendental obstinacy (if I may call it that) would be, as it happens, also at variance with (as I have discussed in my book) the idea of justice that we get from some of the great thinkers who were so preoccupied with removing injustice in the world. In the Enlightenment period, the list would include not only Smith (with his investigation of the role of moral sentiments and public attitudes) and Condorcet (with his particular focus on education, especially of girls, and the importance of open public dialogue), but also Mary Wollstonecraft (and her elaborate discussion of the multitude of changes, including those in public understanding, media coverage and respect for people across the barriers of class, race and gender), and Tom Paine (and his attempts to introduce various state interventions to remove poverty without insisting that the package must be perfect for it to count at all as a justice-enhancing change). Justice depends on many things, and it does not sink or float only with a perfect package of state action.

Varden's second point is that she can "boost [her] arguments for the necessity of states by arguing that rightful resolutions of many of the indeterminacies Sen points to require the establishment of public authorities, including states" (193). As has just been discussed, there is no need for any "boosting" in the need for state action for some critically important enhancements of justice (which is a part of my own claim). So that can hardly be the issue involved here. It is important to recognise that the possibility of "indeterminacies" in the assessment of justice arises, in my analysis, only from residual disagreements between different people—and sometimes even in the mind of the same person—that survive open and informed public discussion. I very much hope that Varden would not like to use the machinery of the state to "eliminate" disagreements that people may continue to have despite serious engagement in public reasoning. I do not believe she is pointing to that authoritarian route, and I must therefore conclude that she is, again, concerned with the necessity of the state for something that she would see as an "ideally just" situation. But that is an argument that I have already addressed.

Varden's third point is that "Kant's suggestion that justice—for ideal, rather than merely prudential reasons—requires the establishment of public authorities constituted by a certain set of institutions is not . . . a drawback for the theory [Kant's "republican" theory]. Quite the contrary, it is a significant strength" (193). It certainly is that for Kant's republican characterization of ideal situations. Having institutions that make people independent of the help others would surely be a part of the picture of an ideal society, but this does not entail that in the absence of such independence, there is no issue of justice left.

So that cannot be a point of difference either, even though we do seem to differ on whether justice is *only* about contractarian perfection or about republican independence, for reasons I have discussed in *The Idea of Justice* (including my argument that we do not get much help from the identification of the ideal to make comparisons of justice and injustice in non-ideal states to which our choices may be actually confined [98–105]). The kind of world with which I am particularly concerned is not one in which everyone can be entirely independent of the actions of others. To be willing to provide help to others is not beyond the demands of justice, even though some commentators have presented the odd argument (this is not Varden, I should explain) that if something could conceivably be a part of "kindly behaviour," then it cannot have anything to do with the justice and injustice in the world in which we live.

Varden is quite right to claim that "even a world in which the rich continuously give money to beggars so that none of them starve still is not a just world" (104). Justice cannot be based only on charity, or even primarily on charity. And yet a world in which, in the absence of adequate public institutions, millions are left to starve, with others, living in luxury, refuse to help the famished in any way, is surely a more unjust world than the one that Varden describes. There is no puzzle in appreciating the distinction when the comparative demands of justice are understood. The vision of a world in which there is no need whatever for what Smith called "sympathy," "generosity" and "public spirit," should not hold us back from seeing *more* injustice in a world in which many people suffer terribly with the others doing nothing to help their fellow human beings. I do not think Kant has ever advocated that extremist position, and that is not a respect in which he differed from his contemporaries like Smith or Condorcet or Wollstonecraft.

Varden's fifth point is that "although I find Sen's proposal that ideal theories should spend more time taking people's bad or non-ideal behavior into account compelling, questions concerning non-ideal-behaviour are primarily important for the institutional design for a theory of justice" (103). They are certainly very important for institutional design, and there is no disagreement between us on that. And I applaud Varden's illustration of the relevance of this issue for Thomas Pogge's visionary initiative of the "Health Impact Fund" (HIF). I would only add that even a fully functioning HIF will not make the world perfectly just, and we have to see what it does to a world that remains non-ideal. The great strength of HIF is that is does not have to assume a world in which the demands of perfect justice (if they could be identified) have been, in other respects, already achieved. The IHF is, happily, not meant to work only in the world of cosmopolitan perfect justice, since it can be expected to do much good—and significant enhancement of justice and reduction of injustice—even in a world that remains very imperfect in many other respects.

If I may take the liberty of ending with a general point of my own, concerning Helga Varden's interesting arguments and engagements. If she were to take the comparative approach more seriously, rather than trying to fit all her justice-related thoughts within the limited world of perfect justice (and even more restrictively, of perfect institutions), she would find, I believe, much greater use for her powerful concerns and commitments, and even for her arguments, liberated from the tight box of transencendental institutionalism. And this applies, I would argue, also to her interesting work on public and private rights. But this reply is far too long already for me to give myself the liberty of following up that quick remark. So I just end by thanking Varden, along with Chatterjee.

Notes

1. Samuel Freeman, "A New Theory of Justice," *New York Review of Books*, October 14, 2010.

2. John Rawls, *A Theory of Justice* (Cambridge, MA: Harvard University Press, 1971).

3. However, in a later essay, presented at a symposium on my book arranged by Rutgers University (in particular, by its Institute of Philosophy and Law), Samuel Freeman has clarified the issue, and has emended his earlier reading in the appropriate direction.

4. *Mind* 74 (1965).

5. *On Economic Inequality* (Oxford: Oxford University Press, 1973; extended edition, with new annexe, written jointly with James Foster, 1997).

6. I hasten to affirm, since the point seems to worry Varden from time to time, that I use the word transcendental in the sense of being unbeatable (as I explained in my book), which is, of course, different from the much more extensive way Kant uses that term (I merely presume that Kant has not put some kind of a "bolt" on any other—including simple mathematical—use of that common word).

Notes On Contributors

Marilea Bramer is an assistant professor of philosophy at Minnesota State University Moorhead. Her research interests include the moral value of personal relationships in Kantian moral theory as well as general moral problems specific to personal relationships, including domestic violence, the obligations children have to parents, and the purpose of apologies between family members and friends.

Deen K. Chatterjee teaches philosophy at the University of Utah and is the editor-in-chief of the forthcoming multi-volume *Encyclopedia of Global Justice* and the series editor of *Studies in Global Justice*. His publications include, most recently, *Democracy in a Global World: Human Rights and Political Participation in the 21st Century* and *Gathering Storm: The Ethics of Preventive War*.

Martin Gunderson is DeWitt Wallace Professor of Philosophy at Macalester College. For the past two decades he has been interested in areas where healthcare, civil liberties and ethics overlap. He has published on informed consent, physician-assisted death, suicide, medical privacy, confidentiality, and human rights. His articles have appeared in a variety of journals including *The Hastings Center Report*, *The Kennedy Institute of Ethics Journal*, the *Journal of Social Philosophy*, *Public Affairs Quarterly*, and *Philosophy and Medicine*, and he is a co-author of *AIDS: Testing and Privacy*.

Ryan Jenkins is a doctoral student at the University of Colorado Boulder. He is interested in normative and applied ethics, with special interests in rule-consequentialism, desert, and justice.

David Kenneth Johnson is professor of philosophy at Massachusetts College of Liberal Arts. He is the author (with Matthew Silliman) of *Bridges to the World: A Dialogue on the Construction of Knowledge, Education, and Truth*, and has published numerous philosophical essays in the areas of ethics, epistemology, metaphysics, and critical thinking. He lives and plays jazz piano in the Pioneer Valley of Western Massachusetts with his wife, Kathleen, and two daughters, Sarah and Laura.

Sean Donaghue Johnston has recently completed his Ph.D. in the Social, Political, Ethical, and Legal Philosophy (SPEL) program at Binghamton University. He is currently writing on the social and political philosophy of John Stuart Mill.

Ryan Long is the Law and Philosophy Fellow at the University of Chicago Law School. His research interests include ethics, political philosophy, free will, philosophy of law, and philosophy of religion.

Alistair M. Macleod (Philosophy, Queen's University) is the author of *Social Justice, Progressive Politics and Taxes* (2004) and of papers on freedom, equality, justice, and democracy in various collections and in such journals as *Canadian Journal of Philosophy, Journal of Philosophy, Journal of Social Philosophy*, and *Archiv fur Rechts- und Sozialphilosophie*.

Jan Narveson is Distinguished Professor Emeritus of Philosophy, University of Waterloo, Ontario, Canada. He is the author of several books, most recently *You and The State, This is Ethical Theory*, and, with James P. Sterba, *Are Liberty and Equality Compatible?*, as well as some hundreds of papers on moral and political matters, from very theoretical to quite hands-on. He is also an avid promoter of music in general and of chamber music especially, in his home cities of Kitchener and Waterloo, Ontario. Jan was made an Officer of the Order of Canada in 2003.

Natalie Nenadic is an Assistant Professor of Philosophy at the University of Kentucky. She teaches in the history of philosophy (especially Heidegger, Arendt, and Hegel), philosophy of law, and social and political philosophy. She enlisted Catharine MacKinnon to represent Bosnian survivors and initiated with her the landmark lawsuit *Kadić v. Karadžić* in New York City that pioneered the claim for sexual atrocities as acts of genocide under international law.

David Schweickart is Professor of Philosophy, Loyola University Chicago. His books include *Against Capitalism* (Cambridge University Press, 1993), *Market Socialism: The Debate Among Socialists* (Routledge, 1998 [co-author]), and *After Capitalism* (Rowman and Littlefield, 2002; 2nd edition, 2011). All three of these works have been translated into Chinese. His work has also been translated into Spanish, French, Slovak, Catalan, and Farse.

Amartya Sen is Thomas W. Lamont University Professor, and Professor of Economics and Philosophy, at Harvard University and was until recently the Master of Trinity College, Cambridge. He has served as President of the Econometric Society, the Indian Economic Association, the American Economic Association and the International Economic Association. He was formerly Honorary President of OXFAM and is now its Honorary Advisor. Born in Santiniketan, India, Amartya Sen is an Indian citizen. He was the Drummond Professor of Political Economy at Oxford University, and is a Distinguished Fellow of All Souls. Sen's books have been translated into more than thirty languages, and include *Choice of Techniques* (1960), *Collective Choice and Social Welfare* (1970), *Choice, Welfare and Measurement* (1982), *The Standard of Living* (1987), *Development as Freedom* (1999), *Identity and Violence: The Illusion of Destiny* (2006), and *The Idea of Justice* (2009). His research has ranged over a number of fields in economics, philosophy, and decision theory, including social choice theory, welfare economics, theory of measurement, development economics, public health, gender studies, and moral and political philosophy. Among the awards he has received are the "Bharat Ratna" (the highest honour awarded by the President of India); the Senator Giovanni Agnelli International Prize in Ethics; the Edinburgh Medal; the Brazilian Ordem do Merito Científico; the Eisenhower Medal; the George C. Marshall Award; and the Nobel Prize in Economics.

Matt Silliman teaches philosophy at Massachusetts College of Liberal Arts. His previously published work includes *Sentience and Sensibility* (Parmenides Publishing, 2006), and co-authored with David Johnson, *Bridges to the World* (Sense Publishers, 2009).

Nancy E. Snow guest edited this volume. She is a Professor of Philosophy at Marquette University. She is the author of *Virtue as Social Intelligence: An Empirically Grounded Theory* (Routledge, 2010), and articles in moral psychology and virtue ethics.

James P. Sterba is Professor of Philosophy at the University of Notre Dame. His previous publications include *Affirmative Action for the Future* (Oxford, 2009), *Does Feminism Discriminate Against Men?—A Debate* (Oxford, 2008 [co-authored with Warren Farrell]), *The Triumph of Practice over Theory in Ethics* (Oxford, 2005), *Terrorism and International Justice* (Oxford, 2002), and *Justice for Here and Now* (Cambridge, 1998). He is past president of the American Philosophical Association (Central Division) and several other organizations.

Helga Varden is an assistant professor in the Department of Philosophy and Women and Gender Studies at the University of Illinois at Urbana-Champaign. Her main research interests are in legal, political, and feminist philosophy, with an emphasis on the Kantian and the Lockean traditions. Her most recent publications include "A Kantian Conception of Global Justice" (*Review of International Studies*), "Kant's Non-Absolutist Conception of Political Legitimacy: How Public Right 'Concludes' Private Right in 'The Doctrine of Right'" (*Kant-Studien*), "Kant's Non-Voluntarist Conception of Political Obligations: Why Justice is Impossible in the State of Nature" (*Kantian Review*), "The Lockean 'Enough-and-as-Good' Proviso—An Internal Critique" (*Journal of Moral Philosophy*), "Kant's Murderer at the Door . . . One More Time: Kant's Legal Philosophy and Lies to Murderers and Nazis" (*The Journal of Social Philosophy*), and "Lockean Freedom and the Proviso's Appeal to Scientific Knowledge" (*Social Theory and Practice*).